D1195661

FIRE ON THE WATER

FIRE ON THE
WATER

SECOND EDITION

★

China, America, and the Future of the Pacific

ROBERT HADDICK

Naval Institute Press
Annapolis, Maryland

Naval Institute Press
291 Wood Road
Annapolis, MD 21402

Library of Congress Cataloging-in-Publication Data

Names: Haddick, Robert, author.
Title: Fire on the water : China, America, and the future of the Pacific / Robert Haddick.
Description: Second edition. | Annapolis, Maryland : Naval Institute Press, [2022] | Includes
    bibliographical references and index.
Identifiers: LCCN 2022000749 (print) | LCCN 2022000750 (ebook) | ISBN 9781682476765
    (hardback) | ISBN 9781682478035 (ebook)
Subjects: LCSH: Sea-power—Pacific Area. | Security, International—Pacific Area. | Pacific
    Area—Strategic aspects. | United States—Military policy. | China—Strategic aspects.
    | China—Military policy. | United States—Foreign relations—Pacific Area. | Pacific
    Area—Foreign relations—United States. | BISAC: HISTORY / Military / Naval | HISTORY
    / Military / United States
Classification: LCC UA830 .H34 2022 (print) | LCC UA830 (ebook) | DDC 355/.03301823—dc23/
    eng/20220331
LC record available at https://lccn.loc.gov/2022000749
LC ebook record available at https://lccn.loc.gov/2022000750

30 29 28 27 26 25 24 23 22   9 8 7 6 5 4 3 2 1
First printing

My impression is that a lot of people sign up to the notion that a military revolution is under way, but very few draw the significant consequences that flow from that belief.

—Andrew Marshall, director of the Office of Net Assessment, Office of the U.S. Secretary of Defense, memorandum for the record, July 27, 1993 (Krepinevich and Watts, *The Last Warrior*)

CONTENTS

MAPS

FOREWORD

At the 2021 Air Force Association Air, Space, and Cyber conference in Washington, DC, new Secretary of the Air Force Frank Kendall relayed that when asked at a congressional breakfast what his top three priorities were, his answer was, "China, China, and China." His response was certainly appropriate given the recent dramatic increases in China's military capability. China's accelerating military prowess in the twenty-first century has been accompanied by alarming land seizures in the South China Sea for the development of military outposts. During 2021, China routinely penetrated Taiwan's air defense identification zone with advanced fighters and bombers, causing concern that the Communist People's Republic of China may not be far from using lethal force against Taiwan.

Visual images from commercial satellites have revealed that China is embarking on a significant expansion of its nuclear arsenal through the building of silo-based intercontinental ballistic missiles. This evidence is significant because it shows that China appears to be shifting from minimal deterrence to a nuclear first-strike capacity with the potential to grow its nuclear forces to levels equal to or greater than those of the United States. Accordingly, dramatic action is called for by the United

States and its allies to achieve an effective conventional deterrent that will dissuade China's leaders from considering either conventional or nuclear aggression in their march toward global power status.

Robert Haddick's *Fire on the Water: China, America, and the Future of the Pacific* has arrived just in time to provide insights toward that objective. He has produced a most timely update to his original work, which was published in 2014. This second edition is not simply an update on China's growing military might since that time. Rather it is an astute look at where China's military is going as well as a thoughtful summary of U.S. moves and reactions to China's growth as a dominant player on the world stage. This book focuses on how the United States and its allies can sustain conventional military deterrence in the Indo-Pacific during what has now been established as a long, open-ended competition with China.

Haddick realistically acknowledges the waning utility of surface warships in the face of China's technological advances, but he also explains the critical roles they will retain in a long-term competition against China—particularly as part of a cost-imposing element of a new Indo-Pacific strategy. Battle networks composed of ubiquitous sensors and long-range precision munitions have fundamentally changed the character of warfare. Consequently, the Indo-Pacific is no longer primarily a naval theater. Henceforth, long-range airpower and space power will be the keys to success in any effective strategy. And yet the U.S. Air Force is the smallest and oldest force it has ever been. Renewing the necessary number of modern, penetrating long-range aircraft and associated maritime-capable munitions should be a priority if the United States is to maintain escalation dominance over China's military forces. Haddick observes that without rapid action to correct the deficiency of modern U.S. bomber forces, escalation dominance may shift into the hands of the Chinese, with devastating consequences for the United States and its allies.

Haddick also recognizes that the greatest barriers to implementing a better military strategy for the Indo-Pacific are the existing bureaucratic and institutional interests that resist changes to the defense program. Overcoming those barriers will require inspired leadership that can surmount the decades of tradition that currently paralyzes innovative strategy in the Indo-Pacific.

Fire on the Water is a must-read for those who recognize that China is no longer a future threat we can worry about tomorrow—it is a real threat we must deal with today. For those who are not aware of that perspective this book is even more important.

Lt. Gen. David A. Deptula, USAF (Ret.)
Dean, The Mitchell Institute for Aerospace Studies

PREFACE

The Naval Institute Press published the first edition of *Fire on the Water* in September 2014. The goal of that book was to raise awareness about the rapid rise of China's military power, the deteriorating security situation in the Indo-Pacific region, and the potential consequences if those trends remained unchanged. Perhaps most important, the book explained why the U.S. government needed to make major changes to its military forces and policies for the region. Concern about trends in the region was rising then among some U.S. and allied national security analysts, but for most, the problem still seemed distant and hardly urgent.

Today, there are very few in Washington or elsewhere among America's allies who do not see the menace in China's military buildup and its markedly more aggressive foreign policy and actions. Seasoned diplomats and senior military commanders now worry that war over Taiwan or elsewhere in the region is looming and perhaps imminent. The first edition described China's military modernization program and predicted the threats those capabilities would pose to U.S. military forces and concepts by the 2020s. Most of those predictions have come to pass.

But much else has changed over the past eight years. As a result, the editors at the Naval Institute Press asked me to write a second edition. This edition discusses the many political, military, and strategic developments that have occurred on both sides of the Pacific Ocean since the first edition was published. This new edition incorporates that new information and extends the forecast horizon through this decade and into the 2030s. It also reaches new conclusions and recommendations on how the United States should reform its defense program to meet the challenges that China's military power and increasingly assertive actions present. With so much new since 2014, readers will find an almost entirely new text, with little carried over from the first edition.

The preface to the first edition asserted that the rapid rise in China's economic, political, and military power would likely be the most consequential national security challenge the United States would face over the next two decades. That now seems to be the consensus view among national security strategists in Washington and elsewhere. China's economic capacity and apparent dynamism will make the magnitude of this challenge as great as that presented by the Soviet Union during the Cold War, another point mentioned in the preface to the first edition. For the United States and its partners, meeting the challenge will be strenuous. But as this edition will make clear, U.S. policymakers and citizens should have confidence that with a good strategy they can achieve a favorable outcome for U.S. interests at a reasonable cost, and that people throughout the Indo-Pacific region, including in China, can enjoy a century of peace and opportunity.

Achieving this outcome will require policymakers to refashion America's legacy defense program and push through significant reforms over the objections of some resistant interests. Many readers will find some of the book's conclusions controversial. If so, good. A healthy debate over America's policies for Asia is welcome because the stakes for the United States are so high. This book will succeed if it sparks further research on these issues and more discussion among policymakers and the public—but hopefully not too much more research and discussion. Almost a decade has passed since the first edition was published, and yet U.S. military forces in the Indo-Pacific region are little better prepared for a Chinese threat that has since compounded. The danger is here, and those in authority need to act.

ACKNOWLEDGMENTS

I have received much support during the process of completing this project. The Naval Institute Press continues its century-long work of publishing history, analysis, and reference books critical to America's security. I am honored to continue my association with this august institution. I thank Adam Kane, the press' director, for taking on the first edition of *Fire on the Water* in 2013 and for engaging me to write the second edition. Padraic (Pat) Carlin expertly managed the second edition's publication process. Mindy Conner skillfully edited this new edition, greatly improving it. I thank Chris Robinson for updating Charles David Grear's maps for this second edition of the book. The U.S. Naval Institute's Emily Martin performed miracles in getting the second edition's images ready for publication. The Naval Institute Press continues to sustain its excellence, a product of the professionalism of these people and their colleagues. Naturally, any shortcomings in the book are my responsibility.

My colleagues at the Mitchell Institute for Aerospace Studies were an invaluable asset to me during this project. Lt. Gen. David Deptula, USAF (Ret.), the Mitchell Institute's dean and author of the foreword, remains a tireless advocate for a better national security strategy and smarter defense policies. I benefited from the insights and support of Doug Birkey;

Maj. Gen. Larry Stutzriem, USAF (Ret.); and Col. Mark Gunzinger, USAF (Ret.), all strategy intellects at the Mitchell Institute.

Finally, my wife, Susan, encouraged me to press on with the second edition and get the manuscript over the finish line. To her and everyone else involved, thanks.

Introduction

In February 2021, the Council on Foreign Relations published a report written by Robert Blackwill and Philip Zelikow that discussed the prospect of a Chinese attack on Taiwan. The authors, both former career U.S. diplomats and senior National Security Council staff members for Democratic and Republican presidents, concluded,

> China is now in a prewar tempo of political and military preparations. We do not mean that we know that China is about to embark on a war. We simply observe that the Chinese government is taking actions that a country would do if it were moving into a prewar mode. Politically, it is preparing and conditioning its population for the possibility of an armed conflict. Militarily, it is engaging now in a tempo of exercises and military preparations that are both sharpening and widening the readiness of its armed forces across a range of different contingencies on sea, air, land, cyber, or in space.[1]

Similarly, Adm. Philip Davidson, the commander of U.S. Indo-Pacific Command until May 2021, reported to Congress in early 2021 that China is likely to attempt an invasion of Taiwan sometime this decade, perhaps in the next few years.[2] And in March 2021, Kurt Campbell, coordinator of

Indo-Pacific policy at the Biden White House and a former U.S. assistant secretary of state for East Asian and Pacific Affairs, explained to a private conference hosted by the University of California at San Diego that China's leaders in Beijing had become "impatient" on the mainland's reunification with Taiwan.[3]

The Indo-Pacific region has long been a challenge for the United States. Over the past century, America fought four wars in the region and struggled with a dangerous four-decades-long competition against the Soviet Union. But with these challenges and tragedies have also come opportunity, trade, wealth, and cultural enrichment for countless millions on both sides of the Pacific Ocean. America's ties with the region have delivered millions of jobs, higher standards of living, growing investments, and cultural interactions that have enriched all.

When the Naval Institute Press published the first edition of *Fire on the Water* in 2014, China had begun pressing previously dormant claims for maritime territory in the East and South China Seas. Since then, China's actions have accelerated and include the establishment of heavily armed air and naval sites in the Paracel Islands and Spratly Islands in the South China Sea; peremptory dismissal of an international tribunal's ruling against China's claims in the South China Sea; ongoing incursions by China's coast guard and "maritime militia" fishing fleets into the exclusive economic zones of Japan, Vietnam, Indonesia, the Philippines, and elsewhere; and regular harassment of Taiwan by Chinese air force bomber and fighter aircraft. China's apparent goal is to demoralize its neighbors and compel them to agree to its unfounded territorial claims over the Near Seas in the western Pacific. If successful, China would tighten its control over some of the world's most vital economic lines of communication and gain control of vast hydrocarbon, mineral, and fishing resources. But these gains would come at the expense of its neighbors, most of whom are now resisting China's increasing pressure.

China's well-designed modernization of its air, naval, missile, and military space power has similarly accelerated over the past decade and has become the most rapid and sustained peacetime buildup of military power since Germany's in the 1930s.[4] According to the Stockholm International

Peace Research Institute (SIPRI) database of military expenditures, China's defense spending rose seventeen-fold between 1995 and 2019, a 12 percent compound annual growth rate.[5] Although China's defense spending growth has slowed during the past few years, its defense budget remains on a pace to double every decade. By one analysis, China's annual procurement of military weapons and defense hardware will overtake that of the United States in 2024.[6] China's massive investment in military power has given it the ability to challenge the United States and its allies for dominance over the air and sea lines of communication in the western Pacific.

The stakes are immense. The Indo-Pacific has long been the most economically dynamic region in the world. A major conflict there would cripple the global economy. Many of America's largest trading partners are there, and more than 10 million U.S. jobs are tied directly or indirectly to the export of U.S. goods and services to customers in the region. From a strategic perspective, the United States has six formal and many more informal security relationships in the Indo-Pacific that benefit U.S. security but are also a measure of America's credibility as an ally. Finally, since its founding the United States has both relied on and defended the freedom of navigation and rights to the global commons. Today's disputes in the western Pacific, tied to China's territorial assertions in the region, place these principles at risk.

The first edition of *Fire on the Water* used the pre–World War I era as the metaphor to describe the building security competition between China and the United States and its partners, citing former secretary of state Henry Kissinger: "The relations of the principal Asian nations to each other bear most of the attributes of the European balance-of-power system of the nineteenth century. Any significant increase in the strength by one of them is almost certain to evoke an offsetting maneuver by the others."[7] In 2013, former Australian prime minister Kevin Rudd described East Asia as "a 21st-century maritime redux of the Balkans a century ago—a tinderbox on water," referring to the nationalist hothouse that sparked World War I.[8] Kurt Campbell similarly compared the ongoing tensions between China and Japan over small islands in the East China Sea with tensions in Europe at the beginning of the twentieth century: "There is a feeling of 1914 in the air. Just as with tensions between European armies at the turn of the last century, both Tokyo and Beijing are absolutely certain of the rightness of their positions. More importantly, both believe that with a little further pressure, the other side is on the verge of blinking and backing down."[9]

In their 2021 report for the Council on Foreign Relations, Blackwill and Zelikow ominously switched the metaphor to the period just before World War II. They described Taiwan as analogous to Czechoslovakia in 1938 and wondered whether the United States and its allies should make their stand against aggression in Taiwan or instead cast Taiwan away to appease China in the hope of avoiding war. In their Czechoslovakia analogy, the United States and Japan represent Great Britain and France, respectively, which in the 1938 crisis were divided on how to respond to Germany's demands. Unable either to rally or to prepare, they chose abandonment. Today's leaders in Washington and Tokyo should take note.[10]

The 2014 edition of *Fire on the Water* described the magnitude of any threat as the product of a competitor's capabilities and its intentions. The book implored strategists to focus on capabilities. Intentions may change from benign to hostile, but that matters little without powerful capabilities to back them. China's military capabilities, already formidable in 2014, now pose an even greater danger to U.S. and allied military forces in the Indo-Pacific region. China's leaders in Beijing know this, and that does much to explain the marked increase in their belligerence since 2014—they now have the military capabilities to back up their intentions.

The views of U.S. national security officials have hardened since 2014. Gone is the time when the top U.S. commander in the Pacific expressed more concern about natural disasters and climate change than the growing power and assertiveness of the People's Liberation Army (PLA). Commanders today discuss when the war over Taiwan might begin rather than whether there will be war. Similarly, following the policy established by President Richard Nixon in 1969, U.S. policymakers until recently had hoped that engagement with China would lead that nation to become a "responsible stakeholder in the international system." In a *Foreign Affairs* article published in September 2019, however, Kurt Campbell and Jake Sullivan, who is now President Joseph Biden's national security adviser, announced the "unceremonious close" of the engagement era.[11] The public national security strategy documents of the Trump and Biden presidencies leave no doubt that China and its challenges to the international system are now the top national security priority of the U.S. government.

But while much has changed since the first edition of *Fire on the Water* was published, America's military culture and the institutions that sustain it have not. The services remain mostly unwilling to implement the innovations that will be required to maintain conventional deterrence in the Indo-Pacific region. As the epigraph for this edition notes, a revolution in military technology and concepts has been under way for more than three decades. In the United States, it began after the Vietnam War and started to bear fruit in the 1991 Persian Gulf War. This military-technical revolution is linking vast arrays of sensors with inexpensive, long-range, and deadly precise missiles. These battle networks, which can span entire regions, have upended legacy military systems and warfighting concepts. The PLA is exploiting the military-technical revolution with lethal efficiency.

The military-technical revolution has created winners and losers inside the immense U.S. defense bureaucracy, and the potential losers are strenuously resisting change. Although the U.S. military services are now finally experimenting with new systems and ideas, they have come late to the game now long afoot in the Indo-Pacific. Senior U.S. defense leaders spanning numerous administrations and Congresses have yet to develop a competitive military strategy to counter the Chinese threat, make the necessary hard choices that any good strategy requires, and impose those results on obstinate defense bureaucracies. The U.S. and allied military posture in the Indo-Pacific is now exposed to the dangerous consequences of this resistance.

This second edition of *Fire on the Water* focuses exclusively on how the United States and its allies can sustain conventional military deterrence in the Indo-Pacific during a long, open-ended competition with China. This single facet of the U.S.-China competition is large enough to merit a book-length examination, and it warrants such an examination because so much disagreement exists among strategists on how to proceed. Other areas of the U.S.-China competition such as trade policy, technology transfer and competition, public diplomacy, finance, cyber espionage, and "gray zone" competition are important as well, but we must leave them for their own book-length treatments.

The conventional military balance is the most important facet of the competition. U.S. failure to maintain conventional military deterrence will lead China's leaders to believe that they possess the military options they need to employ the PLA in decisive fait accompli military campaigns. Believing that, they might choose to employ these options irrespective of how either side might be faring in the other competitions just mentioned. And next to a nuclear exchange, a failure of conventional military deterrence would have the costliest consequences. In testimony to Congress in March 2021 Admiral Davidson warned, "The greatest danger we face in the Indo-Pacific region is the erosion of conventional deterrence vis-à-vis China. Without a valid and convincing conventional deterrent, China will be emboldened."[12]

This edition of *Fire on the Water* will explain how the United States can sustain conventional deterrence against China over the long run and at an affordable price. This is not a facile problem; China is a true peer competitor the likes of which the United States has not faced since it became a great power more than a century ago.

In his landmark book *The Causes of War*, historian Geoffrey Blainey explained that when two countries agree on their relative strength—that is, when the leaders of the two countries agree which is stronger and which is weaker, or when they agree that they are evenly matched—then war is unlikely to occur. But when they disagree on which is stronger or if a balance exists, perhaps both thinking they are the stronger, then war is much more likely to occur.[13] A decade ago, few doubted that U.S. and allied military forces enjoyed superiority in the Indo-Pacific region. That certainty has vanished. On current trends, Washington and Beijing will soon disagree on which is the strongest, and that disagreement will bring a grave escalation in the chance of conflict.

Within the next decade China's leaders might conclude that they, and not the United States and its partners, possess escalation dominance, and that China's leverage would improve during a crisis in the western Pacific.

During such a crisis, the PLA could put into readiness—and perhaps into action—more and more of its land-based air and missile power. U.S. commanders would not relish the prospect of sending their naval and airpower into such tactically unfavorable circumstances. They would presumably have to report this analysis to policymakers in Washington, who would similarly have to ponder the consequences of a visible and substantial military setback. The policymakers would inevitably shift their attention to face-saving de-escalation of the crisis that would sacrifice U.S. negotiating leverage.

U.S. policymakers are unaccustomed to dealing with an adversary in possession of escalation dominance, and that could lead to a costly miscalculation or an embarrassing back-down in a crisis. Most dangerous of all would be a situation where both sides perceived they would benefit from escalation. In that case, a conflict would be virtually certain. That once unthinkable scenario is now plausible. China's leaders and PLA commanders might have great confidence in their naval, missile, and aerospace power, while the confidence of U.S. policymakers in a crisis could rest on comforting, but possibly mistaken, memories of military dominance. Needless to say, it cannot be the case that both sides would benefit from escalation.

This edition of *Fire on the Water* describes a strategy for a more hopeful outcome, a program for preserving peace and security in the Indo-Pacific region. Doing so will require the United States to remain the region's security guarantor. Against a great power like China, this will be a burden, but America's defense institutions can maintain conventional military deterrence against China's military challenge at an affordable price. Perhaps most important, this edition will explain why U.S. policymakers and citizens should be confident that America can sustain this responsibility over the remainder of this century.

Chapters 1 and 2 consider the sources of conflict in Asia and explain why America's best option is to maintain its active forward presence in the region. Chapter 3 discusses the history of America's military presence in the Indo-Pacific and explains why that presence is now vulnerable. Chapter 4 explains in detail China's military modernization program, its shrewd exploitation of the military-technical revolution, and why China now poses a grave threat to U.S. and allied interests. Chapter 5 examines the U.S. responses to China's military modernization over the past decade and explains why these responses fall short of a convincing competitive strategy.

The remainder of the book describes a new approach for sustaining conventional deterrence in the Indo-Pacific region. Chapter 6 explains the principles of strategy as they apply to the problems the United States faces in the region. Chapter 7 examines the critical role of aerospace power in the region and how the United States should urgently refashion its aerospace concepts if it is to deter aggression, focusing on Taiwan, the most difficult case. Chapter 8 considers how the military-technical revolution has drastically changed the potential of naval forces in the Indo-Pacific region and why U.S. policymakers and planners need to adjust their expectations and planning for naval forces there. Finally, chapter 9 discusses what lessons U.S. policymakers can apply from past great-power competitions, examines long-term trends affecting the current competition, summarizes a new U.S. strategic approach to the region, describes how policymakers can overcome institutional barriers that will stand in the way of a better strategy, and explains why policymakers and the public should have confidence about sustaining deterrence and peace in the region over the long term.

The goal of a new American strategy in Asia is to prevent conflict while preserving an existing international order that benefits all. The United States will have to implement specific military reforms to deter China's employment of its military power in a prospective fait accompli assault. This is not a war plan; it is instead a strategy for managing a peacetime competition in a highly dynamic region. Success will be measured in terms of the crises that never occur, the wars that are never fought, and the long continuation of the region's prosperity and development.

The Indo-Pacific region is crucial to the U.S. economy, and yet current U.S. policies for the region are falling short. Getting on the right course will not be easy for policymakers. But the rewards for doing so will be immense. The risk of war in the Indo-Pacific is rising. But the United States and its partners in the region have the power to prevent another tragedy and to shape a better future that will benefit all.

A Four-Decade Drive to a Collision

It was inevitable that China and the United States would collide in a long-term and open-ended security competition. Both countries are now great powers with global and overlapping interests. This fact alone, however, is not reason enough for the diplomatic rivalry, multidimensional arms race, and war planning in which they are now engaged. The additional ingredients required for an increasingly dangerous security competition—the "fear, honor, and interest" Thucydides discussed in his history of the Peloponnesian War—have also appeared. Aside from fearing each other's military and ideological power, the leaders of both nations are under domestic political pressure to protect their country's culture and position in the world. And they understand that defending their nation's global interests is vital if their country is to continue as a sovereign great power.

A decade ago the trends of China's military modernization were clear, even if Chinese military forces had not then achieved the level of capability needed to threaten America's position in the Indo-Pacific region. Most U.S. policymakers then still held out hope that China would largely refrain from challenging the existing global institutional arrangements, which had greatly benefited China itself. It was not necessarily self-evident at that time that China's rise should increase the risk of conflict with either its own neighbors or with the United States. The expanding interactions between China's economy and those of its neighbors, the United States, and the rest of the world greatly benefited all those involved. None would seem to have any incentive to upset this valuable interdependence.

Nevertheless, China's actions have become more aggressive over the past decade, first during the later years of Hu Jintao's reign, and more so under Xi Jinping's leadership. China's leaders have revealed clear revisionist intentions supported by an accelerated military modernization. Increasing confidence, rising nationalism, and new assumptions about weakness and disorder inside the United States and other Western societies have catalyzed China's recent actions to expand its global diplomatic and military reach and to set the conditions for settling what the Chinese perceive as unresolved historical issues.

Whether the two great powers will be able to peacefully manage the resulting friction is one of the momentous questions of this decade. The costs of preventing conflict, preserving the region's gains in freedom and prosperity, and assembling a better security architecture will impose a heavy burden on the United States. Making the case for this obligation requires an explanation of the sources of potential conflict between China and the United States, the consequences of such a conflict, and the choices available to U.S. policymakers. The challenge that China now presents is forcing policymakers in Washington to assess the rising price of maintaining America's position in the region and to wonder whether better and cheaper alternatives to military presence are available. This chapter and the next will explore these topics.

China Rises Again—and Acquires a World of Interests

The economic reforms implemented around 1979 by Deng Xiaoping, and continued by his successors, unleashed one of the largest and most dramatic economic expansions in history. Deng's arrival as China's leader in the late 1970s was a watershed in modern Chinese history of a magnitude few then recognized. Observers of China appreciated China's long history, its former great-power status, and the latent potential of its massive population. But Mao Zedong's long reign of ideological mismanagement and Japan's aggression and brutal occupation in the 1930s and 1940s had reduced China to a low ebb. Given the country's long period of political chaos prior to Deng's accession, and a society for the most part trapped in subsistence agriculture, the economic colossus that emerged over the next four decades exceeded the most optimistic forecasts made at the time Deng assumed power.

Deng's reforms, which began in Guangdong province in the early 1980s and slowly spread across the country, mobilized China's previously unproductive population and created one of the largest and most strategically consequential economic booms in history. In four decades of frenetic expansion, China transformed from a country deliberately shut off from the world into a major power with links and interests in every corner of the globe. The boom likewise provided the resources to pay for one of the most dramatic military modernizations in history.

From the beginning of Deng's reforms in 1980 through 2019, China's annual economic output, adjusted for inflation, expanded more than elevenfold, a 6.4 percent compound annual growth rate (the U.S. economy grew at a 2.7 percent inflation-adjusted rate over the same period).[1] In 1980, China's economy was 24 percent the size of the U.S. economy when measured in terms of purchasing power parity. By 2019, China's economy, at purchasing power parity, was 96 percent the size of the U.S. economy.[2] According to the U.S. Central Intelligence Agency (CIA), China is now the world's largest producer of agricultural products, industrial products, and electricity and has the world's largest labor force.[3]

Perhaps of most importance regarding the clash of global strategic interests, China is the world's largest exporter of goods and services and the second largest importer.[4] China's economy under Mao was guided by the principles of autarky and self-reliance, with very limited trading exposure to the rest of the world. In 1976, when Mao died, exports and imports were each about 2 percent of China's annual economic activity. By 2019, exports and imports were 19 percent and 17 percent, respectively, of China's economic activity, with this outbound and inbound trade flowing to and from nearly every corner of the globe.[5] China's opening to the world after the Mao era vaulted the country onto the top tier of economic powers. But this rise also engendered China's dependence on the security and stability of the trade flows essential for its economy.

These stupendous economic achievements have raised hundreds of millions of Chinese citizens out of poverty and have provided inexpensive goods to consumers around the world. China's imports of raw materials, capital equipment, and consumer goods provide employment to millions of workers worldwide. By the same token, China's emergence as an economic superpower has also displaced workers and investments that could not compete with its cost advantages in the global marketplace. And while the per capita income of China's enormous population is still relatively low, ranking only 128th among countries,[6] China's economy now easily provides its government with the resources to acquire a military able to compete with the United States and its allies in the Indo-Pacific and elsewhere, a goal the PLA has avidly pursued since the early 1990s.

Of particular strategic interest is China's growing reliance on crude oil imports to power its economic expansion. In 2019, China imported more than 10.1 million barrels of oil per day, 70 percent of its average daily oil consumption.[7] Despite various initiatives to increase energy efficiency, develop alternative energy sources, reduce carbon emissions, and transition to a service-based economy, China's consumption of crude oil will continue to grow and outpace its domestic crude oil production. By 2030, China is expected to import 80 percent of its daily crude oil requirement.[8]

The imported oil comes from South America, Africa, the Middle East, Central Asia, and Russia, and that extends China's strategic interests to every continent. Some 77 percent of China's oil imports—more than half its daily consumption—must transit the Strait of Malacca and the South China Sea, making those waterways critical choke points, indeed a "single point of failure," for the daily functioning of China's economy.[9]

China's Strategic Goals

The leaders of China's Communist Party (CCP) determine the country's national objectives and design the strategies for achieving them. The cardinal objective for the leaders of the CCP is to maintain the party's absolute command over China.[10] As we have seen, Deng's decision in

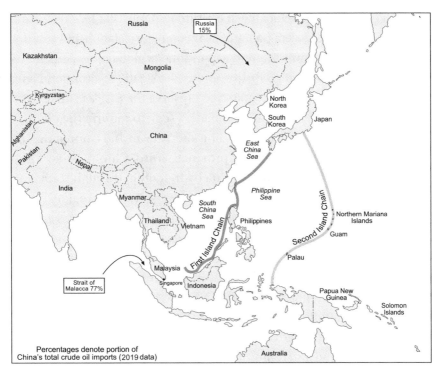

MAP 1. Pacific Island Chains and China's Crude Oil Import Routes. *Map by Charles David Grear*

the late 1970s to open China to the world led to the development of the economic and political colossus that China is today. But it also complicated the party's task of maintaining its control over Chinese society. Foreign economic engagement, while boosting China's prosperity, created new vulnerabilities that require strategies and resources to manage. The Chinese people's exposure to foreign cultures, a consequence of China's foreign trade and large student population studying abroad, similarly requires many more resources expended on internal security and control. Indeed, China's Ministry of Finance has reported that internal security spending exceeds the national defense budget by roughly 20 percent.[11]

Thus, Deng's choice to open China bought immense prosperity at the price of new external and internal vulnerabilities for the CCP. Deng's momentous decision has proven irrevocable; it is unimaginable that his successors might revert to the Mao-era policy of near complete isolation and autarky.

With China thus committed to expanding its global engagement, its leaders have formulated goals to support the strategic situation Deng left to them. Their paramount goal is to preserve the CCP's primacy and expand its power. Second, China's leaders seek to reunify the country by establishing control over Hong Kong and Taiwan and completing the pacification of Tibet and Xinjiang province. Third, China's leaders aim to secure a buffer zone around China by inducing, through trade and coercion, its neighbors to accept China's leading role in the region. Under this vision, there would be no role for U.S. military bases or forces around China's periphery. Finally, China is seeking global influence with the aim of shaping international institutions and norms of behavior to support its other goals and interests. Although China's leaders regularly assert that their focus is on internal development and on managing China's difficult transition to a middle-income country, their fourth goal is to establish authoritarian forms of government as legitimate, and even preferred, choices over elected and representative governance.[12]

Achievement of the CCP's economic and social development goals will be critical for achieving the first strategic goal: maintaining the CCP's control over China. China's leaders have likely concluded that the other three strategic goals, which would secure and stabilize China's regional and global positions, are also necessary prerequisites for ensuring China's continued economic and social development.

The leaders of the small and medium-sized countries in Asia have achieved their economic and social development goals by conforming to existing international systems and norms rather than challenging them. But China's leaders come from an authoritarian tradition that succeeded in ending the long period of political and social chaos that had shattered that nation's position as a great power. These leaders trust the efficacy of direct control over problems. It should be no surprise that they seek to extend such methods to the overseas exposures that they conclude could put at risk China's continued success and thus threaten the party's continued rule.

From the Chinese perspective, China is a divided country. Although Taiwan is the most notable example of a wayward Chinese territory, the island's status is only one of several critical territorial disputes whose resolution remains an important priority for China's leaders.

The leaders' second strategic goal—completing the reunification of China in accordance with the borders claimed by Beijing—would deliver several substantial benefits to the leaders of the CCP and to China generally. Establishing dominion over the remaining territorial claims would greatly boost the prestige of the CCP and reinforce the justification for the party's leading role in the country. There are likely to be substantial rewards in position and prestige for CCP members who bring about such a success.

Equally important are the potential security gains China would accrue if it could expand the breadth of its rule in the Indo-Pacific region, the third strategic goal. Like all great powers, China has an interest in expanding its influence over areas adjacent to its periphery. John Mearsheimer, an international relations theorist at the University of Chicago, developed a theory of "offensive realism" that explains this behavior by great powers throughout history.[13] Mearsheimer concluded that China will follow the strategic logic followed by virtually all other great powers in history (including the United States) by becoming the hegemonic power in its region. The purpose behind achieving this position is to establish a broad zone of security around the country, by either weakening potential rivals in the region or intimidating them into compliance with the regional hegemon's security requirements.

Over its long history, China has suffered from foreign invaders who penetrated Chinese territory from nearly every direction. The history of overland invasions from the north and west extends back thousands of years. Sea battles against Japanese fleets occurred over many centuries. More recent are the harsh memories of the nineteenth century, when an expansionist Europe employed its superior sea power to establish colonies such as Hong Kong from which they projected influence deep into China's interior. The result was social and cultural chaos, economic decline, and a century of humiliation at the hands of foreigners.[14]

The sudden downfall of the Soviet empire in 1991 dramatically changed China's security situation, creating an opportunity that China's leaders were quick to exploit. The Soviet Union's collapse removed the traditional threat of overland invasion from the north and west, and Beijing became free to reallocate defense resources to China's maritime approaches to its east and south. Since 1998, China has settled eleven lingering land border disputes with six of its neighbors, further removing security friction from potential overland threats.[15] Although notable land boundary disputes remain with India, it is China's territorial claims in the East and South China Seas that are currently creating the greatest tensions in the region. China's huge reliance on maritime commerce through these waters and its memories of European maritime exploitation during the nineteenth century are combining to direct its strategic attention in this direction, which is likely the reason why clashes in these waters are becoming more frequent.

China has an additional maritime strategic interest because it is a nuclear weapon state. China acquired a strategic nuclear arsenal because its leaders believed such weapons are an essential deterrent against potential threats from other nuclear powers. Like the other large nuclear powers, China has an interest in establishing a fleet of long-endurance nuclear-powered submarines armed with long-range nuclear ballistic missiles. This sea-based nuclear deterrent was a critical acquisition priority of the United States, Soviet Union, Great Britain, and France during the Cold War, and all these countries maintain it today. Strategic planners have long considered a sea-based deterrent the most survivable and thus the most stabilizing. Like the other nuclear powers, China believes that missile-armed submarines at sea will be a deterrent against attack.

In 2020, the Chinese navy (formally, the People's Liberation Army-Navy, or PLAN) operated six Jin-class (Type 094) nuclear-powered ballistic missile submarines. Each Jin-class boat is armed with twelve JL-2 nuclear-armed ballistic missiles, each with an estimated range of 7,400 kilometers. China is also developing a new ballistic missile submarine class, the Type 096, to be armed with a new and longer-range ballistic missile. The PLAN could have two of these submarines operational by 2030, giving China a significant fleet of eight ballistic missile submarines.[16]

Its ballistic missile submarine force could give China a secure second-strike nuclear retaliatory capability matching the retaliatory capability possessed by the Cold War–era powers mentioned above, but these submarines must have secure patrol areas where they will be relatively protected from adversary antisubmarine warfare efforts. Establishing patrol sanctuaries for its ballistic missile submarines is another motivation for China to extend maritime control into the western Pacific Ocean.

Finally, gaining its fourth strategic goal—to reshape international institutions and norms of behavior to favor China and its goals—would be a decisive step in securing China's global position and ensuring the continued rule of the CCP. The existing international institutions and norms, fashioned mostly by the Western Allies at the end of World War II, seek to protect and expand the rule of law, open economies, human rights, sovereign rights for all countries, democratic values, and the fair application of laws and rules. China's leaders, by contrast, are seeking, either by reshaping current institutions or by building new parallel ones, systems that will tolerate or even support authoritarian governments and norms, such as those practiced by China and its few friends around the world. In addition, China's leaders want new institutions and norms that will tolerate and support a hierarchy that favors the interests of large, dominant countries like China. Naturally, China's leaders intend to have the CCP guide these international institutions and set their norms.[17]

Having set a course forty years ago for rapid growth and attendant deep global engagement, China is now committed to a regional and global strategy of greater influence and control over trade, information, security, norms of behavior, and military power.[18] China's immediate neighbors in East Asia are bearing the consequences most directly.

China's Interests in the East and South China Seas

The First Island Chain, which runs from Japan's home islands to Okinawa, through the Senkaku/Diaoyu Islands to Taiwan, then to the western Philippines, and finally to Borneo (see map 1), would currently present a barrier to unrestricted Chinese naval and air operations in the western Pacific during a conflict. The islands in the chain host several bases for U.S. and allied military forces and could potentially host dispersed allied missile forces that could interdict and impede Chinese military operations and threaten the Chinese mainland. The U.S. and allied presence on the First Island Chain could also threaten the commercial shipping that is critical for the functioning of China's economy.

China thus has a strong interest in establishing its own permanent presence on the First Island Chain, which would break down the barrier to its operations and provide secure passages for its military forces and commercial shipping. Bringing Taiwan under China's control would not only be a great cultural and political victory for the CCP, it would also give China a PLA garrison, naval base, air base, and missile base that would be a large step toward opening unrestricted access to the Pacific for the rest of China's military power (chapter 7 discusses the Taiwan flashpoint in greater detail).

Secure access and freedom of movement for its military forces and commercial shipping are not China's only strategic interests in the seas off its coast. As mentioned earlier, China currently imports more than half its daily requirement of crude oil through the narrow Strait of Malacca between Malaysia, Singapore, and Indonesia and then through the South China, East China, and Yellow Seas (these three seas are collectively called China's Near Seas). With crude oil imports projected to reach 80 percent of China's requirement by 2030, China's exposure to the Malacca "single point of failure" will only worsen.

China's leaders likely see the large potential oil reserves under the South and East China Seas as a potential solution to this problem. The U.S. Department of Energy estimates that the South China Sea could hold up to 33 billion barrels of proved, probable, and estimated crude oil—enough for about 6 years of Chinese consumption. However, the state-owned Chinese National Offshore Oil Company (CNOOC) believes the South China Sea holds as much as 125 billion barrels of oil, enough for up to 23 years of Chinese consumption. Independent studies have not supported the CNOOC's conclusion,[19] but what matters for China's motivation and possible strategy is what its own leaders believe.

MAP 2. The Western Pacific Theater of Operations. *Map by Charles David Grear*

The dispute between Japan and China over sovereignty of the Senkaku Islands (in China called the Diaoyu Islands) in the East China Sea is an ongoing source of friction and a possible conflict flashpoint. These five islands (also claimed by Taiwan) are the site of regular flare-ups between Chinese and Japanese fishing fleets, coast guard vessels, and military air and naval patrols.

Nationalism and still-fresh memories of Japan's harsh treatment of China during World War II intensify and complicate the ongoing dispute between China and Japan over control of the Senkaku/Diaoyu Islands, but strategic factors are equally important. The islands are surrounded by rich fisheries that both countries want to exploit, but perhaps more consequential are the hydrocarbon energy sources under the East China Sea. The ongoing territorial dispute between China and Japan has hindered exploration and development in the area. The U.S. Department of Energy estimates the sea's proven and probable crude oil reserves at only about 200 million barrels, enough for just two weeks of Chinese consumption, but Chinese sources believe the sea holds as much as 160 billion barrels of oil, more than CNOOC's estimate for the entire South China Sea, and enough for thirty years of Chinese consumption.[20]

Thus, we can see strategic, economic, historic, cultural, and security reasons motivating China's claims and assertions across its Near Seas to the First Island Chain and beyond. Mearsheimer's "offensive realism" theory for the behavior of great powers is just a start. Regaining hegemony over its periphery would both provide security and restore China to its former place in Asia as the "Middle Kingdom" at the top of the Asian hierarchy. Seizing control of the East China Sea would settle an old score with Japan, would open access to the Pacific, and would provide what some in China believe would be an energy security windfall. Controlling the South China Sea would provide more of the same and would further reduce China's dependence on the Strait of Malacca. Finally, and perhaps most important for China's leaders, achieving these goals would advance the prestige of the CCP and solidify its rule over China.

U.S. Interests in East and Southeast Asia

In the eight decades since World War II, successive U.S. presidents have articulated a surprisingly consistent view of America's foreign policy interests. Although the degree to which particular administrations were willing to commit U.S. prestige and resources to security in East Asia has fluctuated, U.S. foreign policies for the region have been remarkably consistent.

As the dominant power in the region since 1945, the United States has had a leading role in shaping the international order in the Indo-Pacific. Nearly all the countries in this region have been remarkably stable, and U.S. policymakers point to the region's adoption, in large measure, of the principles and values supported by successive U.S. administrations as one of the main reasons for that. These principles and values have included individual freedom, democratic choice, protection of minorities, and the rule of law. Over the past half century, the economies of a large majority of the region's countries have flourished. All but a few countries in the region have transitioned away from authoritarianism and arbitrary legal systems since World War II.

The broad acceptance of another enduring principle—an open international economic system—has led the Indo-Pacific region to enormous economic success over the past seven decades, with gains in per capita income larger than in any other region in the world.[21] The region has been the best example to the rest of the world of how citizens' lives can improve through the application of the principles and values that the U.S. government has favored during this period. The United States will logically have an interest in preserving what U.S. policymakers will view as a triumph of U.S. values and policy.

The United States has long defended freedom of navigation in the global commons. Unrestricted passage in international waters is particularly important in the Indo-Pacific. About $3.7 trillion in trade—about a quarter of the world's total—passes through the South China Sea each year, constituting a critical connection to the rest of the world both for China and for major U.S. trading partners in the region.[22] Eighty percent of the crude oil shipped to Japan, Taiwan, and South Korea passes through the sea.[23] The global trading system relies on the security the U.S. military provides in the South China Sea and elsewhere, and disruption of the system would be very damaging to the global economy.

Trade through the global commons has been an essential feature of the region's economic success and would not be possible without free navigation through open sea and air lines of communications. It is thus little wonder that keeping those lines of communication open is a basic mission of the U.S. military and a long-standing goal of U.S. policymakers.

The United States has formal security treaty commitments with six countries in the Indo-Pacific region: Japan, South Korea, the Philippines, Thailand, Australia, and New Zealand.[24] These mutual defense pacts obligate the parties to provide military assistance to each other in the case of overt military aggression. In addition, the United States has a growing list of informal security relationships to which Washington is committing resources and prestige. Over the past decade the U.S. government has updated and extended its diplomatic and defense relationships with India, Indonesia, Malaysia, Singapore, Vietnam, and other nations in the region.[25] Defense relationships with these countries include exchange programs, training programs and exercises, visits from naval and air units, and military equipment sales and training.

U.S. presidents and statesmen place great weight on the reliability of U.S. security commitments to their allies and partners, in some cases even when ownership of the territory the United States has obligated itself to defend is ambiguous. The dispute between Japan and China over the Senkaku Islands is an ongoing example. In November 2020, just days after he was elected president, Joseph Biden called Prime Minister Yoshihide Suga of Japan to reassure him that the U.S. defense treaty with Japan would remain in force and that the U.S. defense commitment would explicitly cover Japan's administration of the Senkaku Islands. On the same day Biden gave similar commitments to the leaders of South Korea and Australia.[26] Biden's quick actions after his election are another example of the continuity of U.S. policies in Indo-Pacific region.

America's economic ties to the region bear heavily on Americans' standard of living. In 2019, the United States exported $573 billion in goods and services to its major trading partners in Asia, providing direct employment to about 4.5 million U.S. workers.[27] Indirect trading and economic relationships add millions more jobs to this sum. The Indo-Pacific economy remains the fastest growing in the world, benefiting both the U.S. labor force and those of its trading partners. Losing access to customers in the region due to conflict or a decay in the principle of open global trade would, through both first- and second-order effects, damage the U.S. economy and the standard of living of American workers. U.S. economic prosperity in the future will thus depend on sustained stability in the Indo-Pacific.

In sum, the United States has deep commitments of interests and prestige in the Indo-Pacific. Over the past seven decades, the region (with a few exceptions) has increasingly adopted the values and principles promoted by U.S. policies, improving the well-being of the countries that have done so. This success has advanced U.S. influence and has served as a positive example for other regions. U.S. policymakers have an interest in preserving this success. The preservation of formal and informal security commitments across the region is important to U.S. prestige and credibility, and substantial U.S. economic output and millions of jobs are tied to trade and development there. U.S. policymakers have consistently backed a policy of forward military deployments and engagement as the preferred means of defending U.S. interests in the region and furthering the credibility of U.S. security commitments. The increasingly urgent question, however, is whether China's rising interests, assertions, and military power will be able to coexist with America's.

China's Changing Strategic Behavior under Hu and Xi

The weight of China's new security interests, a by-product of the nation's four-decades-long economic boom, has caused its leaders to revise their views of China's role in the world. In the early 1990s, when China's new growth trajectory was clear but China had not yet become an economic superpower, Deng Xiaoping's dictum guided foreign policy: "Observe calmly; secure our position; cope with affairs calmly; hide our capabilities and bide our time; be good at maintaining a low profile; and never claim leadership."[28] That advice was suitable for a country that was an oil exporter rather than a massive importer and had a small economy and a negligible presence in global commodity, trade, and financial markets. China today is highly dependent on the global commons and has many other commercial and financial connections. The leaders of the CCP count on China's growing economy to provide the legitimacy that leaves their rule of the country unchallenged. The global commons in the western

Pacific and Indian Oceans are patrolled by competitors such the United States and India. At issue is the tolerance future Chinese leaders will have for this perceived vulnerability to their interests.

Under Hu Jintao, Xi Jinping's immediate predecessor, China began discarding Deng's dictum in favor of the openly assertive national security strategy we see today. The new approach takes greater account of global interests and vulnerabilities that were not so widely present in China in the early 1990s and manifests China's greater political, diplomatic, and military power and the confidence these sources of power have given China's leaders.

In 2004, Hu Jintao, then China's president and general secretary of the CCP, announced a new mission statement for the PLA. "Historic Missions of the Armed Forces in the New Period of the New Century" made note of China's global interests and expanded the PLA's responsibilities for protecting those interests. In 2007, the "new historic missions" were codified through an amendment to the CCP's constitution. This amendment reaffirmed the PLA's fundamental role in protecting the party's ruling position in Chinese society, assigned the PLA a lead role in providing a security guarantee during "the period of strategic opportunity for national development," and directed the PLA to "provide a powerful strategic support for safeguarding national interests."[29]

Xi Jinping succeeded Hu in 2012 and immediately began expanding China's overt aspirations and global presence. In his "work report" speech to the Nineteenth Party Congress in October 2017, Xi discussed in detail the CCP's goals and milestones for China's development to the middle of the twenty-first century. By mid-century, Xi declared, China will be a "fully developed nation," a "global leader in innovation," and "a global leader in terms of comprehensive national power and international influence." Xi's speech described a situation in which "international forces are becoming more balanced," implying that the United States and the West are in decline, opening the way for China to assume greater global influence. Xi had high praise for the achievements of "socialism with Chinese characteristics" and held out this system as a model of development for other countries.[30]

Xi commanded the PLA to complete its modernization by 2035 and to be "fully transformed into a first-tier force" by mid-century. "A military is built to fight," Xi asserted, and PLA commanders should "regard combat capability as the criterion to meet all [their] work."[31] To be sure, we should expect national leaders to exhort their military commanders in this way. But in the context of the PLA's rapid expansion (discussed in chapter 4) and Xi's openly declared goal for China to be a leading global power by mid-century, policymakers elsewhere should take care to contemplate the implications of Xi's declared goals and milestones.

Two years later, the PLA issued a new report that responded to the commands Xi had issued at the 2017 Party Congress. The 2019 white paper "China's National Defense in the New Era" combined a defensive tone with bold assertiveness. The paper repeatedly assured readers that China's military modernization had purely defensive intentions and that China's level of military spending was both low and much more reasonable than that of the United States and Western European countries. The report justified the need for the PLA's modernization by describing "uncertainties" in the regional security environment resulting from new U.S. policies and military developments. The white paper discussed some items of China's modernization (a new battle tank and jet fighters) while neglecting to mention China's hypersonic weapons and several new nuclear-capable missiles under development. By contrast, the report was boldly unapologetic about the PLA's air and naval intimidation of Taiwan, its buildup of military forces and operations in the South China Sea, and the PLAN's increasingly global operations and presence.[32]

Why a U.S.-China Security Competition Was Inevitable

A backlash is developing in response to China's changed behavior over the past decade. This backlash is global, multidimensional, and organic, and among both policymakers and ordinary citizens. This backlash, which continues to expand and deepen, will make it more difficult for China to achieve its strategic goals.

China is now paying the price for abandoning Deng's dictum to "bide our time; be good at maintaining a low profile; and never claim leadership."

Why did China's leadership choose an approach that seems contrary to the country's interests, illogical, and perhaps self-defeating? Had China's leaders adhered to Deng's dictum and grown the nation quietly instead, opposition to China would more likely have been confused, disorganized, or perhaps barely existent.

So, what explains China's seemingly irrational strategic behavior? In *The Rise of China vs. the Logic of Strategy*, strategist Edward Luttwak asserted that increased Chinese diplomatic and military assertiveness (which have expanded greatly since his book was published in 2012) is less the manifestation of a tightly coordinated grand strategy than the result of cultural behavior.[33] Within China's vast government bureaucracy, opportunistic and entrepreneurial mid-level officials display aggressiveness as a means of increasing the resources allocated to the agencies they control.[34]

This is likely a common behavior within any bureaucracy, but in the case of China, bureaucrats observe the behavior and goals of their leaders and respond accordingly. Xi Jinping, who is known for his micromanagement of the CCP's sprawling enterprises, must be regarded as the ultimate source of China's strategic behavior. Western policymakers and diplomats who interacted with Xi before his elevation to supreme power in China were surprised when he revealed himself to be a committed Marxist, an admirer of Mao and his methods, and a firm believer that only a strong CCP under his centralized authority can solve China's problems and achieve its strategic goals. This outlook goes far toward explaining Xi's assertive and nationalistic behavior, his confidence in his actions, and his surprising tolerance for risk-taking.[35] Ambitious officials throughout China's vast bureaucracies have followed Xi's lead, compounding China's aggressiveness.

Both internal and external forces will thus exert pressure on China's leaders to be more assertive regarding security concerns. Nationalism, energized by Xi himself, is likely to intensify. China's economic and social development has increased urbanization, education levels, and greater awareness of the world beyond China, although that worldview is filtered and shaped by the CCP's world-class censorship technology. Rising living standards, education, and global awareness inside China have also catalyzed a rising awareness of China's historical grievances. Such expressions of nationalism are common in societies and cultures that have experienced rapidly rising incomes.[36]

It is thus possible that in addition to their own desire to keep the party in their control, China's leaders will come under increasing pressure from an aroused population demanding respect for China's great-power status and may reap political rewards from responding to these nationalist appeals.[37] Conversely, nationalism may be a technique China's elites will use for social control if other forms of their legitimacy falter.[38]

The CCP's analysis of its external security requirements may result in even more assertive behavior than China has exhibited thus far. The starting point of this concern is China's traditional fear of encirclement by potentially hostile powers. The long-standing remedy to this concern has been to increase China's military power and to expand its zone of influence beyond its core territory, creating more defensible space, as Mearsheimer's "offensive realism" theory suggests.

China's leaders are likely well aware of the "paradox of power." That is, the more assertive China is and the more it builds its military strength, the more China's neighbors will respond with their own military buildups and efforts to contain China.[39] Yet when given the choice between military weakness and strength, policymakers invariably choose strength as the least risky option, if only because they are unwilling to bet on the good intentions of potential adversaries. China has clearly chosen the path of increasing military strength.

China's expanding role in the world has created new vulnerabilities that its leaders must mitigate. The first among these vulnerabilities is China's reliance on the Strait of Malacca to provide energy for its economy. Although China is attempting to develop alternate pathways for oil imports, including a pipeline through Burma, pipelines from Central Asia, and perhaps a canal through Thailand's isthmus, these alternatives come with their own vulnerabilities and in any case will not remove China's dependence on the massive flow of tankers and merchant ships through the Malacca Strait.

It is disturbing to note that while China has settled eleven land border disputes with six of its northern and western neighbors since 1998, in

many cases ceding more than half of its original claims,[40] it has accelerated its maritime claims in the East and South China Seas. China is thus
not opposed on principle to settling territorial claims. If, for example,
China's main interest in the Near Seas was the exploitation of the vast
hydrocarbon potential there (an important strategic interest), it would
seem a straightforward matter to set aside sovereignty questions and
instead negotiate deals with Japan, Taiwan, Vietnam, the Philippines,
and others to develop and share the seas' oil and gas. The fact that China
has done little to pursue this course indicates its unwillingness to achieve
mutually advantageous agreements with its maritime neighbors. Instead,
China has chosen to build up its naval, air, and land-based missile power
in pursuit of maritime dominance (see chapter 4). This choice of a con-
frontational path backed by increasing military power rather than the
mutually beneficial negotiated path China has used in disputes with
other neighbors is alarming.

Based on China's recent actions and behavior, we can assume that its
leaders believe that rapid military modernization and the acquisition of
maritime "breathing space" in the western Pacific constitute the proper
way to defend China's expanding interests and hedge against uncertainty.
But this logic has brought China into conflict with the interests of the
United States and its partners in the Indo-Pacific region.

From the perspective of policymakers in Washington and in the Indo-
Pacific, China's assertions in the East and South China Seas are an attempt
to rewrite international law and norms and to settle territorial disputes
by material strength and intimidation—if not overt military force—rather
than by negotiation. The United States has a strong interest in defending
the rules-based international system it helped to establish. That system and
U.S. interests would suffer should China succeed in unilaterally imposing
its will.

Further, U.S. officials must concern themselves with the credibility of
the security promises they have made to their allies, not just in Asia but
elsewhere in the world. Should China be viewed as gradually undermining
the existing security architecture in the Indo-Pacific, the reliability of the
United States as an ally elsewhere would come into question.

The stage is thus set for a security competition in which leaders in both China and the United States will conclude that the least risky hedge for each is to reinforce their military power. Indeed, this competition has been under way since at least the 1990s, when China shifted its military investments from land power toward aerospace and naval power and developed a military strategy designed to exploit U.S. vulnerabilities in the Indo-Pacific while the United States was engaged in the Middle East and Central Asia.

The post–Cold War decline in the U.S. military capability in the Indo-Pacific did not dissuade China's leaders from pushing forward with military modernization. After all, China's policymakers and military planners must reckon with America's potential future military power in the region and the possibility that U.S. intentions—along with those of China's neighbors—could change at any time for any number of reasons. And so it is for U.S. policymakers as well: as long as conflict is at least plausible, they and their military planners should prepare for China's actual and potential military capabilities.

That task will become increasingly complex, especially if it is connected to a strategy that maintains a U.S. presence in the Indo-Pacific. America's forward presence there is a legacy inherited from World War II, but many are beginning to wonder whether there is a better approach.

2

It Matters Who Runs the Pacific

C hapter 1 discussed why U.S. and Chinese interests in the Indo-Pacific region were bound to clash and why a security competition between the two countries was the inevitable result. But why should the region's security be America's responsibility, and why is a U.S. military forward presence there desirable?[1] Can the United States not avoid the expense and risk and leave the region's security to the Indo-Pacific nations themselves?

Indeed, are there alternatives to maintaining a U.S. forward presence in the region, a presence that risks a costly clash with a rising China? As the costs and risks of its forward presence grow, some policymakers in Washington, along with many skeptical constituents, will increasingly ask whether there are other policies that can avoid the burdens and risks of a forward presence. This chapter examines different paths the region's security structure might take, along with alternatives to the current U.S. forward presence strategy.

Four Paths Forward for Asia

Beginning in 1997, and shortly after each U.S. presidential election since, the U.S. intelligence community has published a *Global Trends* update. The purpose of these reports is to "stimulate strategic thinking by identifying critical trends and potential discontinuities."[2] Each *Global Trends* report projects economic, political, social, military, and scientific trends that could create significant transformations for global affairs. *Global Trends* is written by senior analysts in the U.S. intelligence community but relies heavily on contributions from researchers and practitioners in academia, business, finance, science, and other governments. In December 2012, the U.S. National Intelligence Council released *Global Trends 2030: Alternative Worlds*. *Global Trends 2030* described four possible pathways for Asia's strategic order over the next several decades.[3]

The first pathway was an extension of the present order, with the United States continuing its forward presence and engagement in the region. Under these conditions, the scenario assumed a continuation of rules-based cooperation and peaceful competition within existing regional structures. The scenario envisioned the continued expansion of Chinese military power, various mischief created by North Korea, and the potential for other security competitions. However, the U.S. presence in the region, and the cooperative security architecture the United States would maintain with its partners in the region, would continue to mitigate the consequences of these problems.

The second pathway, the most ominous and a focus of this chapter, envisioned a U.S. retreat from its security presence sparking a Hobbesian scramble for security among the region's major and minor powers. In this scenario, the Indo-Pacific countries would struggle to establish a stable balance of power, resulting in rivalries, shifting and re-forming alliances, and internal and external maneuvers to find security. Nuclear weapon and missile races would be likely as countries strive to compensate for the security vacuum left in the wake of America's departure from its previous security role.

The third pathway for the region envisioned the development of a pluralistic and peaceful Indo-Asian community resembling the better aspects of the European Union. This scenario assumed substantial political liberalization in China, universal respect across the region for the autonomy of Asia's smaller countries, and a dissipation of nationalist sentiments. If Western Europe's political and social development over the past six decades is the model, this scenario also implied acceptance of the region's existing security structure (presumably still largely guaranteed by the United States), some demilitarization, and a focus on economic integration fostered by the buildup of EU-like regional institutions.

The fourth pathway was a hierarchical Sinocentric order, with China establishing a sphere of influence over the region. Under this scenario, the countries around China would support a regional political and economic structure designed and coordinated from Beijing. This structure would be centered on Asian trade, development, and cooperation rather than on the open trans-Pacific and global trade and engagement that have been the norm since World War II. This scenario assumed an end to America's forward security presence in the region, with security and the region's foreign policy now under the direction of Beijing. This scenario would be a return to the Middle Kingdom system that existed in China's ancient past, with China's small neighbors as harmonious subordinates to China's leadership. In this fourth scenario, China's neighbors would lack independent security options and would thus "bandwagon" with Beijing to obtain protection.

Which Path Will the Region Take?

The first pathway, the current rules-based system, characterized by increasing security competition but defended by forward U.S. power, is the familiar base case. However, China's rising military power, confidence, and assertiveness will require renewed and reenvisioned political and military commitments from the United States. This pathway creates numerous problems for U.S. policymakers, who must convince U.S. partners in the region that the United States will not abandon them, while also avoiding the underwriting of risky behavior by these partners that could ensnare the United States in an avoidable conflict. Some constituents in the United States will complain about "free riding" and ask why these wealthy countries are not doing more for their own security and defense. Others will view China's increasing power as so compelling that it seems quixotic to attempt to resist or balance it. Given the costs, risks, and difficulties of the current U.S. approach, it is little wonder that many are looking for alternatives.

The report's third pathway, a peaceful and demilitarized region focused on development and regional institution building, would seem to be an ideal long-term goal for U.S. policy. Such an outcome would represent the triumph of the model the United States has promoted since World War II, with rules-based institutions, respect for rights and autonomy, and peaceful development. It would also permit a gradually declining U.S. security burden in the region as a more cooperative political culture takes hold, as it has in Europe.

Regrettably, this third scenario is the least likely to occur, at least within any relevant planning horizon. The catastrophe of World War II did not burn out national and ethnic grievances in Asia as it did in Western Europe. These grudges still linger, with rising living standards in China possibly fueling some of these feelings to burn hotter.[4] The Soviet threat catalyzed Western European unity after World War II, with the U.S. security presence also aiding the continent's unity on security matters. Old adversaries in Europe cooperated on building the North Atlantic Treaty Organization (NATO) along with trade and economic institutions that eventually led to the European Union. The Indo-Pacific region has no similar accomplishments in its postwar record. Asia's security structure after the war was much more complicated, involving not just the USSR but also Mao's China, a hot war in Korea, and postcolonial struggles in Southeast Asia that went on for decades. The U.S. security presence in Asia kept the Soviet Union at bay but did not eliminate many of the region's other lingering grievances.

China's political liberalization, denoted by pluralism and a truly open society, would seem to be a necessary (if insufficient) condition before China's neighbors could overcome their anxiety about China's burgeoning power. But Western-style political liberalization is hardly the goal of the CCP. Indeed, in one of his first speeches to PLA generals after assuming his position as leader of party in 2012, Xi Jinping discussed the Soviet army's failure to protect the Soviet Communist Party before the Soviet Union's breakup in 1991. Xi vowed that would never happen in China.[5] With authoritarianism in China, and arms races, nationalism, and unresolved grievances still present across Asia, the Kantian future described by the report's third path seems an unlikely dream.

Nor do the odds favor the smooth arrival of the report's fourth scenario, the reestablishment of the Chinese Middle Kingdom, with the region's other nations a supporting cast in a Sinocentric hierarchy. This scenario is essentially a restatement of China's third strategic goal (described in chapter 1), namely, control and pacification of a broad area around its periphery. China's stated aspirations call for "building a community of common destiny for mankind."[6] Many in China view a Sinocentric hierarchy as the natural result of five millennia of Chinese culture.[7] Japan, India, Russia, Vietnam, and others, however, would resist the establishment of a new Middle Kingdom. Should the United States reduce its security role in the region, that resistance would still occur, only in more unstable and dangerous forms.

It is important to discuss why China's neighbors tolerate—indeed, even welcome—U.S. security hegemony in the region and at the same time resist Chinese hegemony. Simply put, China is a large and powerful neighbor, and the United States, while also large and powerful, is not nearby. The United States requires the permission of most countries in the region to continue its role as the security guarantor. It requires bases, access rights, and negotiated agreements with local governments to project its military power across the Pacific Ocean and perform its security functions. If these governments withdrew their permission due to, say, bad American behavior, the United States would find it difficult and costly to sustain a presence there.

China, by contrast, is a permanent presence in the region that its neighbors can never dislodge. Should China engage in bad behavior, these countries cannot make China go away. They can only fight or accept China's treatment. Having security contracts with an outside power gives China's neighbors some bargaining leverage as well as an escape clause should they decide to end the contracts. When dealing with a powerful neighbor like China, the only way to achieve that same bargaining leverage is to match that neighbor's power, especially its military power. And that implies arms races and spiraling security competitions.[8]

Thus, hegemons are not all created equal. It is easier to strike a bargain with an outside hegemon than with a local one, an immutable reason why the U.S. security presence will be welcome in the region. Even more crucially, America's service as the region's security guarantor is much more likely to result in stability than would be the case if the region was left alone to find its own stable structure (more on this next). It helps that the United States has a seven-decade record of keeping the region's commons open for all and, unlike China, does not have territorial disputes with countries in the region. The logic behind why most countries in the region welcome the United States as the security guarantor, and why most would resist China attempting to play the same role, is a strong argument for maintaining this arrangement.

Which brings us to *Global Trends'* second pathway, the Hobbesian scramble for security, as the most likely outcome should the United States choose to reduce its costs by withdrawing from the region. As this chapter will explore, this outcome would likely trigger multisided missile and nuclear arms races across the region, with unpredictable and unstable consequences. The risk of military disaster inside the most important economic region in the world would rise abruptly. The U.S. economy and standard of living would not escape the consequences of these developments.

It is easy to see how the absence of the United States as an outside security guarantor could result in a dangerously unstable security competition in the Indo-Pacific. The rapid rise of China's military power will create the logic for an offsetting alliance by most of its neighbors. Some, however, may choose to bandwagon with China instead, especially if historical grievances make allying with some of China's adversaries politically unacceptable. Bandwagoning by some will increase the security anxiety of those that do not. Finally, some significant powers (e.g., Russia or a future united Korea) may choose to remain unaligned, which would compound the region's uncertainty as the players would have to ponder how these neutrals would act during a regional crisis. Should one or more countries conclude that stability is unachievable and conflict inevitable, the calculation would then turn to the logic of security trends, time pressures, and the possible advantage gained by striking first rather than waiting for adversaries to grow even stronger in the future.

Critics of this line of analysis will note that the region's high degree of economic interdependence would make such a security competition illogical and therefore unlikely (although their economic interdependence did not prevent war among Europe's belligerents in 1914). They will also point out that awareness of the destructive power of modern armaments should be all leaders need to avoid provoking a conflict. Finally, state-on-state war is widely thought to be passé, an artifact of a thankfully bygone era.

Even if these notions are true, they do not remove the serious security concerns that Japan or the Southeast Asian countries would feel should China and the PLA obtain hegemony over the western Pacific and the commerce that runs through it. China, Korea, Russia, and others would likewise become alarmed should Japan, in its perceived self-defense, become a substantial missile and nuclear weapon state and expand its navy to protect its overseas interests. The result would likely be several multisided and unstable security competitions that would leave decision-makers in the region with great uncertainty and little response time during crises.

One would hope that the destruction caused by the twentieth century's wars, and the even greater destructive potential of modern weapons, would deter aggressive behavior by today's statesmen. But while fear of the modern capacity for destruction might restrain some leaders, others might use this same fear as leverage against adversaries during a crisis. We hope that we live in a more enlightened era. But that hope may be a consequence of the post–World War II Pax Americana in Europe and the Indo-Pacific, which many now seem to take for granted.

U.S. policymakers will thus have to choose between the costs of maintaining its forward presence opposite China's military expansion and allowing the Indo-Pacific region to construct its own self-enforcing stability, knowing that if that effort should fail, the consequences to the United States and the rest of the world would be ruinous.

Nuclear Asia—It Could Get Much Worse

Of the ten known, suspected, and impending nuclear weapon states (the United States, Russia, the United Kingdom, France, China, India, Pakistan, North Korea, Israel, and Iran), seven continuously keep military forces in the Indo-Pacific region. Should the *Global Trends* Hobbesian scenario occur due to a withdrawal of the U.S. forward security presence, the number of nuclear weapon states would almost certainly rise. That outcome would assuredly result in greater instability, as multisided security competitions would likely break out. Military planners in the region would have to defend against multiple and possibly shifting adversary alliance combinations. The addition of more nuclear players would result in the need for greater preparation and stockpiling by all, since previously sufficient levels of nuclear munitions would no longer be enough. New players would mean further reductions in warning time during crises. Some leaders may view striking first at the hint of crisis as the only way to survive. Under the Hobbesian pathway, the odds of nuclear disaster rise substantially.

Should the United States withdraw its forward military presence, Japan has the capacity to rapidly become a powerful nuclear weapon state. Japan has decades of experience with its nuclear enterprise, having operated fifty electrical generation reactors and fully developed nuclear fuel reprocessing facilities and expertise.[9] Japan already possesses roughly nine tons of weapons-usable plutonium, enough for about two thousand nuclear weapons—more than the number of strategic nuclear weapons allowed on active service by the United States and Russia under the New START treaty.[10] Japan's nuclear industry intends to operate the Rokkasho reprocessing facility, one of the largest such nuclear fuel processing plants in the world. Although full operation has been delayed several times due to safety concerns, the plant will have the capacity to produce an additional eight tons of plutonium annually from spent fuel at Japan's nuclear power plants.[11]

As a world leader in industrial machining and electronics, there is no doubt that Japan could also manufacture the other exotic components of nuclear weapons. Japanese officials remind those concerned about its nuclear capacity that its nuclear enterprise is closely supervised by the International Atomic Energy Agency (IAEA). But the fact remains that Japan has all the ingredients required to quickly become a major nuclear weapon state should a change in the security environment in the region compel its leaders to make that decision.

Japan also already possesses the means to deliver nuclear warheads to targets anywhere in the region. Its civilian space agency has operated since 1955 and has extensive experience with liquid and solid fuel missiles. Japan put its first satellite into earth orbit in 1970 and has recorded scores of successful space launches, from low earth orbit to deep space. Its experience with satellite construction and its participation in the International Space Station program demonstrates the country's expertise with payloads, sensors, telemetry, and space maneuvering.[12] Japan's current boosters, capable of lifting almost five tons into geosynchronous orbit, easily exceed the capacity required for military intercontinental ballistic missiles.[13] In sum, Japan possesses the technical expertise and capacity to become an intercontinental missile power in short order should a security vacuum created by a U.S. withdrawal from the region make that necessary.

Although not quite as well prepared as Japan, South Korea could also become a nuclear weapon state. Indeed, some political leaders there have recently argued for this course, perhaps responding to the public's wishes. Public opinion surveys in 2017 showed that 60 percent of the public supported South Korea obtaining its own nuclear weapons, and 68 percent supported the return of U.S. tactical nuclear weapons, which were withdrawn from South Korea in 1991.[14]

In 2013, South Korean leaders pressed the U.S. government to modify an agreement between the two countries so that South Korea could build the same nuclear fuel reprocessing capacity that has been allowed to Japan since the early 1980s. Such a capacity would allow South Korea to reprocess the spent fuel from its twenty-two nuclear power plants into weapons-grade plutonium.[15] In 2015, U.S. and South Korean negotiators agreed to a twenty-year extension of the Korea-U.S. Atomic Energy Agreement. This agreement provides for uranium supply for South Korea's operating nuclear power plants but prohibits South Korea from nuclear enrichment or reprocessing nuclear waste to extract plutonium. Even so, South Korea's nuclear enterprise has the expertise to perform these functions, and many South Korean officials have complained that the restrictions under the agreement are too onerous.[16] As with Japan, South Korea possesses the industrial and electronics expertise to fashion the other components required for deliverable nuclear weapons. South Korean officials deny that the government is interested in nuclear weapons and remind observers that the country's nuclear enterprise remains under the IAEA's supervision. But the country is just a few steps away from having the capacity to produce substantial amounts of bomb-grade nuclear material, something a large majority of the public seems to support.

South Korea has eight types of land-attack ballistic and cruise missiles in service; two of those have a 1,500-kilometer range that can reach nearly all of Japan and much of eastern China. A new cruise missile under development will have a 3,000-kilometer range, enough to reach all but the far west of China.[17] When the new missiles are deployed on South Korean submarines, an even greater number of targets come into range. During the 1980s, the United States fitted similar cruise missiles with nuclear warheads, and Israel is thought to have done the same with its submarine-launched cruise missiles.[18]

Thus, although it would take longer than Japan, South Korea already has most of the nuclear enterprise and missile capacity it needs to become a nuclear weapon state. Perhaps equally important for political leaders responsible for making such a decision, the South Korean public backs such a move. It seems rational to surmise that the intensity of such a view would only increase should the United States reduce its security presence or Japan acquire its own nuclear arsenal.

India is already a substantial nuclear and missile power and has the capacity to further expand its capabilities and inventories. It is currently thought to have 130–140 nuclear weapons based on indigenously designed and produced plutonium cores (India conducted three underground nuclear tests in 1998). India also possesses enough plutonium and unprocessed nuclear fuel for hundreds more nuclear weapons.[19]

India has numerous nuclear-capable ballistic and cruise missiles in service and is developing new missiles with longer ranges and new basing options. The new Agni-5 ballistic missile, for example, has a range of five thousand kilometers—sufficient to reach targets throughout China and into the western Pacific. India is also testing a submarine-launched ballistic missile whose deployment would increase the survivability of

India's nuclear capacity.[20] India will thus soon have the capability to deliver military power into the western Pacific should its interests require it to do so, a development policymakers and military planners in the region will have to account for.

Taiwan presents perhaps the least likely, but also the most provocative, case of nuclear weapons potential in the region. In the 1970s and again in the 1980s, Taiwan launched clandestine nuclear fuel reprocessing programs aimed at producing its own nuclear deterrent against mainland China. On both occasions the United States forced Taiwan to abandon these programs.[21] Taiwan has stored spent nuclear fuel at three two-unit nuclear power plants that could be reprocessed into bomb-grade plutonium if a facility were built to do that. Taiwan also possesses the industrial and electronics expertise to assemble a deliverable nuclear weapon.

Taiwan is developing a long-range land-attack cruise missile which in theory could be armed with a nuclear warhead. The missile, named Yun Feng, has a range of 1,200 and possibly 2,000 kilometers, sufficient to strike nearly all of eastern China.[22]

The leadership in Beijing would view a decision by Taiwan to acquire nuclear weapons as highly provocative and quite possibly as a casus belli. Such a development would be tantamount to a declaration of independence from China, something that Beijing in the past has stated it would resist with force. Under current circumstances, Taiwan appears to have no interest in acquiring nuclear weapons. But a withdrawal of the U.S. security presence, especially if it led to nuclear and missile races elsewhere in the region, would create a different situation. In that event, a Taiwanese nuclear program could go from being a highly remote possibility to perhaps the most likely path to war in the region.

The Case against Offshore Balancing

Several well-respected scholars view nuclear proliferation in the region, especially for Japan, as a favorable path. These scholars argue that the United States should reduce its costs and risks by extracting itself from its commitments to the region. Should Japan and other Indo-Pacific nations then require a large nuclear weapons capability to establish an intraregional balance of power, such an outcome would be both logical and laudable.

In *The Peace of Illusions: American Grand Strategy from 1940 to the Present*, Christopher Layne, professor of international affairs at Texas A&M University, made the case for a policy of offshore balancing. The offshore balancing strategy assumes that America's only strategic interest in Eurasia is preventing the emergence of a Eurasian hegemon that could (but might not) threaten U.S. interests.[23] Wars between Eurasian great powers should not otherwise draw in the United States. Under a policy of offshore balancing, the United States would extract itself from its present security commitments in the Indo-Pacific region (and from Europe also) and then expect the countries in Eurasia to manage their own security. This strategy would isolate the United States from the effects of conflicts in Eurasia and preserve its freedom of action.[24] To some observers, offshore balancing appears to offer an attractive alternative to the rising costs and risks of forward engagement, especially as China's military capacity and geopolitical interests expand.

Offshore balancing would, however, require U.S. policymakers to take on a different set of risks and to accept some questionable assumptions. For example, Layne expressed little concern that multisided and destabilizing nuclear and missile races would occur in the wake of a U.S. withdrawal from the region. His view that "great power wars in Eurasia don't happen often" dismisses the stabilizing role the United States has played over the past seven decades and ignores the much greater destructive potential that would reside in the region should the United States withdraw and another war occur.[25] Layne similarly downplayed the consequences to the U.S. economy from a catastrophic war in Asia,[26] disregarding the millions of U.S. jobs that come from trade with the region, let alone the second- and third-order effects to the global economy from a great power conflict there.

As mentioned, offshore balancing is premised on the possibility that the United States might need to intervene in Eurasia to prevent a hegemon from establishing a position that would threaten U.S. interests. Such a strategy would not only increase the likelihood that the United States would have to return during a conflict to restore stability (because without a U.S. forward presence, the likelihood of conflict rises), it would also ensure that the United States would have to act under very unfavorable circumstances because it would intervene only if it appeared that an undesirable hegemon might triumph. The United States performed this task three times during the twentieth century (World War I and the two ends of Eurasia in World War II), and the costs of doing so were very high. In all three cases, U.S. intervention occurred after the potential hegemons had weakened the allies the United States intervened to support and after the potential hegemons had built up their military power and captured forward positions. In these cases, an offshore balancing policy sacrificed an opportunity to prevent conflict in the first place and ensured that the subsequent U.S. military campaigns to restore balance from offshore were costly and bloody.

Those painful experiences have led all U.S. presidents since World War II, along with a vast majority of U.S. policymakers from all political persuasions, to reject offshore balancing and support forward presence instead. Proponents of offshore balancing assert that the strategy reduces America's risks, but in fact it merely exchanges one set of risks for another. U.S. policymakers since the 1940s have found the risks of forward engagement more subject to their management and adjustment than voluntarily opting out of any influence on international events and then playing catch-up. When offshore balancing actually was employed during the first half of the twentieth century, the results were horrific. The proliferation of nuclear weapons and missiles (a policy supported by advocates of offshore balancing) could make the results of a hypothetical offshore balancing strategy even more catastrophic. It is no wonder that most U.S. policymakers across the political spectrum have shown little enthusiasm for the approach.

Can the United States and China Reach an Enduring Accommodation?

Is there an arrangement the United States and China could reach that would satisfy each side's security concerns and result in an enduring reduction in the security competition? What terms and conditions might lead to a stable and mutually satisfactory agreement in the Indo-Pacific region? As this chapter has argued, that is a question that China and the United States cannot wholly decide by themselves; the other powers in the region will have their say, whether they are included in the conversation or not.

In *The China Choice: Why America Should Share Power*, Hugh White, a professor of strategic studies at Australia National University and former official in the Australian government, proposed a framework for accommodating China's rising power.[27] White asserted that China's growing power and its desire to use that power to guarantee its security interests will make it impossible for America to sustain primacy in the Indo-Pacific region. He pointed out that China is already the most formidable country the United States has ever faced and concluded that an attempt by the United States to defend an untenable position in the Indo-Pacific will lead to an unnecessary conflict that will cripple America's interests. At the same time, White rejected offshore balancing and U.S. abandonment of the region, insisting that the United States, China, and other great powers in the region need to fashion a new and sustainable security order.

White proposed a "concert of powers" that would negotiate a stable arrangement that would satisfy the security interests of the region's great powers.[28] His proposal that the United States, China, India, and Japan negotiate "spheres of influence" is loosely modeled on the great powers' negotiation after the Napoleonic wars that stabilized Europe's security for much of the nineteenth century. White conceded that the Indo-Pacific's medium and small powers—including his own Australia—would be left out of the process and would be forced to accept their position in any new structure. But this outcome would be better for these countries than the great-power conflict that is the likely alternative. White argued that U.S. leaders will have to accept equality with the three other great powers rather than primacy, a reckoning he admitted will be exceptionally difficult for the United States politically. Equality for Japan would also mean the end of the U.S.-Japan alliance and Japan's emergence as a nuclear and regional missile power.

White's formulation makes several rather optimistic assumptions. It assumes there will be a convenient convergence between what each of the four great powers is willing to concede as nonvital regarding each prospective sphere of influence and what the other great powers will find acceptable for their security interests. The hoped-for outcome is mutually acceptable and nonoverlapping spheres of influence.

For example, White suggested that the Japanese and American spheres of influence would center on maritime interests in the western Pacific, while India and China would be satisfied with purely continental domains. But China's economy requires access to the South China Sea, the Strait of Malacca, the Indian Ocean, and far beyond. Indeed, the vital interests of most of the region's powers, great and nongreat, overlap and cannot be neatly divided up into contiguous geographic spheres of influence. This is especially the case for the region's vast maritime areas and is a cardinal reason for the concept of the global commons and free international transit through them.

White admitted that implementing his "Concert of Asia" would entail immense practical difficulties. He proposed it because he viewed the alternative, attempting to sustain U.S. primacy, as even more difficult and dangerous. But White's proposal still does not resolve the underlying conflicts. On the one hand, he assumed that China cannot be persuaded to accept the current rules-based international system in the region, even though China had done so until Xi acceded to power, and greatly to its benefit. On the other hand, White assumed that China would find its security interests satisfied with the concession of a sphere of influence that does little to advance the interests that Chinese leaders see as vital.

White's attempt to accommodate China would achieve little good while inflicting great harm. The result, as with offshore balancing, would be the region's descent into a multisided, Hobbesian security competition resembling the pre–World War I instability that finally resulted in a great-power war. With vital interests overlapping in so many areas, there is no chance of negotiating stable spheres of influence. Although White saw the 1815 Congress of Vienna as his model, the 1938 Munich Agreement, where Europe's great powers agreed to dismember Czechoslovakia on the eve of World War II, is a more fitting comparison. Asia's middle and small powers are highly unlikely to accept an arrangement that hands them their fate without their consent. Resistance and destabilization would likely result. Finally, the pullback of U.S. security guarantees combined with Japan's emergence as a nuclear weapon state would surely catalyze disruptive arms races that would thwart the very stability White's concert of powers envisioned. White is right to ask whether the status quo, guided by the U.S. presence as the regional security guarantor, is sustainable. Unfortunately, his proposed solution would only increase the region's instability.

Another issue is whether the United States and China, with such differing political cultures and governing ideologies, can comfortably coexist over an enduring period. Hal Brands, among other scholars, argues "no." According to Brands, China's leaders fear the prospect of democratic ideas taking hold among China's population, especially the growing middle class, leading to questions about the legitimacy of the CCP's authoritarian rule. China's leaders see the United States as the original and most threatening source of this prospective democratic "infection" and thus conclude that they must engage in a permanent and increasingly energetic ideological struggle against the United States.[29]

"Document No. 9," formally titled "Communiqué on the Current State of the Ideological Sphere," encapsulated the CCP's fear of a Western democratic infection. The document was a secret memorandum written by the CCP's Central Committee General Office and approved personally by Xi Jinping in 2013 that was leaked to Western media outlets. Document No. 9 warned that seven ideological "perils"—including "Western constitutional democracy," "universal values" of human rights, media independence, civic participation, and pro-market "neo-liberalism"—threaten to undermine the CCP's rule and must therefore be eradicated from Chinese society.[30]

Fear of these "perils" is the reason why the CCP and the Chinese government, represented by the "wolf warrior" diplomats at China's foreign ministry, unashamedly boast about the virtues of Chinese authoritarian governance while mocking U.S. democracy and its domestic shortcomings.[31] It also explains why the CCP and the Chinese government are now executing a strategy to promote China's authoritarian governance model to prospective partners and to a global audience. Apparently believing that the best defense is a good offense, China's leaders have concluded that rebuking democracy and legitimizing authoritarianism will reduce the odds of a regime-threatening democratic movement arising at home, as it almost did at Tiananmen Square in 1989.

The behavior of China's leaders is a clear indication that they do not believe they can peaceably coexist with an America that is still a global democratic power. Such an America poses an intolerable threat to the CCP. Leaders in Washington will have no choice but to deal with an ever more revisionist, aggressive, and well-armed China that is engaged in a constant effort to break down America's alliances, impair human rights, tilt the global economy in China's favor, and repeal the liberal international order the United States and its partners have defended and deepened since World War II. It is very unlikely that the United States could reach an enduring settlement with such a challenger.

The Taiwan Flashpoint

Taiwan illustrates many of the concepts discussed in this chapter. For decades, U.S. policymakers have faced a prospective decision on whether to commit U.S. military forces to defend Taiwan should the PLA attempt a blockade or a fait accompli–style assault of the island. These considerations have recently changed from hypothetical to much more tangible.

The CCP's long-standing position is that Taiwan is a province of China and that resolution of its governance (from Beijing's perspective, the removal of the current government on Taiwan) is an internal Chinese affair. The Chinese government will point to the numerous "One China" declarations and diplomatic agreements extending back to the Nixon administration as evidence of international legal support for its position.[32] Some Western observers find Beijing's presumed legal claim over Taiwan's sovereignty convincing.[33]

If the PLA could seize and pacify Taiwan at a reasonable cost, enormous benefits would accrue to China. Geographically, Taiwan is at the center of the First Island Chain. This island chain is currently occupied by military forces from China's potential adversaries that pose a barrier to the PLA's access to the broader Pacific Ocean. They are also latent threats to the nearby Chinese mainland, including China's most economically productive region extending from Hong Kong and Guangzhou to Ningbo, Shanghai, Nanjing, and to Shandong province. Capture of Taiwan would open a broad passage for the PLA's air and naval power into the Pacific Ocean and would break the line of adversary military positions threatening eastern China. A pacified Taiwan would provide bases from which the PLA could project its air and naval power against—and displace—U.S. and allied military positions along the Second Island Chain (Guam, the northern Marianas, Palau, etc.), giving China control of the major sea and air lines of communications in the western Pacific. This would give China immense coercive leverage over Japan, South Korea, the Philippines, Vietnam, and Singapore.

Access to crude oil is a central issue in China's planning in the region. East Asia (including China) will become increasingly dependent on the maritime crude oil traffic that runs from the Middle East, across the Indian Ocean, through the Strait of Malacca and Indonesia's other straits, and up through the South and East China Seas and the western Pacific. Although renewable energy sources such as solar and hydroelectric power will provide a rising proportion of the Indo-Pacific nations' energy needs, eastern Asia will continue to depend heavily on crude oil from the Middle East and Africa for many decades. The U.S. Energy Information Administration (EIA) forecasts that in 2050, Asia's daily requirement will be 51 million barrels per day, with daily Asian production just 6 million barrels per day, leaving a daily import requirement of 45 million barrels. China's daily import requirement in 2050 will be 12.6 million barrels. China will benefit from the development of renewable energy such as solar power, but in 2050, crude oil and other energy liquids will still constitute almost 16 percent of China's energy consumption, including 63 percent of its transportation energy usage.[34]

In sum, by mid-century, the Middle East will remain Asia's essential crude oil source. This means that for the next three decades, East Asia— both America's allies there and China—will depend on access to the Strait of Malacca and the South and East China Seas. The capture of Taiwan and, with it, control over the western Pacific's shipping routes would give

China dominant coercive leverage over Japan, South Korea, the Philippines, Vietnam, and Singapore.

For this reason, among others, Japan's leaders and citizens would likely view China's capture of Taiwan as an existential threat to Japan's sovereignty. Indeed, Japanese political and military leaders are stepping up preparations for a potential Taiwan conflict.[35] Taiwan might fall either because U.S. military forces attempting to defend it were defeated or because U.S. policymakers decided to forfeit Taiwan to Chinese control and abandon the western Pacific. In either case, the likely result would be a rapid cultural change in Japan toward strong rearmament, likely including nuclear and theater missile capabilities.[36] India's political leaders could also view China's capture of Taiwan as a step toward hegemony in eastern Eurasia. This is an outcome India would likely resist as an ally of a now nuclear-armed Japan.

Thus, the failure to deter a PLA attack on Taiwan could lead to the Hobbesian scenario described in *Global Trends 2030* and a high risk of war between major nuclear-armed states, with Japan and India resisting Chinese hegemony and attempting to protect their sovereignty.[37] This outcome would be a disaster for the entire global economy, with painful consequences for the United States and its workers.

The Taiwan flashpoint illustrates the beneficial consequences of America's role as the Indo-Pacific's security guarantor and the importance of continuing to deter prospective aggression by the PLA, including against Taiwan. Besides the economic impacts, the subjugation of a free and democratic Taiwan would be a human rights tragedy. U.S. prestige is also as stake. Most observers believe the United States would employ its military power to defend Taiwan, even if the U.S. government has not openly committed to do so.

The strategic consequences of Taiwan's fall dwarf issues such as the legality of China's sovereignty claim or whether Taiwan is doing enough for its own defense. It is up to the Taiwanese people to decide on their defense preparations. Whether U.S. and allied policymakers decide to resist China's possible moves to become eastern Eurasia's hegemon is a separate issue with ramifications far beyond the Taiwan Strait. A PLA fait accompli lunge for Taiwan would force the United States and its allies to make that decision. Chapter 7 will discuss military considerations regarding Taiwan and the western Pacific.

Despite the Costs, U.S. Forward Presence Is the Best Approach

With an enduring settlement between the United States and China so unlikely, current and future generations of U.S. leaders face an open-ended competition against a strong and persistent China. The United States will have to devise a strategy that can sustain this competition over an unknown period. The current U.S. policy of forward military presence and deterrence against aggression is the least risky and ultimately the least costly of the alternatives.

America's forward presence strategy in the Indo-Pacific region is not charity work. The United States has performed this task for seven decades to protect U.S. security, to avert more costly great-power wars that would inevitably involve the United States, and to strengthen America's standard of living by promoting the security and economic growth of its trading partners in the region. As an outsider to the region with no territorial claims, the United States is trusted to be the security guarantor, a role the countries in the region are reluctant to grant to one of their neighbors. That is why the forward presence approach has worked so well for so long.

The challenges involved in continuing this success will increase. China's rise has shaken the region's long-standing security structure. As mentioned above, a majority of South Koreans believe their country should have nuclear weapons. Parliamentary elections in Japan over the past decade reveal a public that is supporting nationalist governments that are expanding Japan's defense spending and its military doctrine. Outside China the region's defense spending has surged over the past decade, a trend likely to continue.[38] These may be early signs that the *Global Trends* Hobbesian scenario is unfolding, perhaps in response to faltering confidence in America's security commitment to the region.

When all the alternatives are considered, the United States has no choice but to sustain its forward presence strategy. Sustaining a forward presence, however, will require making major changes to how the U.S.

military equips, trains, and deploys its forces in the region. The most important role for U.S. military forces is to deter conflict by compelling potential adversaries to conclude that they would lose if they used force against U.S. interests. China's military modernization combined with a bungled U.S. response over the past two decades is now calling America's ability to sustain deterrence and stability into question. Why this happened and what the implications will be for U.S. strategy are subjects of the next three chapters.

The Origins of America's Archaic Military Machine in the Pacific

C hapter 2 explained why a forward presence of U.S. military forces in the Indo-Pacific region—the strategy the United States has consistently implemented since the end of World War II—is the least costly and least risky strategy for protecting U.S. interests. The history of how U.S. policymakers, military commanders, and planners have implemented this strategy reveals remarkable stability in doctrine, equipment, training, and tactics, even as adversaries have changed and disruptive military technologies have appeared.

The extraordinary constancy in how the United States has implemented its forward presence in the region can be attributed to the simple axiom, "If it ain't broke, don't fix it." The goal of forward presence has been to protect stability and prevent the outbreak of a war between major powers. Since the region has not experienced a significant war between major powers since 1945, the U.S. approach over the past seven decades can be said to have been successful. Considering the grave national importance of maintaining that success, it is natural to conclude that the United States should continue with the approach that has brought such good results.

This chapter and the two that follow will explain why that conclusion is now dangerously wrong. This chapter examines the historical background of U.S. military basing and operational concepts in the western Pacific, beginning with a planning document written in 1943 and ending around a decade ago, when policymakers in Washington began to finally take China's growing military threat seriously. In the meantime, a basing and operational concept developed for post–World War II contingency planning ossified into an institutional culture that is nearly impervious to significant adaptation.

While the United States maintained its steady presence, secure in its superiority, China's leaders began a military modernization program (the subject of chapter 4) based on PLA planners' studies of the 1991 Persian Gulf War, the 1995–96 Taiwan Strait crises, and subsequent U.S. military operations. This program is specifically designed to exploit vulnerabilities in the stagnant U.S. force structure, doctrine, and planning for the Indo-Pacific region. Assumptions that U.S. commanders have long taken for granted are no longer sound. Under these conditions, U.S. military forces in the region will be vulnerable to frustration and defeat in a potential conflict against China.

Should China's policymakers and military planners gain sufficient confidence in their forces and plans, the result will be greater Chinese aggressiveness during a crisis and an increased chance of conflict. There is an urgent need for U.S. policymakers and military planners to implement bold reforms in defense acquisition, strategy, and doctrine if they hope to maintain deterrence in the region. Long-ingrained service cultures and defense acquisition practices have resulted in U.S. military forces that are far too heavily weighted toward short-range weapon systems unsuited for the vast operational distances in the Indo-Pacific. Military command-ers and planners assume that lines of communication between forward theaters and the continental United States will remain as unchallenged as they have been since 1945. Finally, U.S. military planners assume that they will be able to sustain the "American way of war" centered on maximizing the number of combat aircraft sorties from centralized air bases and aircraft carriers, as their predecessors have consistently done since 1945.

Over the past decade, U.S. military planners finally recognized that Chi-na's carefully designed military modernization was placing the moribund

U.S. position in the Indo-Pacific at risk. China's military planners had studied U.S. operating methods and were fielding weapon systems and concepts to thwart them. China now has the capacity to hold U.S. forces at risk in the western Pacific out to the Second Island Chain, about three thousand kilometers from China's coast.[1] U.S. policymakers now realize that China's carefully designed strategy threatens to overturn the assumptions and doctrine that U.S. planners have taken for granted for many decades. But they face the immense difficulty of remaking an institutional culture that has spent those decades resisting meaningful reform.

The Origins of U.S. Military Strategy in the Western Pacific

To understand why U.S. forces in the Indo-Pacific became increasingly vulnerable, we should examine the history of America's forward presence there. The current array of U.S. bases and patterns of operations in the region traces its origin to the middle of World War II when U.S. and Allied forces were about to begin their bloody march across the Pacific toward Japan and eastern Eurasia. Almost eight decades later, and in the face of remarkable changes in alliances and military technology, the current U.S. basing and operational architecture in the region still resembles the postwar vision outlined by military planners during that war.

In 1943, planners at the Joint Chiefs of Staff in Washington prepared a classified study on postwar basing. Titled JCS 570/2 and approved by President Franklin Roosevelt on November 23, 1943, the study identified sixty-six foreign sites where access was required to meet the postwar mission requirements contemplated at that time.[2] Roosevelt's approval of the basing plan occurred immediately prior to the Tehran Conference where he discussed postwar planning with Prime Minister Winston Churchill and Soviet leader Joseph Stalin.

In the Pacific region, the authors of JCS 570/2 foresaw basing requirements across the main island chains in the central Pacific and then all the way to the Eurasian mainland itself. At the western perimeter, the list included sites in Bangkok, the Philippines, Formosa, Hainan Island, mainland China, the Ryukyu Islands, Japan, Korea, and the Kurile Islands.[3] The planners' stated assumptions included the defeat of the three Axis powers, the continued postwar solidarity of the anti-Axis alliance (which in 1943 included the Soviet Union and China), and the requirement to conduct postwar peace enforcement missions. The planners also assumed that the United States would have ongoing postwar security interests across the Indo-Pacific region.[4]

The designers of JCS 570/2 and its successor plans did not envision establishing large basing hubs and garrisons at these locations. Rather they sought access rights, mainly for U.S. airpower, that would place U.S. forces in a position to project power if needed and yet retain the flexibility to respond to uncertain contingencies. The planners also sought to deny these sites to others by gaining access rights first.[5] The broader strategy behind the basing plan was to establish a "perimeter defense in depth" whose border would roughly correspond to the Allies' military positions in Central Europe, the Middle East, South Asia, and the Far East at the conclusion of the war. The U.S. planners expected to have complete control inside this perimeter, especially over the Atlantic and Pacific Oceans.[6]

As early as November 1943, then, policymakers and military planners had disposed of offshore balancing as a future security strategy for the United States. At that point in World War II, Allied gains in the Pacific were limited to New Guinea and the Solomon and Gilbert Islands, with the bloodiest fighting still ahead. In the European theater, Allied forces still struggled to suppress Germany's two access-denial threats: its submarine fleet and its air defense network over northwest Europe. Ground fighting for the U.S. Army was confined to southern Italy. As in the Pacific, the worst fighting had yet to occur in western Europe.

But U.S. policymakers and planners had seen enough to conclude that they were not willing to forfeit the sea and air control the United States was currently paying so much to achieve. They further concluded that in the future, America's first line of defense would be on Eurasia itself; the nineteenth-century notion of oceanic protection had proved meaningless in the increasingly interconnected world visible as early as 1943. Finally, U.S. policymakers at that time already perceived that U.S. military power in the postwar era must be ready to respond to unknowable contingences on both ends of Eurasia. These planning assumptions reflected their conclusion that the United States would better protect its interests if it maintained a forward military presence on the perimeter of Eurasia. World War II had killed the concepts of "splendid isolation" and offshore balancing as credible national strategies.

In October 1945, a month after the end of the war, JCS 570/40, a successor to JCS 570/2, added basing requirements in Indochina, India, and Pakistan. The updated plan also recognized that the Soviet Union's occupation of the Kurile Islands would rule out U.S. bases there.[7] But this plan and its successors remained out of reach to U.S. military commanders and planners in the five years following the Axis defeat. Resistance from both the U.S. State Department and several of the Allied nations prevented the U.S. military from immediately establishing the perimeter-defense-in-depth approach first laid out in 1943.[8]

The Soviet Union's break with the West, the triumph of the PLA in China's civil war in 1949, and the outbreak of the Korean War in 1950 resuscitated the Joint Chiefs' overseas basing vision. Rather than the archipelago of largely ungarrisoned accessed rights envisioned in JCS 570/2 and JCS 570/40, however, the war in Korea and the standoff against the Soviet army in Central Europe resulted in the construction of large main operating bases in Germany, South Korea, and Japan. Large supporting bases in the United Kingdom, Italy, Turkey, and the Philippines sustained the expected front lines in these two theaters. While JCS 570/2 and JCS 570/40 had contemplated an array of air and naval access points that would support flexible and responsive expeditionary forces, the Korean War and the Cold War face-off in Europe resulted in massive garrisons of ground forces on the terrain where they expected to fight the next war.[9] This arrangement of bases, alliance relationships, and associated training operations remained largely unchanged for the next four decades.

Coagulation around Korea

The Cold War, and particularly the Korean War, swept away any remaining resistance in Washington and most of the host nations to the strategy of U.S. forward presence in Eurasia.[10] By the mid-1950s, the United States had either permanent bases or base access to support two broad missions. The first mission was strategic nuclear deterrence against the Soviet Union. This mission required access to air bases that would support U.S. Air

Force bombers, refueling aircraft, and reconnaissance aircraft around the USSR's long periphery.[11] The second mission was defending Western Europe from a possible surprise attack by the Warsaw Pact forces based in Central Europe. In Asia, U.S. forces remained on watch in South Korea and Japan in the wake of the Korean War's murky ending.

The second mission, the ground defense of Western Europe, South Korea, and Japan, resulted in the permanent basing of hundreds of thousands of U.S. troops on both ends of Eurasia. The specific tactical missions in both theaters resulted in these forces being concentrated in a few frontline countries. By 1957, more than 244,000 U.S. troops were based in Germany, more than 150,000 in Japan (including Okinawa), and more than 71,000 in South Korea. Substantial garrisons in Great Britain, France, and the Philippines supported the two fronts.[12]

In East Asia, U.S. military power began the Cold War era overwhelmingly concentrated in the northwest corner of the Pacific Ocean, poised for renewed combat in Korea. These forces remain concentrated there. The one substantial deviation from this basing pattern was the U.S. intervention in Vietnam, which saw large commitments from all four military services from 1965 to 1972.[13] The U.S. decision to fight in Vietnam was guided by the perimeter-defense-in-depth theory first drawn up in JCS 570/2 in 1943, which identified ongoing U.S. security interests in Eurasia and called for flexibility to respond to unpredictable security contingencies.[14] Although the military campaign in Vietnam failed to achieve U.S. strategic objectives, no U.S. administration since has given serious consideration to abandoning the concept of perimeter defense and forward presence in Eurasia.

The end of the Vietnam War brought the pattern of U.S. military positioning in East Asia roughly back to the status quo antebellum—namely, highly concentrated in South Korea and Japan. In addition to concentrating ground and tactical air forces for South Korea's defense, commanders and military planners began developing plans to employ the U.S. Pacific Fleet to strike Soviet military facilities in Russia's far east in the event of a wider NATO–Warsaw Pact war.

In the late 1970s, Adm. Thomas Hayward, the commander of the Pacific Fleet (and former commander of the Seventh Fleet, responsible for the western Pacific), promoted Project Sea Strike, which would greatly alter the wartime strategy of the Pacific Fleet. Previous war plans called for the Pacific Fleet to transit to the Atlantic to reinforce naval operations there in the event of a NATO–Warsaw Pact war in Europe. During his time as Pacific Fleet commander, Hayward argued for keeping the Pacific Fleet in the Pacific and employing its aircraft carriers for conventional strike operations targeting Soviet military facilities in Petropavlovsk, Vladivostok, and the Kurile Islands.[15]

Hayward reasoned this horizontal escalation of a Europe-centered conflict would stretch Soviet military resources, prevent redeployment of Soviet assets from the Far East to the European theater, absorb Soviet decision-makers' attention, and degrade the ability of Soviet forces in the Asian theater to conduct offensive action. Sea Strike strongly influenced the development of the Navy's overall maritime strategy that appeared in 1986.[16] Both strategies added forces to the already high concentration of U.S. military power in the northwest Pacific.

The collapse of the Soviet Union in 1991 did not lessen the concentration of U.S. military power in the northwest Pacific, it paradoxically increased it. In 1992, the Philippines government ordered the United States to vacate the large air and naval bases on the western side of Luzon Island that had served as critical support facilities during the Vietnam War. These bases were well located to support U.S. air and naval patrols of the sea lines of communication in the South China Sea, the value of which would greatly expand in the decades to follow. While the Cold War persisted, Filipino policymakers had reason to be wary of Vietnam, a Soviet client and frequent host of detachments of Soviet naval and airpower. But after the USSR collapsed in 1991, domestic hostility to a perceived quasi-colonial American presence at the bases became the top priority for these leaders. The ejection of U.S. forces from those facilities inevitably reduced the frequency and magnitude of U.S. forward presence in the South China Sea, and further increased the concentration of U.S. forces around Korea and Japan.

But as chapters 1 and 2 discussed, conflict flashpoints are now apparent in the East and South China Seas, in some cases more than three thousand kilometers south of the main U.S. military concentration around Korea.

Equally problematic is the easy proximity of these flashpoints to China's air and naval power. China has numerous basing options to project military power over these disputed territories, while U.S. options are comparatively constrained.

During the 2010s, U.S. diplomats and military planners worked to improve basing options for U.S. military forces in the southwest Pacific. But the resulting U.S. military capability operating from locations near the South China Sea is modest: a few patrol ships and aircraft in Singapore and a battalion-sized Marine Corps air-ground task force in Darwin, Australia. U.S. military forces conduct numerous small bilateral training exercises with the Philippines,[17] but the Philippines government does not allow the permanent basing of U.S. combat forces.

Farther east, the Defense Department continues to expand its basing capacities on Guam and neighboring islands Tinian and Saipan to support additional submarines, aircraft, and a brigade-size Marine Corps air-ground task force to be relocated from Okinawa.[18] But the concentrated U.S. military buildup on and around Guam only illustrates the fundamental problem U.S. military planners face in the western Pacific, namely a vast, empty ocean nearly devoid of usable islands and land on which to build ports, airbases, barracks, supply depots, bunkers, and all the other facilities necessary to support substantial modern military forces. China, with its continental position, does not suffer from this strategic shortcoming.

The recent efforts to diversify U.S. basing options in the western Pacific and to expand the U.S. military presence in the southwest Pacific will not be enough to staunch the deterioration of the U.S. military position in the region. The U.S. forces concentrated in and around Korea and Japan are clearly misplaced to deal with the increasing security problems and flashpoints well to the south.

The congealing of U.S. military power in bases in the northwest corner of the Pacific Ocean would not matter so much if that military power itself was more flexible and able to deliver its effects from longer ranges. Alas, that is not the case. Institutional cultures and preferences that became ingrained during the Cold War combined with basing geography inevitably led to the strategic problems policymakers and commanders now face.

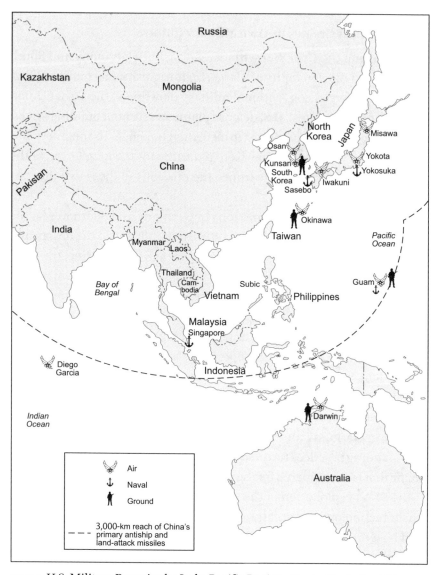

MAP 3. U.S. Military Bases in the Indo-Pacific Region. *Map by Charles David Grear*

Cold War Stasis Creates Its Own Military Culture

Tasked during the Cold War with defending both Germany and South Korea against the possibility of a large, high-intensity, mechanized blitz-krieg (the preferred conventional military doctrine of the Soviet Union and most of its satellites), U.S. defense planners set about building forces, doctrine, and training programs to meet this challenge. The planners also soon came to realize that they were planning for the long term. As the Cold War congealed on these fronts, the missions in these two theaters became open-ended.

During the long military missions in Germany and South Korea, the U.S. military developed a specific culture that influenced the design and procurement of generations of weapons, warfighting doctrine, training, and personnel selection and promotion policies. Over time, these ingrained cultural habits produced a joint military force that displayed impressive tactical and operational competence, at least when deployed against adversaries that mimicked the anticipated high-intensity Soviet threat.

U.S. joint and combined arms operations in Panama in 1989, the Persian Gulf in 1991, and Iraq in the spring of 2003 displayed this tactical and operational (if not strategic) competence. Those three missions were well suited for the particular military force the United States established for combat in Germany and South Korea during the Cold War. But these long-standing practices resulted in a U.S. military posture in the western Pacific that is not prepared for the military challenge China now presents.

The PLA's exploitation of the revolution in conventional missile and sensor technology has greatly expanded the ability of its forces, mostly land based, to hold at risk even well-defended warships and military targets thousands of kilometers from its territory. The naval dimension of this military-technical revolution began in the Soviet Union in the 1970s, with worrying consequences for U.S. naval planners and others in the 1980s.[19] As chapter 4 will explain, the rapid maturation and falling costs of the technologies associated with this military-technical revolution have allowed the PLA to greatly expand on the techniques and tactics the Soviets began developing five decades ago.

To cope with China's emerging capabilities to dominate land and naval targets far into the Pacific Ocean, U.S. military forces need the ability to strike effectively at greater ranges themselves. Regrettably, the trend across the U.S. military services over the past six decades has been heavily weighted toward highly capable but short-range weapon platforms at the expense of long-range strike capacity. These harmful trends have left U.S. forces in the Pacific highly vulnerable.

The origin of the current U.S. military culture—and its resulting preferences regarding weapon systems procurement, warfighting doctrine, training, and personnel policies—can thus be traced back to JCS 570/2 and the assumptions and policies imbedded in that plan for post–World War II basing and operations. JCS 570/2 and its successors assumed that the United States would have command over the Atlantic and Pacific Oceans and would thus be able to move and sustain continental forces to forward bases in Eurasia unhindered.

Under this assumption, the starting point for tactical operations would be any of the numerous U.S. bases around Eurasia's periphery. Tactical forces operating from the archipelago of bases around Eurasia that the U.S military created in the decade after World War II would normally have to travel a relatively short distance from a base to combat. These assumptions were sound at one time; from Korea in 1950 through to the military campaigns in Iraq and Afghanistan, U.S. forces for the most part operated at short distances from logistics hubs and tactical air bases and had unimpeded access to these bases across the oceans. As these assumptions were repeatedly confirmed over many decades and conflicts, U.S. procurement, doctrine, and training increasingly conformed to these conditions, eventually becoming a part of the services' cultures.

How the Air Force's Reach Got So Short

Airpower has played a major role in U.S. military doctrine since World War II. U.S. military commanders and planners view airpower as a competitive advantage worthy of considerable funding, and both long-range and short-range airpower were once substantially represented in Air Force budgets. Long-range strike capacity has declined sharply, however, while short-range tactical airpower capacity has become overwhelmingly dominant in policymakers' attention and resources allocated. This outcome is a result of the assumptions behind JCS 570/2 and its successors and the habits formed from access to overseas bases close to required action. Commanders and planners have formulated decisions based on these largely unquestioned assumptions and cultures even as the strategic situation in the Indo-Pacific region has made a stark departure from these expectations.

In 1960, the Air Force operated 5,488 short-range fighter and attack aircraft and 2,194 bombers, a fighter-to-bomber ratio of 2.5 to 1. The arrival of long-range Air Force and Navy strategic nuclear missiles in the 1960s allowed the Air Force to retire the medium-range bombers that had performed nuclear deterrence up to that point. By 1980, the number of bombers had dropped to 414, resulting in a fighter-to-bomber ratio of 9.2 to 1. The end of the Cold War in the 1990s, strategic arms control agreements, and the association of the bomber with then-déclassé nuclear weapons resulted in a further withering of the bomber fleet, which was down to 158 aircraft in 2016, with a resulting fighter-to-bomber ratio of 12.5 to 1.[20]

The 1991 Persian Gulf War, interventions in the Balkans later in the 1990s, the intervention in Iraq between 2003 and 2010, and the few large air bases the Air Force and Marine Corps established in Afghanistan after 2001 reinforced planners' perception that future conflicts would be fought from large, modern, and secure air bases close to the conflict. The U.S. military's recent aircraft investment plan assumes more of the same, with the number of bombers in 2028 holding nearly steady at 157.[21] That plan was written before the Air Force decided to retire an additional seventeen bombers (discussed further in chapter 7).

The assumption that its planes would have access to close-in bases was not the only reason the Air Force decided to focus on short-range fighter aircraft. One of the main goals of airpower doctrine is to establish air superiority, giving friendly air forces the ability to attack the enemy without serious opposition while simultaneously denying enemy air forces the ability to mount serious attacks on friendly forces.[22] U.S. military doctrine views air superiority as a necessity, because "no country has won a war in the face of enemy air superiority, no major offensive has succeeded against an opponent who controlled the air, and no defense has sustained itself against an enemy who had air superiority."[23]

Since World War II, the Air Force has looked to its fighter aircraft as the principal tools for establishing air superiority. They are flexible platforms for destroying adversary aircraft in the air and on the ground, and for defending airspace against adversary air attack. Missiles and bombers are also useful for establishing air superiority, but the Air Force views superior fighter aircraft able to achieve dominance over second-ranking opponents as the crucial tools.

Until the 1990s, airpower planners considered adversary aircraft the most serious threat to their own air operations. Before long-range precision-guided missile technology began to proliferate, missiles armed with conventional warheads were not deemed to have the accuracy necessary to threaten air bases that hosted tactical fighter-attack aircraft within a combat theater; only enemy aircraft employing pilot-aimed bombs and rockets could pose such a threat. For this reason, the U.S. services and planners put great weight on having the best fighters and antiaircraft missiles to establish air superiority and preserve airpower as a U.S. competitive strength. U.S. air bases in Vietnam, Iraq, and Afghanistan did occasionally come under ground attack from mortars or infiltrators, but such attacks were viewed as nuisances, not a significant threat to continuing air operations.[24]

Having emphasized the acquisition of first-rate fighter aircraft and keeping them at secure bases accessible to close-by targets, the Air Force's next logical priority was to establish a command and logistics system that would support a high and sustainable rate of combat sorties. Sustaining tactical fighter units at a high operating tempo requires a high-capacity supply chain that flows fuel, ordnance, spare parts, and other provisions to the bases. The logic of economies of scale, as well as host nation limits and better physical security, have typically resulted in the Air Force preferring a few large bases over smaller, more widely dispersed bases, which would be more difficult to supply for high sortie rates.

The current Air Force basing position in the western Pacific reflects that preference for concentrating forces at a few large bases. The Air Force has consolidated its operations at six bases—two in South Korea, two on Japan's home islands, one on Okinawa, and one on Guam. (Chapter 5 discusses recent conceptual thinking that departs from these practices.) Although the bases host aircraft of all sizes that cover the full range of functions, other than Guam they are all within fighter range of the Eurasian landmass, a requirement for an Air Force heavily weighted with short-range fighter aircraft. Navy and Marine Corps airpower in the western Pacific is located on Japan and Okinawa or on aircraft carriers, with all these strike aircraft being short-range fighters.

The current structure and basing of land-based U.S. airpower in the western Pacific is thus a product of its history in the region and the service cultures that hardened over the post–World War II era. Until very recently U.S. airpower strategy assumed that U.S. airpower would have access to bases near Eurasia and that there would be little or no constraint on supplying those bases across the oceans. Air commanders planned to generate high sortie rates through centralized logistics and by maintaining air superiority. Enemy aircraft were thought to be the only substantial threat to these bases. Air planners believed that they could thwart even the most serious threat to their forward bases so long as the United States had the best fighter aircraft. The rapid proliferation and falling costs of precision-guided missiles and munitions coupled with the expanding range of these weapons have dramatically changed the operating conditions under which the Air Force must function. Such weapons now pose a grave threat to the service's operating procedures, especially in the western Pacific.

The Navy's Range Comes Up Short, Too

Just as the Air Force's culture, inferred from its institutional behavior, is centered on its fighter community, the Navy's culture places a very heavy weight on its aircraft carriers and associated carrier air wings. The Navy's submarine fleets are also a prominent part of Navy culture; indeed, the deterrence provided by the Navy's ballistic missile submarines is arguably the most consequential mission the Defense Department carries out every day. But the Navy's own institutional behavior suggests that Navy culture, built up over decades of experience in a particularly stable and unthreatening maritime environment, values aircraft carriers above all else. In 1989, at the end of the Cold War, the Navy battle fleet numbered 592 ships, 14 of which were aircraft carriers.[25] In 2021, the Navy has 297 ships, a 50 percent reduction from 1989. Eleven are aircraft carriers, a 21 percent fall from the number in 1989.[26] The Navy's cruisers, destroyers, and supply ships exist to defend and support the aircraft carriers in wartime. Ranking lower in priority is their support to amphibious forces and the Marine Corps.

The Navy's aircraft carriers won the Pacific war during its critical early phases, when there were few alternatives. Decades later, the aircraft carrier proved itself highly effective at projecting power against land targets. Aircraft carriers have seemed to be excellent investments, with service lives running up to five decades. Navy planners have adapted them to changing times by altering and recapitalizing the air wing with constantly improving aircraft. For these reasons, Navy commanders and planners have reasonably concluded that the aircraft carrier is a dominant U.S. competitive advantage and a proven benefit worth sustaining into the future.

But just like the Air Force, the Navy's assumptions and institutional culture are facing new challenges. China's expanding ability to project its shore-based military power far out to sea is already forcing the Navy to reconsider the ways it conducts its business.

Aircraft carriers convincingly displaced battleships as the decisive warship after the 1942 fleet battles against Japan in the Coral Sea and near Midway Island. During those battles, carrier-based aircraft from both navies proved their ability to find and sink warships from much longer ranges than battleships could. The lesson the U.S. Navy took from this was that maintaining superiority in aircraft carriers and their aircraft would ensure superiority over adversary fleets, and thus control of the seas.

But in the postwar era the U.S. Navy found itself without any naval challengers, and thus without an apparent justification for maintaining a strong aircraft carrier force. The pressing strategic task at the start of the ensuing Cold War was deterring the Soviet Union, and it was the Air Force that proposed the solution: a large fleet of long-range bombers armed with nuclear weapons. The Air Force requested and received postwar defense resources to build this capability.[27]

The Navy was on its way to losing this interservice funding squabble when North Korea's surprise invasion of South Korea in June 1950 presented an opportunity for aircraft carriers to demonstrate their utility. The North Korean army quickly overran most of the friendly air bases in the south, leaving the beleaguered U.S. and South Korean defenders trapped inside the Pusan perimeter. The Seventh Fleet quickly arrived to provide the airpower the ground forces inside the perimeter needed to repel the North Korean assault.[28] During the remaining three years of the Korean War, eleven different large-deck aircraft carriers served in combat. Naval air crews from the Seventh Fleet's Task Force 77 flew 275,000 sorties, amounting to 53 percent of the close air support and 40 percent of the interdiction sorties flown by U.S. combat aircraft from all four services.[29]

During the Vietnam War the Navy once again demonstrated its capacity to project power ashore from aircraft carriers. Task Force 77 was re-formed at Yankee Station in the South China Sea to participate in sustained air campaigns such as Rolling Thunder and Linebacker.[30] From 1964 to 1973, Task Force 77 aircraft flew hundreds of thousands of attack sorties against targets in North and South Vietnam and had major roles in the war's air campaigns.

Operation Desert Storm, the 1991 campaign to drive the Iraqi army out of Kuwait, presented another opportunity for the Navy's aircraft carriers to demonstrate their power projection capabilities. In January and February 1991, the Navy gathered six aircraft carriers and more than four hundred aircraft into the Red and Arabian Seas as part of the coalition air campaign.[31] The Navy's aircraft carriers remained in the region afterward and participated in both the Iraq and Afghanistan conflicts of this century.

In these naval air campaigns, aircraft carriers were able to sail close to the adversary's coast virtually uncontested. Once in this position, the priority for commanders and planners shifted to maximizing the task force's sustainable sortie rate, the same operational imperative for Air Force planners operating from ostensibly secure air bases ashore. In the Navy's case, supply ships, sailing across oceans unchallenged, continuously resupplied the carrier task forces with fuel, ordnance, spare parts, and other required supplies.

Only once during the long era between World War II and the rise of the China threat did the Navy have to plan for a significant hazard to this familiar routine. Beginning in the 1970s, the Soviet Union appeared to be mastering the elements of the "reconnaissance-strike complex," a development that might have menaced the Navy's aircraft carrier strike groups before they could come within range of prospective Soviet land targets.

The USSR's long-range and land-based threat to the Navy's aircraft carriers entailed three components: ocean surveillance satellites, submarines, and reconnaissance aircraft that would find the American aircraft carriers; the Tu-22M Backfire maritime strike bomber; and the Kh-22M Kitchen supersonic antiship cruise missile. Operating from land bases near Murmansk in the North Atlantic Ocean and the Soviet Far East on the Pacific Ocean, the Backfire had a combat radius (i.e., the maximum range an aircraft can fly from its base or last aerial refueling point before it must either return to its base or to a refueling tanker aircraft) of about 5,000 kilometers. The Kitchen antiship missile added about 460 kilometers to this range. U.S. aircraft carrier strike group commanders thus had to reckon with a Soviet adversary that outranged the carrier's strike aircraft by a factor of at least four.[32]

In the late 1970s and extending into the Reagan administration in the 1980s under then–Secretary of the Navy John Lehman, U.S. Navy commanders and planners acquired platforms, weapons, and tactics to fight the threat presented by the Soviet reconnaissance-strike complex. These included the F-14 air superiority fighter, armed with the long-range Phoenix air-to-air missiles; the Aegis combat system and new surface-to-air missiles on cruisers and destroyers for fleet air defense; and tactics designed to find and shoot down the Backfires before they could launch their antiship missiles.[33] Since the Cold War ended without a shootout between the Backfires and the U.S. Navy, we will never know which side had the advantage.

The Navy plans to continue designing its fleet primarily around aircraft carrier strike groups. Navy officials assert that the next-generation aircraft carrier, the *Gerald R. Ford* class, will generate more combat power at a lower lifetime cost than the *Nimitz*-class carriers it will replace.[34] They point to the responsive and flexible roles aircraft carriers have played over many decades and maintain that carrier air wings will continue to adapt to changing circumstances.

For the military balance in the western Pacific, the issue for the future of aircraft carrier–based airpower is whether these improvements, while notable, will keep pace with the dramatically improved sensor and missile battle networks the PLA is now fielding (discussed in chapter 4). The carrier air wing needs to greatly increase its operations range to keep the carrier strike group away from these adversary battle networks. Unfortunately, U.S. aircraft carriers are designed to host short-range tactical fighter aircraft that are fated to be out-ranged by land-based aircraft and missiles. The institutional culture inside the Navy that promoted the aircraft carrier's role as an effective platform for projecting power ashore must now reckon with a military-technical revolution that previous commanders did not have to face in combat.

Indeed, the aircraft carrier's range problem is likely intractable. Aircraft range is highly correlated with aircraft size (the Air Force's large bombers have a far longer range than fighter aircraft), and the Navy's carrier-based aircraft have reached their size and range limits. There is no more space on aircraft carriers to accommodate aircraft large enough to have the range they will need to strike land-based targets while also keeping their aircraft carrier host out of the range of the PLA's battle networks. If aircraft carriers could accommodate substantially larger and therefore longer-ranged aircraft, the Navy would have already acquired them. Nor is it practical to build larger aircraft carriers to accommodate larger, longer-ranged aircraft. Midair refueling to extend the range is not a solution, because it would have to occur in airspace patrolled by adversary aircraft. To continue being useful in the western Pacific, aircraft carriers need aircraft with theater-wide or even strategic range, not the tactical range that is now the permanent limit. The Navy does not have a solution to this enduring problem.

In addition to its carrier-based aircraft, the Navy can strike land targets with Tomahawk cruise missiles. The Navy is also modifying this missile to attack surface ships at long range. Navy submarines, cruisers, and destroyers can launch Tomahawk missiles at targets up to 1,600 kilometers away.[35] U.S. Navy surface ships launching Tomahawks against Chinese targets would thus have to approach within China's antiship-missile perimeter to bring their missiles in range (more on this in chapter 4).

Navy cruisers and destroyers launch the Tomahawk from Mark 41 Vertical Launch System (VLS) cells (there are 127 VLS cells on each Navy cruiser, 96 cells on each *Arleigh Burke*–class destroyer, and 80 cells on each *Zumwalt*-class destroyer). VLS cells are also used for missile and air defense interceptors and antisubmarine weapons. The Navy's attack submarines can each carry up to 12 Tomahawks, and the 4 guided missile submarines (2 of which are assigned to the Pacific Fleet) each carry 154 Tomahawks.[36]

The number of VLS cells in the Pacific Fleet represents the maximum theoretical long-range cruise missile capacity of the Navy. According to the Navy's official website, the Navy currently assigns 12 cruisers, 36 destroyers, 25 attack submarines, and 2 guided missile submarines to the Pacific Fleet.[37] The Pacific Fleet thus has a total of 5,556 VLS cells for air and missile defense, antisubmarine warfare, and Tomahawk land-attack missiles.

The Navy does not openly report how it actually allocates VLS cells among its various missions. By one report, the "baseline" loading of VLS cells allocates just four cells on cruisers or destroyers to Tomahawks, with the remaining cells, almost 92 percent, allocated instead to air and missile defense.[38] Such an allocation reflects the main task of the Navy's surface combatants: defending the aircraft carriers against air and missile attack. If baseline loading is standard routine, the Pacific Fleet would have about eight hundred Tomahawk missiles available across all its ships and submarines, each able to strike one aim point. The VLS system affords commanders and planners the flexibility to alter this load-out, but substantially increasing the allocation to Tomahawks would come at greatly increased risk to surface forces operating within range of adversary antiship weapons. In addition, Navy ships do not have the capability to reload VLS cells while the ship is at sea.[39]

Although a highly useful weapon when used as part of a larger air operation (Tomahawks have been employed against adversary air defense systems at the start of air campaigns), the Navy's Tomahawk capacity by itself is insufficient for a sustained campaign against a significant opponent. During the six weeks of the 1991 air war against Iraq, for example, coalition air forces attacked 35,085 targets (often consisting of more than one aim point), of which 11,655 were "strategic" targets (targets other than Iraqi ground forces).[40] It is reasonable to presume that the potential target set in a conflict with China will be larger than the target set in Iraq in 1991. Thus, although the Navy's Tomahawk inventory would be a critical tool during a conflict with China, the potential target set in China will certainly be at least one and perhaps as much as two orders of magnitude greater than the Tomahawk inventory available in the Pacific.

With no significant adversary since 1945 to challenge it on the high seas, the Navy found a mission for its aircraft carriers in power projection against land targets. None of the Navy's adversaries after the Korean War had the means to prevent aircraft carriers from coming close to shore and setting up for long bombardment operations. Opponents occasionally had other ways of resisting; for example, North Vietnam's dangerous air defense system claimed 900 carrier aircraft and 881 naval aviators killed or captured.[41] But over the decades and numerous engagements, the Navy perfected a method for sustaining air campaigns from its aircraft carriers that orchestrated task force tactics, an ocean-wide logistics chain, and integrated training and personnel systems.

This meta-system for naval power projection, combined with repeatedly favorable operating conditions, established an institutional culture supporting the aircraft carrier. That culture now seeks to sustain itself with new and improved components such as the *Ford*-class aircraft carriers and the F-35C fighter-attack aircraft. Most of the Navy's senior leaders understand that the conditions that have supported this institutional culture for so long are now rapidly deteriorating. Chapter 5 will discuss how the Navy over the past decade has attempted to adjust to the Chinese threat.

A Treaty Removes the Army's Long-Range Punch

Beginning in the 1950s, the U.S. Army developed and maintained a variety of battlefield and theater-range ballistic missiles. The Army's missile capability reached its apogee in the 1980s when it deployed 108 Pershing II intermediate-range ballistic missiles in Europe. Pershing and ground-launched cruise missiles (the latter based on the Navy's Tomahawk missile design) provided an effective and inexpensive way of holding at risk targets that an adversary valued highly. Both missiles were mounted on mobile transporter-erector-launchers, allowing them to disperse and relocate during crises, making enemy targeting of the missiles much more difficult. During the Cold War, the United States armed them with nuclear warheads to allow them to attack hardened and deeply buried targets. The nuclear-armed Pershing II missile was highly accurate and was designed to hold Soviet leadership and command bunkers at risk. At the same time, the Air Force deployed 464 equally accurate ground-launched cruise missiles in Europe with the same mission as the Pershings: pinpoint attacks on Soviet command bunkers. A parallel purpose for these deployments was to compel Soviet leaders to agree to a treaty that would bilaterally remove intermediate-range nuclear forces from the European theater. Post–Cold War interviews and documents revealed that Soviet leaders were apparently so agitated by the prospect of the missiles launching pinpoint nuclear strikes aimed at them personally that they agreed to the treaty soon after the United States completed deploying the missiles.[42]

In December 1987, the U.S. and Soviet governments concluded the Intermediate Nuclear Forces (INF) Treaty, which banned the two countries from possessing land-based missiles with ranges between 500 and 5,500 kilometers. By 1991, both countries had complied with the treaty by dismantling their land-based medium- and intermediate-range missiles and support equipment.[43]

In the decades that followed, U.S. (and Russian) military planners were left in the odd position of merely observing while China built and deployed thousands of land-based short-, medium-, and intermediate-range ballistic and cruise missiles. The planners were relatively unconcerned initially that the INF Treaty prevented the United States from deploying land-based, theater-range missiles in the Pacific. The long-standing ability of U.S. airpower to roam widely was considered all the capability the United States would need should a conflict arise there. China's military modernization disrupted those assumptions, however, with major consequences for U.S. strategy.

China's military buildup combined with evidence that Russia was developing new intermediate-range missiles in violation of the INF Treaty led the Trump administration to exit the treaty in 2019.[44] Chapter 7 discusses what the end of the INF Treaty might mean for U.S. strategy in the Indo-Pacific.

Why Did the Pentagon Neglect China?

China's military modernization now places U.S. military forces, doctrine, and plans in the Indo-Pacific region under great duress. Ambiguity is growing about the U.S. military's capabilities and options relative to the PLA. As this ambiguity grows, so does the confidence China's leaders have in their military options. The U.S. Defense Department has a large budget, access to leading technology, and experienced commanders and planners, so why is this disturbing outcome occurring?

Planners at the Pentagon and at Indo-Pacific Command headquarters in Hawaii have arguably had three decades of warning about China's military potential. The Persian Gulf War in 1991 was the first large-scale demonstration of the damage a modern battle network composed of sensors and precision munitions can inflict on adversary military forces. Analysts at the Defense Department's Office of Net Assessment (ONA) afterward visualized what would happen to U.S. military forces and operational concepts if an adversary acquired similar capabilities. ONA research completed in the early 1990s concluded that when adversaries acquired the precision-guided munitions and targeting capabilities U.S. forces had used against Iraq's military, U.S. forward bases and the ability of U.S. forces to project power in traditional ways would be compromised.[45]

Subsequent reports from Pentagon analysts also discussed the looming challenge to U.S. forces and concepts; increasingly, China was named as the main threat. The 2001 *Quadrennial Defense Review* (QDR), a long-term strategy document Congress at that time required Pentagon planners to prepare every four years, followed up on ONA's research. The 2001 report warned: "Maintaining a stable balance in Asia will be a complex task. The possibility exists that a military competitor with a formidable resource base will emerge in the region. The East Asian littoral—from the Bay of Bengal to the Sea of Japan—represents a particularly challenging area."[46] The report went on to warn:

> Future adversaries could have the means to render ineffective much of our current ability to project military power overseas. Saturation attacks with ballistic and cruise missiles could deny or delay U.S. military access to overseas bases, airfields, and ports. Advanced air defense systems could deny access to hostile airspace to all but low-observable aircraft. Military and commercial space capabilities, over-the-horizon radars, and low-observable unmanned aerial vehicles could give potential adversaries the means to conduct wide-area surveillance and track and target American forces and assets. Anti-ship cruise missiles, advanced diesel submarines and advanced mines could threaten the ability of U.S. naval and amphibious forces to operate in littoral waters. New approaches for projecting power must be developed to meet these threats.[47]

The PLA did in fact develop and field all these capabilities in the two decades after the Pentagon published this report. Unfortunately, the 2001 QDR was written just before al Qaeda's September 11, 2001, attacks and was published a few weeks after the attacks. With attention understandably focused on the crisis then at hand, the report was lost in the confusion, in Washington if not in Beijing, where the PLA has seemingly used it as a blueprint for its force development.

The 2006 QDR explicitly mentioned the potential Chinese threat. Under "Shaping the Choices of Countries at Strategic Crossroads," the report stated, "Of the major and emerging powers, China has the greatest potential to compete militarily with the United States and field disruptive military technologies that could over time offset traditional U.S. military advantages absent U.S. counter strategies."[48]

The 2010 QDR was even more explicit. It listed eight areas of concern regarding China's military modernization that were "raising a number of legitimate questions regarding [China's] long-term intentions."[49] The 2010 report directed the services to develop a "joint air-sea battle concept" in response to the threat adversary missiles posed against the U.S. military's freedom of action.[50]

Despite these repeated warnings of China's potential—and then actual—military threat, the consistent policy of U.S. political leaders after the Cold War was to engage Chinese leaders in efforts to deepen political, commercial, and cultural ties between China and the West. The theory was that engagement would convince China to cooperate with the existing international system, since China's leaders and citizens would benefit from doing so. After that, the thinking went, China's leaders would be compelled to liberalize China's authoritarian political system because the Chinese people would demand it, and because liberalization would be necessary to get the most out of China's immense human capital.[51]

Former president Bill Clinton discussed the issue of bringing China into the World Trade Organization in his memoir: "I was strongly in favor of doing so, in order to continue China's integration into the global economy, and to increase both its acceptance of international rules of law and its willingness to cooperate with the United States and other nations on a whole range of other issues."[52] After a meeting in 1997 with President Jiang Zemin, Clinton wrote, "I went to bed thinking that China would be forced by the imperatives of modern society to become more open, and that in the new century it was more likely that our nations would be partners than adversaries."[53]

Former president George W. Bush described his theory, which matched Clinton's and the long-standing consensus in Washington, as follows: "Expanding American access to China's one billion potential customers was a high priority for me, just as access to the U.S. market was essential for the Chinese. I also saw trade as a tool to promote the freedom agenda. I believed that, over time, the freedom inherent in the market would lead people to demand liberty in the public square."[54]

In a 2015 speech at Georgetown University, Susan Rice, then President Barack Obama's national security adviser, defended continued engagement with China: "The United States welcomes a rising China that is peaceful, stable, prosperous, and a responsible player in global affairs.

It's natural that China take on greater leadership to match its economic development and growing capabilities. When China is invested in help-ing resolve regional and global problems, the United States—and the world—benefits. . . . We will continue taking steps to build a productive, cooperative relationship with China that delivers benefits for both our peoples. That's a central pillar of our strategy in Asia."[55] Rice did not men-tion China's rapid military modernization, which by then was both obvious and well known. The PLA's buildup and militarization of seven atolls in the Spratly Islands in the South China Sea was also well under way when she made these remarks. Her speech made clear the Obama administration's view that continued engagement with China would yield "a responsible player" that accepted the existing rules of the international system. In 2015, China was already pursuing an assertive, revisionist course in the opposite direction. But the Obama administration was committed to its assumptions, and Rice saw no need to discuss penalties or alternative courses of action.

Donald Trump was the first U.S. president in perhaps a half century to describe China as a serious geopolitical challenge, even as he began his administration under the hope that his personal relationship with Xi Jinping would lead to a settlement of differences, particularly regarding trade issues. Unfortunately, Trump's chaotic staffing of the Pentagon's senior civilian offices and his personal disinterest in deepening alliances with allied leaders undercut implementation of an effective U.S. strategy countering China's belligerence, which accelerated during his term.

Top civilian leaders responsible for U.S. national defense over the past several decades either did not perceive an urgent need to adjust to the growing PLA threat or did not have the ability to institute the reforms required for an effective response. In his memoir, Robert Gates, the U.S. secretary of defense from 2006 to 2011, described his efforts to divert some of the resources the Pentagon was using to prepare for future high-end conventional adversaries such as the PLA toward fighting in irregular and unconventional conflicts such as those in Iraq and Afghanistan that the United States was waging during his tenure.[56] Indeed, during the drafting of the 2008 National Defense Strategy, Gates expressed to his subordinates his willingness to take risks with preparations for future conventional adversaries to provide resources for unconventional conflicts.[57]

Gates repeatedly stated in his memoir that he took the growing threat of the PLA and other conventional trends seriously and supported programs and plans that prepared for them. But he also noted that U.S. forces actually fought in low-end, irregular conflicts during his long career and that the United States always seemed to enter these conflicts unprepared. He did not mention that the United States has avoided fighting high-end conventional wars over the past seven decades because it is these big, consequential wars that the Defense Department has done the most to prepare for and thus deter.

In any case, it is clear that Gates and his immediate successors underestimated the velocity of China's military modernization and overestimated the time the U.S. defense establishment had to prepare for the PLA once it became clear that such preparation was critically needed. For example, although the Air Force assigned the development of its new urgently needed bomber aircraft to its Rapid Capabilities Office (Gates permitted the program start in 2010), the first of the new B-21 bombers will not be ready for combat until the late 2020s.

Gates' successors at the Pentagon lacked the ability and experience to implement the needed reforms. Since Gates left the Pentagon in 2011, ten defense secretaries have occupied the post; none of them served as long as two years, and some served for just months or even days. While some of these defense secretaries might have had strong views on how the U.S. military should organize for the PLA threat (few did), none served long enough to shape the massive department to their strategy.

Senior military leaders similarly took their cues from their presidents and civilian masters and followed along with the "engage and cooperate" approach to China. In June 2012, for example, reflecting long-standing guidance from civilian policymakers to engage cooperatively with China rather than be antagonistic, Gen. James Cartwright, USMC, the recently retired vice chair of the Joints Chiefs of Staff, said that "AirSea Battle [a conceptual response to the PLA mentioned in the 2010 QDR] is demonising China. That's not in anybody's interest."[58]

In March 2013, Adm. Samuel Locklear, USN, then the commander of U.S. Pacific Command, provided another example of a senior military leader responding to the guidance of his civilian masters. During an interview in Cambridge, Massachusetts, Locklear said that significant upheaval related to climate change "is probably the most likely thing that is going to happen . . . that will cripple the security environment, probably more likely than the other scenarios we all often talk about." When asked about recent encounters between Chinese and Japanese warships near the Senkaku Islands, Locklear said, "We have an ongoing number of disputes. It is not just about China and everybody else, because there are disputes between other partners down there, too. Sometimes I think the Chinese get handled a little too roughly on this."[59]

Locklear, Cartwright, and other senior military leaders during this time were arguably following guidance and signals from their civilian masters at the Pentagon and the White House, an entirely appropriate and unsurprising response given the long U.S. tradition of civilian control over military policymaking. These policymakers concluded that there was little justification, and some risk, in spending resources on a hedge should China choose differently than was widely expected. But the result was the loss of several decades that could have been spent preparing for the Chinese military threat, a regrettable outcome for which the top civilian policymakers are ultimately responsible.

Beyond presidential policymaking, there are additional reasons why the Pentagon slept while the PLA built its military power. These reasons trace back to bureaucratic culture. The armed services' entrenched cultures reward officers who support their traditions and maintain continuity with the "installed base" of current programs, organizations, and policies. This is especially true when those programs, organizations, and policies are commonly accepted as having worked. The Air Force's fighter aircraft rule the skies while the Navy's aircraft carriers rule the seas; to argue against this success from inside the institution is to risk being branded an eccentric, even if the conditions that led to that success are quickly changing.

Economic and political interests also reinforce inertia regarding military programs and doctrine. Local political interests and defense contractors will seek to maintain current military bases and operational patterns, along with the defense industrial base that supports them.

An additional problem for the officials and planners responsible for designing U.S. military forces involves the broad range of tasks assigned to these forces, which range from strategic nuclear deterrence to providing humanitarian relief after natural disasters. Military forces designed and funded for such a wide range of geographic and functional responsibilities are generally capable of many things but are not optimized to be the best at certain narrowly focused tasks.

The PLA, by contrast, can focus its energy and resources, at least at this moment in China's history, on a very specific mission: preventing U.S. military forces from operating in or near China's Near Seas. China has concentrated on that specific task for three decades and now fields well-designed forces to accomplish that discrete mission. There is an urgent need for the United States to design an equally specialized response. But paying for that unique response will subtract resources needed for responsibilities currently assigned to the services elsewhere in the world.

The design that planners chose for U.S airpower three decades ago illustrates the effects of bureaucratic inertia and a lack of decision-making agility. In retrospect, a mistaken focus on contingencies in Europe resulted in the recent acquisition of combat aircraft that are unsuited for the vast distances in the Indo-Pacific theater.

In the 1980s, for example, the Air Force began designing a replacement for its F-15 air superiority fighter.[60] The Cold War military competition with the Soviet Union was climaxing at that time, and the NATO Central Front was the focus of contingency planning. That front was characterized by a relatively small geographic area and access to dozens of potential air bases for fighter operations. The result of these planning assumptions was the F-22, a highly capable but short-ranged fighter that suited the requirements of the European theater.

But what was adequate for Europe is not adequate for the Indo-Pacific region. If we defined the NATO Central Front as a rectangle extending from the Bay of Biscay to Warsaw and from Rome to Copenhagen, we would have a rectangle that would fit inside the Philippine Sea, which is just one portion of the massive Indo-Pacific theater with which U.S. airpower must cope. The Air Force operates from just six main air bases in the western Pacific rather than the potentially dozens that would have been available in Europe during the Cold War. Cold War Eurocentrism, as it related to airpower design, thus detracted from the U.S. military position in the Indo-Pacific.

The F-35 Joint Strike Fighter program illustrates several of the institutional maladies discussed above. In the 1990s, the Air Force, Navy, and Marine Corps pursued plans to replace their legacy fighter aircraft models: the F-16 and A-10 for the Air Force, older F/A-18s for the Navy, and the F/A-18 and AV-8B for the Marine Corps. Acquisition officials at the Pentagon perceived an opportunity to reap large economies of scale, in both acquisition and sustainment, by using a common design for all these replacements. The F-35 program gave officials and planners the opportunity to make a fresh assessment about what capabilities would be required for future post-European conflict areas. The vastness of the Indo-Pacific theater should have indicated a need for strike aircraft with vastly more range than the four strike-fighters that were being replaced. Instead, the three services agreed to the F-35 that, while much more sophisticated than the legacy aircraft, has inadequate range for the Indo-Pacific region.

There are essentially two reasons why the F-35 emerged as the planners' choice. First were the incentives to perpetuate the services' institutional cultures: the F-35 provided continuity for each service's fighter community. Second, and related, is the cultural supremacy of the aircraft carrier inside the Navy. As mentioned above, conforming to the size restrictions imposed on carrier aircraft meant that the Navy's F-35C could not exceed a certain size and would thus be limited to a combat radius of about 1,100 kilometers. After Defense Department officials opted early on for a joint program to achieve economies of scale, the Air Force and the Marine Corps had to use the same air frame for their versions of the F-35.

For the Air Force, this removed the option of a larger medium-range strike aircraft such as a replacement for its current F-15E (combat radius of about 1,600 kilometers) or its retired F-111F, which had a combat radius of about 2,300 kilometers, more than twice that of the F-35.[61] As a result of these pressures for conformity, the three services are getting a highly sophisticated strike aircraft with a range too short for the Indo-Pacific theater.

Prior to the 1991 Persian Gulf War, air planners relied on fighter-attack aircraft to deliver precisely aimed bombs, either through pilot skill in a low-altitude attack or by using a laser to designate the target for a guided bomb. Large bombers like the B-52 still delivered conventional bombs in long, unguided "carpet bomb" strings. But later in the decade, that changed. In the late 1990s and into the 2000s the Air Force repeatedly modified its three large bomber types to deliver conventional munitions precisely at short and long ranges through satellite, inertial, and laser guidance.[62] After these modifications, small fighter-attack aircraft no longer had a monopoly on precision strike capability. Long-range strike aircraft can now perform all the air-to-ground missions that fighter-attack aircraft perform, but with more than five times the combat radius.

ONA's research during the 1990s and the 2001 QDR made it clear that shortcomings in the U.S. force design in the Pacific were looming and should have obligated U.S. defense officials to think about airpower design from first principles. The late 1990s, when the bomber upgrades began and the first decision on the Joint Strike Fighter approached, was an opportunity for these officials to think about airpower in creative ways. Regrettably for the current balance of power in the Pacific, they and their successors did not take advantage of the opportunity.

Complacency, institutional cultures, and unwillingness to confront the situation have caused the United States to get a dangerously late start on preparing for the security competition in the Indo-Pacific region. But all is not lost. The history of U.S. strategy during the Cold War shows that when U.S. policymakers and the defense community focus their attention and resources on an important security issue, they can usually achieve a favorable outcome. The concern for security in the Indo-Pacific is whether U.S. policymakers and military planners can fix the problems in time.

4

China's Strategy

The Missile Revolution and Political Warfare

During the first two decades of the twenty-first century, China has executed a three-pronged approach to achieve dominion over its maritime frontier to the east and south of the Chinese homeland, one of its four strategic goals. The first part of this effort involves "salami-slicing" to gradually acquire territories in the Near Seas. Salami-slicing is the slow accumulation of small changes, none of which in isolation amounts to a casus belli, but which can add up over time to a significant strategic change. China successfully used salami-slicing to build up and militarize without any effective resistance the features it occupies in the Paracel and Spratly Island chains.

Political warfare campaigns constitute China's second approach to dominating the Near Seas. These campaigns employ economic trade; financial assistance; information operations; subversion of media, universities, and business networks; and support to friendly nongovernmental organizations with a goal of undermining resistance. Salami-slicing to expand its perimeter and political warfare to pacify potential resistance to its efforts have been kept below a level that would spark a military response.

The third prong of China's approach to maritime dominion in the western Pacific is its carefully designed military modernization program, aimed toward "counter-intervention" ("anti-access" in U.S. military parlance), to thwart any prospective military intervention led by U.S. military forces to roll back the dominion China has established beyond its periphery. China's military buildup over the past quarter century is among the most rapid in history. Just as remarkable is the program designers' thorough study of the U.S. military's vulnerabilities (discussed in chapter 3) and the program's design to exploit these vulnerabilities.

This carefully thought-out approach has put the United States and its partners in the region in a quandary. They are going to have to summon the stamina to match China's persistence and the will to risk brinkmanship with another great power. Meanwhile, they will have to understand the threat China's military modernization poses to U.S. and allied forces in the Indo-Pacific and then be willing to make substantial reforms to these forces to defuse China's plan. Neither of these efforts will be easy.

This chapter describes China's military modernization and discusses why it has so effectively exploited U.S. military vulnerabilities in the Indo-Pacific. China is reaching the limits of what it can accomplish through salami-slicing and political warfare, and going forward, it is going to use an increasingly militarized strategy, which will increase the region's dangers in the decade ahead.

The Origin and Goals of China's Military Modernization

The Chinese military force emerging in the 2020s traces its origins to the early 1990s, when several incidents guided China's subsequent force planning and catalyzed its pace of modernization.[1] The first catalyst was the 1991 Persian Gulf War, which displayed for China's military planners and policymakers the stunning battlefield effectiveness of airpower, precision-guided munitions, and a modern intelligence and command infrastructure. The PLA of that period was still dominated by a bloated and largely immobile army that was supported by obsolete aircraft and warships. After witnessing the rapid and lopsided rout inflicted by the U.S.-led force against the Iraqi army, PLA leaders knew they needed to implement drastic reforms.

Next came the Taiwan Strait crises of 1995–96, prompted by China's attempts to influence Taiwan's election through PLA missile tests aimed into waters off the island. The Clinton administration countered this attempt at intimidation by sending two U.S. Navy aircraft carrier strike groups near Taiwan, confident that China's antiship capabilities could do nothing to stop them. China's impotence at this American show of force was a further accelerant to PLA modernization.

Since then, the PLA has embraced the current military-technical revolution and applied it to modernize its forces. The goal of this modernization program is to build forces and supporting infrastructure that will give China the military capacity to dominate a deep air and maritime buffer zone beyond China's coast. In wartime, this capacity would prevent an adversary's strike and expeditionary forces from entering the Near Seas.

China's leadership has taken several steps since the 1990s to achieve these results. According to the Stockholm International Peace Research Institute (SIPRI) database of military expenditures, China's defense spending rose more than seventeen-fold between 1995 and 2019, a 12 percent compound annual rate.[2] This tremendous growth in military spending by a major power, sustained during peacetime and over twenty-five years, is nearly unprecedented and shows that China's leaders believe in the utility of military power. Next, China reallocated defense resources during this period from its land forces to its naval, air, space, and missile forces. As mentioned earlier, China settled territorial disputes to its north and west, which permitted it to focus on naval, air, space, and missile modernization. Finally, China's industrial development has enabled the establishment of a high-technology research and industrial base to support its military modernization.[3]

Studies of past military modernization programs during military-technical revolutions such as the current sensor and missile revolution indicate that the most successful programs are those whose planners had a specific future adversary to study and a specific operational task to achieve.[4] That describes China's current military modernization program, which is focused on preventing U.S. naval and aerospace power from operating effectively in or near the Near Seas during a conflict. The specificity of China's task contrasts with the broad and vague set of missions for which U.S. military forces must prepare. As chapter 3 discussed, this lack of focus has left U.S. forces unprepared for the military challenge China presents.

China has concentrated its modernization program on achieving its security objectives in the Indo-Pacific region. Its plans to acquire aircraft carriers and large cargo and refueling aircraft, and its various out-of-region naval missions such as those off Somalia likely foreshadow global ambitions. Even so, China's most dramatic military developments to date encompass its capabilities to exert growing naval and aerospace power within its home region.

Although thus far locally focused, China's emerging military capabilities will have global consequences. An attempt to achieve hegemony in the Indo-Pacific would create a dangerous and destabilizing security competition among the region's large and small rivals that could result in conflict and great damage to the global economy and security system. So even though China's military modernization largely retains a regional focus, that should be no comfort to U.S. and allied policymakers.

China's Vision to Rule the Sea from the Land

China plans to defend its interests in the western Pacific with a military doctrine it calls "active defense" or "counter-intervention" (military analysts in the United States term this doctrine "anti-access/area denial," "A2/AD," or "access denial").[5] This doctrine and related acquisition programs foresee using a wide variety of ballistic and cruise missile types, land-based aircraft, missile-armed coastal patrol craft, submarines, surface warships, and naval mine warfare to dissuade U.S. and allied naval forces and airpower from approaching the Near Seas during a conflict.

China will use its continental position to achieve the discrete goal of controlling the seas beyond its shores. The success of this "antinavy" approach will thus not depend on the PLAN achieving operational parity with the U.S. Pacific Fleet.[6] Elements of the PLAN, specifically its submarines, missile-armed surface ships, and mine warfare capability, will make specific contributions to the PLA's overall counter-intervention, or access denial, war plans. But most of China's access denial capacity will reside in land-based platforms and capabilities. In this sense, China will attempt to rule the sea from the land.

The hypothetical battle China's air and naval modernization is preparing for pits China, a continental power, against the United States and its allies, expeditionary powers attempting to project their air and naval power against China's positions on the continent and in the Near Seas. The game-changing technological advance favoring China in this duel is China's now-mature capability to project precise and high-volume missile power into the western Pacific, a threat the U.S. Navy has not had to worry about since the height of the Cold War more than three decades ago. China's force design combines these technological developments with its advantageous continental position in a way that creates a great challenge to legacy U.S. forces and plans.

Its position as the continental power in this competition gives China several important advantages. The continental position offers a much wider variety of basing options than those available to the United States, the expeditionary power. China's airpower can take advantage of basing options along the entire length of its long coast and deep into the interior. U.S. commanders in the region will have far fewer options.

China's continental position similarly supports its land-based missile strategy. Most of China's land-based ballistic and cruise missiles are mounted on mobile transporter-erector-launchers (TELs), truck and trailer combinations that allow missile commanders to move, hide, and constantly relocate their forces inside China's vast and complicated terrain. This ability to disperse and hide, combined with China's integrated air defense system, will make it difficult for U.S. forces to suppress the Chinese missile threat.

China's military forces also have the advantage of land-based logistic and communication networks. As the "home team" operating from interior lines, China's military supply network can be resilient, redundant, and positioned for enduring operations. Its military communications system can make use of terrestrial links, including underground fiber-optic cable, while U.S. forces will rely largely on satellite and radio links that are more vulnerable to disruption.

In the matchup of continental versus expeditionary forces, the land-based power will usually be able to employ weapon platforms with longer ranges and heavier payloads than those the expeditionary naval forces can support. China has invested heavily in its navy and now has the largest inventory of combat warships in the world (discussed more below), but its land-based antinavy missile power is the most dominant and challenging threat to U.S. and allied military forces in the western Pacific.

Finally, its missile-based strategy (here encompassing all of China's land-attack, antiship, and air defense missile systems) allows China to take advantage of its status as a low-cost industrial producer. For example, an advanced long-range cruise missile costs the U.S. Defense Department about $1.4 million; China's production costs for similar models are probably the same or lower. But a modern U.S. destroyer or amphibious ship costs $1.2–1.7 billion,[7] while China can acquire scores of antiship missiles and dozens of launch platforms for the same cost. Marginal costs similarly favor offensive missiles over missile defense interceptors, which cost at least an order of magnitude more than the attacking missiles they aim to intercept.[8] In a race between China's missiles versus U.S. platforms and missile defenses, it will be easier for China to stay in the lead.

The Mission of China's Missile Forces

The United States can rightly claim to have the best tactical combat aircraft in the world. The Air Force's F-22 air superiority fighter has no peer in air-to-air combat. The Air Force, Navy, and Marine Corps are receiving and building new squadrons of the F-35 fighter-attack jet, a multirole aircraft that will improve the air combat power of those services. Several U.S. allies in the Pacific are also purchasing the F-35 with the intention of integrating their future airpower capabilities with those of U.S. forces.

As chapter 3 discussed, however, the excessive allocation of short-range tactical aircraft in the U.S. aircraft inventory has created substantial handicaps for U.S. operations in the vast Pacific theater. Most crucial for the design of China's military strategy, these excellent aircraft are of no value if they are unable to get into the air to fight. China's adoption of the sensor and missile revolution over the past quarter century is specifically

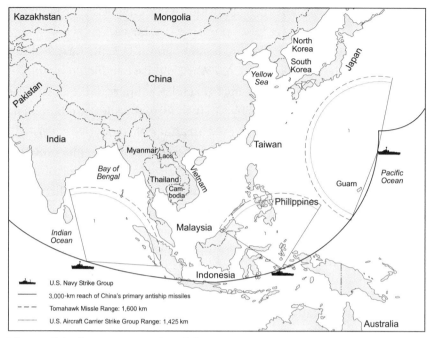

MAP 4. China's Anti-Access Capability. *Map by Charles David Grear.*

designed to attack the handful of air bases and aircraft carriers in the western Pacific on which the advanced U.S. tactical aircraft depend. If successful, China's strategy could nullify the technological advantage U.S. combat aircraft possess and leave China, operating from its continental position, in command of the skies over the Near Seas.

In 2010, the U.S.-China Economic and Security Review Commission concluded that China's land-attack missile forces had the capability to overwhelm the defenses and shut down all the U.S. air bases in the western Pacific except the one on Guam.[9] Since then, China has added new longer-range ground-launched and air-launched land-attack missiles to its arsenal, putting the U.S. bases on Guam at the same risk. China could use a portion of its land-attack ballistic and cruise missiles in coordinated attacks on the U.S. bases to suppress their operations. With surviving U.S. aircraft grounded, China's fighter and bomber aircraft could execute other combat missions without much opposition while employing air-launched land-attack cruise missiles to suppress the U.S. bases.

The China Commission's conclusions about U.S. air base vulnerability match the findings of a Cold War exercise conducted by the Air Force. Called "Salty Demo," the 1985 exercise at Spangdahlem Air Base in Germany simulated strikes by thirty to forty missiles and bombs on the base, which the Air Force termed an attack of "moderate severity."[10] The result was severe degradation of sortie generation, an outcome that came as a "shock" to Air Force officials. Salty Demo's conclusion of severe degradation from thirty to forty impacts on the base was confirmed by similar findings from the China Commission study and from a 2011 RAND Corporation study on challenges to U.S. airpower in the Pacific.[11] Those studies concluded that thirty to fifty missile impacts would render even a large U.S. air base unusable. Another study published in 2015 concluded that forty-five missiles armed with dispersing submunition warheads would destroy more than 80 percent of the aircraft parked in the open (the Marine Corps air base at Iwakuni, Japan, was examined).[12] Salty Demo also tested the ability of air base personnel to repair damaged facilities and restore sortie generation. China will have the missile inventories to periodically restrike the six Pacific bases on Japan, South Korea, and Guam, its task made easier by having such a small target set.

Chinese missile attacks on U.S. air bases in Japan and South Korea would result in horizontal escalation, a result China's decision-makers may in some circumstances wish to avoid. To the extent this is the case, the forward presence of U.S. airpower at these bases enhances regional deterrence. However, it is also possible that in a conflict with China, a nonbelligerent (South Korea, for instance) may prohibit U.S. forces from engaging in military operations against China from its territory. In this case, such bases would be "knocked out" with no missiles fired. Forward bases are a deterrent to expanding aggression but also potentially an unreliable asset for military operations.

The first mission of China's missile forces is to suppress U.S. and allied land-based and sea-based airpower near China's Near Seas. Without airpower, U.S. and allied expeditionary forces would have little prospect of intervening effectively in a conflict against the PLA.

China Becomes the Dominant Missile Power

China operates the most active missile program in the world. This wide-ranging program is developing and fielding many classes of land-based ballistic missiles as well as cruise missiles based on land, surface warships, submarines, and aircraft. According to the Department of Defense, China in 2019 launched more ballistic missiles for testing and training than the rest of the world combined.[13] The basic purpose of this missile program is to develop and deploy missile forces that will deter adversary expeditionary forces, such as U.S. aircraft carrier strike groups, other naval forces, and tactical airpower based near China, from threatening China's military forces, territory, and interests. China's missile-based strategy, employed from a wide variety of launch platforms, exploits its continental position and the basing and range advantages that position provides. The steady construction of sensor and missile battle networks has given the PLA the capability to strike land and ship targets out to and beyond the Second Island Chain, three thousand kilometers from China's coast.

The PLA's top investment priority is missile development. China's ballistic and cruise missiles already match or exceed those produced by the United States in range, speed, performance, and lethality. Even as the PLA upgrades its aircraft and warships to match U.S. standards more closely, PLA planners have concluded that possessing the world's best missiles for these platforms is the shrewdest path to achieving a military advantage.

The PLA Rocket Force (PLARF) fields more than 1,350 short-, medium-, and intermediate-range ballistic and cruise missiles on mobile transporters. These missiles have the range to precisely strike aim points on Taiwan, Japan, South Korea, and Guam and on ships in the Near Seas and other targets in the western Pacific. At least two types of the PLARF's ballistic missiles are armed with maneuvering warheads that can track and strike moving warships, a capability no other country has mastered. In August

2018, the PLARF tested a hypersonic maneuvering warhead designed for precision strikes and to thwart adversary missile defense systems.[14]

China could use its high-speed ballistic missiles in a variety of ways. Principal targets would include the U.S. air bases on Okinawa and Guam, with priority targets being the bases' air and missile defenses, command centers, engineering and repair equipment, and aircraft parked in the open. With the bases' defenses weakened by a ballistic missile volley, follow-up attacks with air-launched cruise missiles would add to the destruction. Successful ballistic missile attacks against U.S. aircraft carrier strike groups would cripple U.S. combat power and demoralize U.S. policymakers and military commanders.

The PLA possesses a wide variety of land-attack (LACM) and antiship cruise missile (ASCM) types. These missiles add hundreds of kilometers to the strike range of the PLA's aircraft, surface ships, and submarines. The PLA could employ large volleys of such missiles either in an independent mission or to follow up a ballistic missile barrage on an adversary base or warship squadron. The PLA's ballistic and cruise missile warheads employ satellite positioning, radar, electro-optical, imaging infrared, laser, and radar and electronic emissions homing for guidance, matching all the missile guidance capabilities of U.S. and allied missiles.[15]

The YJ-12 antiship cruise missile is especially dangerous. The missile began as an air-launched model, but the PLA subsequently deployed variants for land-based transporters and warships.[16] The YJ-12 has a range up to 400 kilometers and sprints to its warship target at speeds up to Mach 4, or 4,900 kilometers per hour.[17] Missiles like the YJ-12 approach their targets at wave-top heights to avoid detection and execute sharp terminal attack maneuvers to thwart ship defense systems. Flying at supersonic speeds, they emerge over the horizon into view of the target's defensive radar only a few seconds before impact, giving the fleet's terminal defense systems little time to react.

China's acquisition of long-range air-launched ASCMs like the YJ-12 has greatly increased the danger to U.S. aircraft carrier strike groups. When China's air-launched ASCMs had ranges under 100 kilometers, U.S. aircraft carriers and their air defense escorts could prepare for the incoming attackers and employ the full range of the strike group's air and missile defenses. The carrier's early warning aircraft and combat air patrols could detect incoming formations of enemy aircraft many hundreds of kilometers from the strike group and intercept them before they reached the launch point for their ASCMs. That launch point was well within the range of the strike group's surface-to-air missiles, which are directed by the powerful Aegis combat system.

But the YJ-12 and missiles like it have shifted the advantage to China. The four-hundred-kilometer range of this missile places its launch point beyond the range of the Aegis system and allows little time for the aircraft carrier to launch interceptors to battle the inbound enemy aircraft before they reach the four-hundred-kilometer launch point. Groups of attacking aircraft could approach a carrier strike group from several axes. The strike group cannot keep more than a few interceptor aircraft aloft at any given time. Although the strike group could rush a few more interceptors to the air defense perimeter before the attackers reached their missile launch points, the attackers would heavily outnumber the defenders and would likely approach from more directions than the Navy fighters could defend.

An aircraft carrier strike group would be a very high-value target for the PLA; China's leaders would likely believe that crippling or destroying such a symbolic target would inflict not only a military blow on the United States but also a shock to morale that could end a conflict on terms favorable to China. Believing this, PLA leaders would organize a large strike force against this target if given the opportunity.

Accepting that the aircraft carrier strike group would shoot down some attacking aircraft before they could launch their antiship missiles, the PLA would likely send one hundred or more ASCMS on wave-top, supersonic approaches to the U.S. ships. In past engagements of antiship missiles against alerted surface warships, 32 percent of the attacking missiles scored hits.[18] If, due to improved defenses, only 10 percent of the ASCMs scored hits, the carrier strike group's ships would still receive ten or more missile impacts, likely causing enough damage to render the group ineffective and possibly defenseless against another attack. Even if few or no ASCMs achieved hits, the carrier strike group would still likely have to retreat, having exhausted its defensive missile magazines to fend off the first missile salvo.

A clever and audacious U.S. carrier strike group commander might be able to execute a single surprise air strike on the Chinese mainland.[19] But an extended campaign, in which the Navy's carriers lie off China's coast for weeks or months launching thousands of strike sorties, will be out of the question. Nor, as we have seen, will the Navy's limited number of Tomahawk land-attack cruise missiles be an effective replacement for carrier strike groups.

In a conflict with China, the Navy as it currently exists is largely out of the power projection business on a significant scale. China's continental position, its ability to generate land-based maritime reconnaissance and strike capabilities despite U.S. attempts at disruption, and its dispersed, mobile, and relatively inexpensive missile and airpower will make it too dangerous in a conflict for U.S. and allied surface naval forces to sail for sustained periods close enough to China to employ their aircraft and missiles.

China's antiship missiles and their launch platforms thus present a substantial challenge to the Navy's long-favored method of projecting power and controlling the seas. From the closing months of World War II up through the carrier-based strikes on Afghanistan, U.S. fleet commanders have enjoyed the freedom to sail their aircraft carriers close to an enemy's shore, confident that their adversaries could do little to interrupt the carriers' flight operations. The military-technical revolution has now changed the rules. In a conflict with China, it would be highly dangerous for U.S. aircraft carrier strike groups to operate within three thousand kilometers of China, placing them well beyond the range of their strike aircraft. We should expect the military-technical revolution to continue, with ASCM ranges increasing and pushing the Navy's airpower capability even farther from shore.

China's Reconnaissance and Targeting Networks

China's land-attack and antiship missile systems and strategies are only as good as the sensor, intelligence, targeting, and command systems that support them. For this, the PLA operates complementary and redundant command and reconnaissance networks that fully support China's missile forces. Together these components constitute the integrated battle networks the PLA would employ in a possible fait accompli assault on Taiwan or to fend off U.S. and allied attempts to roll back China's territorial gains.

China's space program, operated largely by the PLA's Space Systems Department, is currently the most important provider of reconnaissance, overhead imaging, space-based navigation, meteorology, and communications support to the PLA's missile, airpower, and naval strike forces. China's space capabilities are world class, nearly matching those of the United States in breadth and sophistication. The Space Systems Department operates from at least eight bases and in 2019 conducted thirty-two successful launches that placed more than seventy new satellites into orbit.[20]

China's numerous satellite constellations match U.S. military space capabilities in providing a full range of services supporting military operations. China's BeiDou-3 satellite navigation constellation, for example, consists of 45 satellites that provide PLA military forces with global navigation and communication coverage.[21] As of May 2018, China's reconnaissance and remote sensing fleet consisted of 120 satellites, with more units added every year since then. These satellites provide PLA forces with real-time location data on adversary military forces and movements.[22] China's reconnaissance and remote sensing satellites are capable of electro-optical, synthetic aperture radar (SAR), and electronic and signals intelligence gathering.[23] All these intelligence-gathering methods are important, with SAR capability being perhaps the most crucial because it functions day and night and through clouds, allowing the operator to observe and target ships and vehicles on the earth's surface anywhere at any time. Finally, China has in orbit communications and communication relay satellites that give PLA commanders over-the-horizon command and control of their forces and that provide data connections to China's long-range aircraft, ballistic and cruise missiles, and unmanned reconnaissance and strike systems.[24]

China's space program is preparing for the future military environment in space. This environment will require competitors to distribute their space capabilities over wide networks of dispersed, small satellites.

For example, in 2022 a Chinese state-owned company began deploying a new SAR constellation in space that will consist of ninety-six small satellites, each capable of producing images with one-meter resolution, for PLA and commercial imagery analysts.[25] Competitors will similarly require dispersed terrestrial launch platforms, away from main launch centers that could come under attack, and also mobile solid-fuel rocket boosters that can launch payloads into orbit from quickly established nondedicated sites. China is developing all these capabilities, including new, smaller solid rocket boosters; micro-satellites for reconnaissance and communication; and spontaneous launch capabilities, including from sea-based platforms.[26]

Finally, the PLA operates what is likely the world's most active counterspace program, designed to degrade and disrupt adversary space reconnaissance and communication networks. The PLA's counterspace program includes capabilities such as space reconnaissance and situation awareness sensor networks; antisatellite kinetic kill vehicles launched from the surface; surface-based lasers for disrupting adversary space-based sensors; and orbiting space robots for nonkinetic attacks on adversary space systems. China demonstrated a direct-ascent kinetic kill antisatellite weapon in 2007 against a target in low earth orbit and is developing similar weapons to attack satellites at distances out to geosynchronous orbit.[27]

Summing up, China's space-based reconnaissance, navigation, and communications systems provide PLA commanders and planners with the intelligence, targeting, and command capabilities they will need to employ their missiles, aircraft, and naval forces against U.S. and allied military forces operating throughout the Indo-Pacific region and beyond. China's counterspace capabilities increasingly place at risk the legacy space assets of the United States and its allies. China's space operations and capabilities will continue to advance and will make the PLA's space capabilities more robust, redundant, and difficult to counter.

The PLA will supplement its space-based reconnaissance and communication systems by expanding land-based unmanned aerial vehicle (UAV) capabilities. These UAVs will take advantage of China's continental position to patrol the Near Seas and conduct other military operations such as data relay, electronic warfare, deception, and direct attack. The PLA is fielding several classes of UAVs for both reconnaissance and strike missions. For example, high-altitude, long-endurance UAVs currently patrol the South China Sea and western Pacific from Hainan Island.[28] The CH-5 is a medium-altitude, long-endurance UAV that is similar to the Air Force's MQ-9 Reaper UAV and is armed with air-to-surface missiles.[29]

PLA commanders could employ squadrons of CH-5s on armed reconnaissance missions over China's Near Seas and the western Pacific. The PLA could also modify these platforms for data relay and electronic warfare missions. Finally, the PLA is developing and acquiring UAVs with flying wing designs to avoid detection by adversary radar and antiaircraft systems.[30] When fielded in large numbers, these designs will multiply the threat to U.S. naval and land-based forces operating near China. The PLA's land-based UAV capabilities supplement and provide critical redundancy for China's space-based systems and possess capacity and resilience that expeditionary U.S. and allied forces will have trouble matching.

China's Emerging Air Superiority in the Western Pacific

Air superiority is a well-known requirement for military success. China intends to achieve air superiority over the Near Seas and into the western Pacific through the employment of its land-attack missile power and by exploiting the U.S. military's overreliance on relatively short-range tactical aircraft, a weakness discussed in chapter 3.

According to the Department of Defense, China possesses the largest airpower inventory in the Indo-Pacific region. This force comprises about two thousand combat aircraft, including fighters, strategic bombers, tactical bombers, multimission tactical, and attack aircraft.[31]

The PLA's Flanker-series fighter-attack aircraft is an example of the threat facing U.S. and allied forces in the Indo-Pacific region. In 2020, the PLAAF and the PLAN operated 634 Flankers in several variants.[32] The Flanker aircraft originated in Russia (the Su-27/Su-30/Su-33 models), and China acquired its first Flankers in the 1990s. China now assembles its own variants, such as the J-16 and J-11B, while continuing to acquire new upgraded variants from Russia such as the Su-35. China's Flankers have a combat radius of 1,400 kilometers and can employ a wide variety of cruise missiles.[33] The Flanker-ASCM combination can thus attack targets 1,750–1,900 kilometers from the Flanker's last refueling point, giving this fighter-attack force the capability to strike air bases and surface ships well beyond the First Island Chain, where all the large U.S. air bases except Guam are located.

The PLA is now fielding the J-20, a large, stealthy air superiority fighter aircraft.[34] The J-20 is thought to have a combat radius of two thousand kilometers.[35] A primary mission for the J-20 will be to attack large U.S. support aircraft such as command-and-control and tanker aircraft that heretofore have operated in ostensibly safe airspace behind the main battle front. China is developing a very long-range air-to-air missile which the large J-20 will presumably carry internally to preserve its stealthy profile. This air-to-air missile could have a range of four hundred kilometers, far longer than any U.S. air intercept missile, and will be equipped with a multimode guidance sensor to overcome jamming and countermeasures.[36]

U.S. tactical aircraft—such as the F/A-18 E/F and the F-22 and F-35 in their stealthy configurations—have combat radii after their last refueling point of about 1,100 kilometers. If the United States did operate these tactical aircraft from bases in the Second Island Chain, roughly on the same longitude as Guam, Air Force tanker refueling aircraft could in theory sustain them on long flights toward China from the east. But the PLAAF's stealthy J-20s, armed with 400-kilometer-range air intercept missiles, would disrupt this concept. China's J-20s will place at risk large, vulnerable U.S. tanker aircraft flying over the Second Island China and points to the west. This would place the last safe refueling point for U.S. tactical aircraft far beyond their combat radii to targets inside China and much of the area west of the First Island Chain.

China's bomber aircraft, again operated by both the PLAAF and the PLAN, add more range and firepower to China's strike capacities. Between the two services, in 2020 the PLA operated 221 H-6 bombers in several variants.[37] The H-6 derives from the Soviet-era Tu-16 Badger bomber, which China has modernized and upgraded, just as the United States has done with its Cold War–era B-52 and B-1 bombers.[38] Each H-6 can carry six cruise missiles such as the long-range CJ-20 land-attack missile and the YJ-12 antiship missile.[39] H-6 formations can launch large volleys of precision-guided missiles against U.S. bases on Guam and U.S. and allied warships out to the Second Island Chain.[40] A raid by just 10 percent of the H-6 force could launch more than a hundred missiles against a U.S. aircraft carrier strike group or air base.

The PLA's airpower capacity is thus now positioned to launch high volumes of precision missile attacks against land, maritime, and air targets out to 3,000 kilometers from China's coast. The PLA's 221 bombers and 1,382 fighter-attack aircraft (Flankers plus other attack aircraft) can launch land-attack and antiship cruise missile volleys against bases in South Korea, Japan, Vietnam, the Philippines, the South and East China Seas, and out to Guam and other targets along the Second Island Chain.[41] Assuming a daily employment of one-third of the PLA's combined bomber and fighter-attack forces, the PLA could launch about 1,400 missiles a day from its strike aircraft alone and sustain this rate over a long campaign. This daily volume of missiles would be sufficient to keep U.S. and allied air bases in the western Pacific suppressed and to attack aircraft carrier strike groups and other naval formations west of the Second Island Chain with saturation missile volleys. After establishing air and maritime superiority beyond the First Island Chain and thwarting any possibility of U.S. intervention, the PLA could then focus its airpower on campaign objectives such as Taiwan.

China Builds the World's Largest Navy

According to the U.S. Department of Defense, China now has the largest navy in the world.[42] A report for Congress prepared using data supplied by the Navy's Office of Naval Intelligence listed 360 "battle force," or combat, ships in the PLAN in 2020. The U.S. Navy's battle force total was 297 ships. Naturally, the two sums are not directly comparable. China's fleet includes large numbers of diesel submarines and small surface combatants such as frigates and corvettes, while the U.S. Navy has many more aircraft carriers, nuclear-powered submarines, and large surface combatants such as destroyers and cruisers.[43]

Even so, the "bottom line" shows the rapid growth in China's naval power, which is concentrated in the western Pacific, compared to a numerically smaller U.S. Navy that is dispersed around the world attending to global responsibilities. In addition, China's shipyards, the most productive in the world, produce a steady stream of modern new warships for the PLAN—ships that in most cases, such as cruisers and destroyers, match their Western counterparts in both quality and capability.[44]

China's leaders have assigned several missions to the PLAN. The first is to establish an overwhelming Chinese maritime presence in the Near Seas, reinforcing China's territorial claims over these features. China's enormous and growing coast guard and its "maritime militia" of state-sponsored fishing fleets add to China's maritime presence in the Near Seas and western Pacific.[45]

Second, the PLAN now has the task of "showing the flag" elsewhere in the world to demonstrate China's arrival as a global power. The Chinese government's 2019 Defense White Paper assigned the PLAN "protection missions on the far seas."[46] In addition to simply displaying Chinese military power at ports around the world, specific tasks include antipiracy operations in the western Indian Ocean, humanitarian assistance and disaster relief, defending China's sea lines of communication from the Persian Gulf, and evacuating Chinese nationals abroad.[47]

Third, and most relevant to the discussion of the military balance in the Indo-Pacific, is the additional firepower the PLAN's surface ships and submarines can contribute to strikes on U.S. and allied bases and expeditionary warship formations during a conflict. Of note, over the next decade the PLAN will have more than forty submarines and thirty cruisers and destroyers that could be armed with the YJ-18, a new antiship missile with a range exceeding five hundred kilometers.[48] These ships and submarines could add scores of additional long-range missiles to coordinated saturation attacks on U.S. aircraft carrier strike groups led by PLARF missiles and PLAAF and PLAN strike aircraft. The PLAN's surface warships and submarines will also be armed with land-attack cruise missiles. This will give the PLA the capability to precisely attack land targets nearly anywhere in the world in support of China's national security objectives.[49]

China is also steadily building a large-scale amphibious assault capability. The PLAN is acquiring large amphibious assault ships that can carry and deploy helicopters, landing craft, unmanned aircraft, naval infantry, and support equipment. The PLAN has some forty large amphibious ships and is replacing older models with modern ships comparable to large Western designs.[50] In addition, the PLA has expanded its marine corps to eight brigades of naval infantry, special operations forces, and supporting arms. The PLAN marine corps is training for island defense and assault operations in the Near Seas and crisis response operations across the Indian Ocean, the Gulf of Aden, and Africa.[51]

The PLA has militarized the seven features it occupies in the South China Sea's Spratly Islands. Three of these features—Fiery Cross, Mischief, and Subi Reefs—each have a long aircraft runway and shelters for a twenty-four-aircraft fighter-attack regiment.[52] The PLA has installed radars along with surface-to-air and antiship missile batteries and electronic warfare–jamming equipment on the features it occupies. Additional facilities on the Chinese-occupied Spratlys include port facilities, fixed weapon positions, barracks, administration buildings, warehouses, sensor emplacements, and communications facilities.[53]

Militarization of the features China has claimed in the Spratlys achieved several goals for China's leaders. First, it displays China's dominance to all the other players in the Spratlys. The sensors and weapons emplaced on these features surveil broad reaches of the South China Sea and hold at risk ships and aircraft passing through. Second, China's military presence intimidates the smaller claimant countries and inhibits their ability to exploit the sea's resources as they are entitled to do under international law. Finally, the infrastructure China has built in the Spratlys is ready to receive additional advanced military equipment such as fighter-attack aircraft and warships should the PLA decide to reinforce its military power in the sea during a crisis, an advantage no other player currently possesses.

It is important to note that the decision by CCP leaders to commission hundreds of manned surface warships into service could ultimately be a mistake they will regret, because these ships are just as vulnerable to long-range antiship missiles as U.S. and allied surface ships are to the PLA's missiles. China's now-great battle fleet is arguably a symbol of national pride. But such a symbol can turn into a political and cultural "center of gravity" in a war should an adversary target it for destruction (later chapters will discuss this topic). The PLAN surface fleet could be a notable flaw in an otherwise well-designed Chinese military modernization program.

What Has China Achieved?

The tremendous buildup of Chinese military power over the past quarter century has revealed that China's leaders believe in the utility of military power. Chapter 1 explored the insecurities and vulnerabilities China's leaders labor under, which would seem to explain their choice to achieve military parity and then superiority over U.S. military power by 2049, if not long before, according to Xi Jinping's 2017 report to the Nineteenth Party Congress.[54]

It is worth noting that only China's leaders have taken this path. Other substantial powers such Japan, Europe, and India, which are just as dependent as China on global trade and energy imports, have accommodated themselves since the collapse of the Soviet Union to the existing international order that has the United States and its partners providing protection for the free flow of global commerce. No other power has concluded that its vulnerabilities and exposures require a military buildup to challenge U.S. stewardship of the global commons. Instead, these powers reduced the resources they committed to defense and directed them to other social needs. China's new economic power gave its leaders the option to challenge U.S. stewardship, but they did not have to exercise it. They made their choice on the basis of their ideological views, their views of China's culture and history, and their impulse to use force to control what they perceive as vulnerabilities and insecurities.

China's military buildup has created a classic security dilemma. Its regional neighbors are responding to the increased military threat with internal and external balancing actions. Japan, Taiwan, Australia, and India are now engaged in extensive and long-term defense reform efforts and have recently increased their defense spending. Regional military diplomacy is now much more active. For example, the Quadrilateral

Security Dialogue, or "Quad," consisting of the United States, Japan, India, and Australia, is now reinvigorated, with senior foreign ministry officials from the four founding members meeting bimonthly.[55] Key to the Quad's newfound energy is the growing concern in India over China's military power and assertiveness and the resulting willingness of Indian government officials to cooperate with the United States, Japan, and others on security issues and concerns. We should expect to see regular Quad meetings at the head-of-government level and the eventual expansion of the Quad into a "Quad+" as other countries seek to participate.

A formal, NATO-type multilateral security alliance in the Indo-Pacific is unlikely in the near future. Even so, bilateral and multilateral defense cooperation across the region, usually involving the United States but also frequently not, will expand and deepen. Concern about China's military power is catalyzing this cooperation, which will display itself in more sophisticated multilateral training exercises, officer exchanges, intelligence sharing, contingency planning, cooperation on command arrangements, arms sales, and other measures that will improve cross-national military coordination.

China's military modernization has unquestionably increased that nation's capacity to use military force to achieve its security goals. In doing so, however, it has sparked a security backlash and a gradually hardening multilateral security shell around China in the Indo-Pacific region. Some leaders in Beijing may therefore rightfully question whether the PLA's buildup has improved China's security. Nevertheless, we should expect the PLA's modernization to continue, and even accelerate.

The CCP Sparks a Global Backlash, Crippling Its Political Warfare Campaign

During the first two decades of this century China successfully employed salami-slicing to achieve a commanding military position in the South China Sea. According to a former commander of U.S. Indo-Pacific Command, China's slow, patient buildup on the features it occupies in the Paracel and Spratly island chains has made it "capable of controlling the South China Sea in all scenarios short of war with the United States."[56]

Over the same period, the CCP also employed political warfare to weaken the resolve of policymakers around the world to resist China's pursuit of its strategic goals. China's political warfare strategy had several lines of effort. These lines of effort have included

- generating influence favorable to China at Western universities through the use of grants, visas, research exchange programs for scholars, and the Confucius Institute program;
- stimulating pro-Chinese messaging from media and cultural institutions such as Hollywood, and using market access, joint ventures, and work visas as influence tools;
- gaining influence over Western business and finance leaders using trade access and business partnerships as tools;
- using grants and other rewards to achieve pro-Chinese messaging from nongovernmental organizations;
- inserting Chinese officials into leadership positions in international organizations and then shaping the policies of those institutions in a pro-China direction;
- attempting to shape the views of current and future Western policymakers by achieving influence over Western think tanks and research organizations; and
- influencing local political attitudes through outreach to Chinese diaspora communities.[57]

But salami-slicing and political warfare have now reached the end of their effectiveness, nullified by China's belligerence under Xi Jinping. During his decade in power Xi Jinping has abandoned the Deng-era policy of restraint in the strategies he has chosen to achieve China's four strategic goals, and in doing so has sparked a regional and global backlash against China.

In pursuit of the first strategic goal—maintaining and deepening the CCP's control over Chinese society—the CCP and the Chinese government have expanded the country's internal security forces, increased surveillance of the Chinese population, tightened control over the population's access to information, and increased control over the private sector of the economy. As mentioned earlier, China's internal security forces have grown, and internal security spending now exceeds spending on the PLA's conventional and nuclear forces.

China's internal security forces collect mobile telephone tracking data, mobile payments data, content from messaging and chat services, facial recognition, and other related electronic monitoring and analyze these data with increasingly sophisticated artificial intelligence algorithms. These databases and analyses empower the internal security forces to closely monitor the population's behavior and anticipate threats to the CCP's rule. A "social credit system"—a system of rewards and punishments imposed on individuals according to this monitoring—aims to reinforce the CCP's powers of social control.[58] China's domestic economic policy under Xi's administration heavily favors state-owned enterprises at the expense of private-sector businesses.[59] The CCP's goal with these and similar actions is to ensure that no organization arises that could challenge the party's authority over Chinese society. The wider world has noticed the repressive nature of the CCP, and this has undermined China's soft-power approach and its popularity around the world.

The CCP under Xi has also taken strong action to reunite and pacify territory it claims is Chinese, the second strategic goal. In addition to the highly intrusive security force presence and surveillance technology described above, the CCP has employed mass arrests, confinement, and forced labor in Xinjiang province. China's internal security forces over the past decade have constructed more than 380 detention facilities in that Muslim-majority province and have detained more than a million ethnic Uighurs and Kazakhs in them. Private-source satellite imagery has revealed that China's security forces demolished a third of the province's mosques between 2017 and 2020.[60]

In 2020, the CCP and China's internal security forces responded to pro-democracy protests in Hong Kong by implementing the mass arrest of Hong Kong's remaining pro-democracy leadership.[61] With political opposition to Hong Kong's pro-Beijing administration removed and silenced, the CCP now controls the formerly independent territory.

China has stepped up its pressure on Taiwan by implementing attempts at political subversion on the island, more aggressive naval and air patrols around Taiwan, and a buildup of PLA military forces across the Taiwan Strait, including amphibious naval shipping. Chapter 7 will cover the Taiwan flashpoint in more detail.

China has similarly acted over the past decade to implement the CCP's third strategic goal—establishing hegemony over the periphery around China. These actions have included building and militarizing land features in the South China Sea (discussed above); increasing its militia, coast guard, and military presence near the Senkaku Islands in the East China Sea; and building military encampments, air bases, and support facilities along China's Himalayan frontier, where PLA and Indian army soldiers occasionally clash.

China's fourth strategic goal is to reshape international institutions and norms of behavior to support its expanding presence in global affairs. Over the past decade, China has installed dozens of Chinese officials in senior positions in UN principal organs and programs, the International Monetary Fund, the World Trade Organization, Interpol, and others.[62] With these officials in place, the CCP hopes to influence the policies of these institutions toward outcomes the CCP desires, at the expense of other countries and their interests if necessary. China has increased its use of information and influence operations through global media outlets, academic institutions, nongovernmental organizations, the Chinese diaspora, and other channels in an attempt to strengthen overseas support for its actions and weaken opposition to them.

These actions have provoked a backlash from both policymakers and public citizens around the world. For example, the Biden administration aims to follow up on the Trump administration's hawkish China policies by organizing regional and global ad hoc and issue-specific international coalitions to counter China's adventurism. Counter-China coalitions are forming around problems such as military security, trade, cross-border investment, infrastructure investment, technology standards, human rights, democracy promotion, and more. The Biden administration, with its greater emphasis on coalition building and global legitimacy, may be more effective at pursuing this policy.[63]

Efforts to counter China's aggression are mounting in the Indo-Pacific region. The global economic crisis created by the coronavirus pandemic of 2020 did not prevent Japan from enacting its largest ever defense budget, which focused on the purchase and development of new stealth aircraft and long-range antiship missiles designed to counter the PLA.[64] In Australia in 2020, Prime Minister Scott Morrison announced a ten-year stepped-up defense program that, like Japan's, will focus on stealth aircraft, long-range antiship missiles, and antisubmarine warfare. Morrison described the security environment in the Indo-Pacific region as the most uncertain "since the existential threat we faced when the global and regional order collapsed in the 1930s and 1940s."[65] The response to China's behavior extends to Europe, where NATO leaders are now focusing the military alliance's attention on the challenge from China.[66]

Finally, and perhaps most notably, global public opinion about China took a sharp negative turn between 2019 and 2020. Surveys in Europe, Japan, South Korea, Australia, Canada, and the United States indicated that seven to eight out of every ten people interviewed had unfavorable views of China overall and of Xi Jinping in particular, a notable increase over the preceding year. The coronavirus pandemic may explain much of that abrupt change. But even those whose believed China and Xi had done well at managing the pandemic still had negative views of China and its leadership, reflecting increased concern at the public level about China's actions and intentions.[67]

From the end of the Cold War until less than a decade ago, the mainstream and near-consensus hope among U.S. and Western policymakers along the political spectrum was that China's leaders would accept and conform to the long-existent global system of open markets, U.S. and Western stewardship of the global commons, and the existing international institutions that set rules and norms of behavior and adjudicated disputes. It seemed logical to expect China to conform because it had profited so immensely from this international system. As a part of that compliance these policymakers expected China to liberalize internally, presuming that would be necessary for China's population to achieve its full intellectual and economic potential.[68]

Those hopes, which for many policymakers became a planning assumption, have collapsed under Xi's decade of rule. Very few U.S. policymakers and advisers anywhere on the political spectrum still hold out hope that China will become a cooperative, nonthreatening, "responsible stakeholder" in the international system. Views have hardened around a new consensus that China is a revisionist power, a growing military threat, and a country seeking to build a world that legitimizes authoritarianism.

The CCP's behavior under Xi has crippled attempts to build up and display Chinese soft power as a means of disarming resistance to the party's revisionist program. Instead, global public views of China have plunged. Political leaders across Europe, Asia, and North America now view China at a minimum as a worrisome competitor and, for most, an increasingly dangerous and aggressive adversary. That is clearly the case in the United States, Australia, and Japan, where politicians across the political spectrum now must oppose China to sustain their political careers.

Expect an Increasingly Militarized CCP Strategy

With its political warfare tactics now spent, China's leaders will be compelled to rely on their ultimate "hard-power" tool—the PLA's military power—to advance toward their strategic goals. China's leaders are likely to be comfortable doing this. They view the PLA modernization program thus far with satisfaction and pride, and they will likely conclude that the PLA is gaining on, and even surpassing, the U.S. military in several dimensions. CCP leaders have always preferred direct control over problems, something they believe the PLA can give them. As a result, we should expect CCP leaders to continue, and even accelerate, the PLA's modernization.

The ongoing modernization of the PLA over the next decade and beyond will gradually increase its global reach while adding firepower and lethality to existing offensive strike capacities. China's space-based reconnaissance and communications capacities will add coverage, fidelity, and resilience. The trend for space-based sensor, communication, and navigation design is toward constellations composed of scores or hundreds of small satellites. These highly dispersed constellations will provide near real-time observation of the surface below. Small synthetic aperture radar satellites will distinguish objects down to a meter in size or less continuously, day and night and through all weather. Redundant communication relays in space, using lasers to securely transmit massive data volumes, will transmit collected imagery to processors. These processors will employ artificial intelligence to rapidly extract the conclusions commanders and target planners will require for rapid coordinated military operations. This widely distributed network of sensors, relays, and analytical nodes will be difficult for adversaries to attack, jam, or disrupt. China has the engineering skills and experience to build this capability nearly as quickly as the United States.

By the end of the decade, the PLAAF's J-20 stealth fighter will be operating in large numbers, holding at risk U.S. aerial tanker and command aircraft flying near the Second Island Chain. Far greater numbers of unmanned aircraft will fly armed reconnaissance patrols of the Near Seas, out to the Second Island Chain, and into the Indian Ocean. The PLA will increase its capacity for midair refueling of several types of strike aircraft, expanding the range of its airpower. PLA fighter-attack aircraft operating from air bases in the Spratly Islands will project PLA air operations into the eastern Indian Ocean. New antiship and land-attack missiles will have longer ranges and better sensors, and will be more difficult to intercept or even detect. And the PLA could establish additional overseas bases to facilitate its global air operations.[69]

The Chinese navy will similarly continue to expand its global reach and the lethality of its platforms. China's submarine fleet will be larger, more modern, and armed with more dangerous antiship missiles and torpedoes. The PLAN is improving its ability to operate aircraft carrier strike groups and has more aircraft carriers under construction. It has taken delivery of fleet replenishment ships to sustain aircraft carrier operations at long distances from Chinese ports and support bases.[70] During this decade we should expect regular PLAN aircraft carrier operations in the Indian Ocean and the central and even eastern Pacific Ocean. The PLAN's amphibious assault capacity will similarly increase as it takes delivery of large, multimission amphibious ships and as the PLAN marine corps refines its training in large-scale amphibious operations.[71] The PLAN's increases in amphibious assault capacities pertain not only to Taiwan but also to possible contingencies in the Near Seas and Indian Ocean.

Over the next decade, the PLA Rocket Force will continue testing the four-thousand-kilometer-range DF-26 ballistic missile for precision attacks against land targets and underway warships. More generally, the PLARF will continue testing hypersonic and maneuvering reentry vehicles with a goal of perfecting capabilities to thwart missile defense systems and to strike high-value and fleeting targets of opportunity at ranges up to and beyond the Second Island Chain, including Guam and deep into the Indian Ocean.[72]

Finally, the PLA Strategic Support Force will continue to build out and deepen various functions that provide essential support to the PLA's other branches. The PLA space forces will develop the distributed reconnaissance, communication, and navigation satellite architectures described above, which in turn support a modernized command and control system for PLA commanders. The PLA's counterspace and antisatellite capabilities will continue to develop and will enter regular service. The PLA's offensive electronic warfare and cyber-attack capabilities will continue to improve and will integrate more effectively with the PLA's conventional forces. Of note, the U.S. Department of Defense expects the PLA to emphasize the development of, and perhaps even to demonstrate, its ability to disrupt adversary critical civilian infrastructure such as power utility grids and telecommunications as part of an overall political-military campaign.[73]

In sum, over the coming decade the PLA in all its dimensions will become much more lethal, not only inside the First Island Chain but across the Indo-Pacific region and beyond. The CCP's leaders will be rightly proud of how far and how quickly the PLA has advanced over the past quarter century. They will also be anxious for the PLA to overcome its enduring shortcomings, which include the recruitment of skilled and motivated soldiers, training up to Western standards, occasionally weak officer leadership and decision-making, deficiencies in interservice cooperation and joint operations, and seemingly endemic corruption in the ranks.[74] With the CCP's political warfare campaign having run its course and with the United States and its partners now organizing a more effective security response, China's leaders will rely even more on the PLA as one of their few remaining tools of influence. These leaders will direct even more of their attention on the PLA and its officers to urge the acceleration of the military modernization effort.

U.S. defense officials and planners have noticed all this and have belatedly elevated the rapid modernization of the PLA to the top of their threat list. But it is one thing to finally recognize a grave problem and another to implement an effective response.

5

America Pivots to Asia, Then Stumbles

By 2010, officials and military planners at the U.S. Department of Defense were fully engrossed with China's military modernization and the potential threat it posed to the U.S. military's ability to succeed in the western Pacific during a war. The 2010 edition of the *Quadrennial Defense Review*, the department's periodic strategy assessment, explicitly discussed the military threat posed by China and directed the Air Force and Navy to establish a coordinated response.[1] In January 2012, under the signature of Joint Chiefs Chair Gen. Martin Dempsey, the Pentagon's Joint Staff issued the Joint Operational Access Concept (JOAC) as a capstone, all-service response to the access-denial problem.[2] As the Obama administration "rebalanced" America's strategic focus to the Asia-Pacific region and the Pentagon focused on maintaining military access to the western Pacific and elsewhere, the Pentagon scrambled to respond to China's exploitation of the sensor and missile revolution.

The Pentagon's responses were at first controversial and then became increasingly unconvincing. This was a surprise. The challenge posed by China's missile-centered military strategy was a familiar problem for U.S. military planners and one well suited for the Defense Department's traditional strengths in technology and weapon platforms. The United States had overcome an equally virulent adversary in the Soviet Union, in the process developing a research and technology defense culture that should have been equal to the problems posed by China. Further, China is much more involved in global commerce than the Soviet Union was and should thus have been vulnerable to apparent U.S. advantages in naval and airpower.

But as we will see, the U.S. responses to China's military challenge over the past decade revealed a Defense Department and Congress still unwilling to commit to the measures the problem required. Today, all the military services are eager to offer their solutions to the China challenge. This is an encouraging display of enthusiasm and creativity, if not also an expected response to protect their budget allocations. But given China's military strategy and the realities of technological trends, not all the responses proffered by the Pentagon's military services are practical. Some good ideas are neglected orphans while a few faulty concepts are receiving undue attention.

Leaders at the Pentagon over the past decade have finally taken China's military challenge seriously and have worked hard to formulate an effective response. Unfortunately, bureaucratic and political limitations continue to prevent the formulation of a fully effective strategy. As a result, the United States has wasted time while the PLA has continued to develop its strength. If we are to formulate an effective strategy in response to China, we must first understand what is wrong with the current U.S. defense program. This chapter explains the shortcomings of current U.S. defense concepts and clears the way for a better strategy.

Worrying Once Again about the "Reconnaissance-Strike Complex"

Using military power to deny an adversary access to a region or territory is a strategy as old as warfare itself. In naval history, epic engagements such as Salamis (480 BCE), Gravelines (1588), and the campaign against the German submarine fleet in World War II (1939–45) are notable examples of adversaries clashing over theater access to enable, or prevent, further decisive operations ashore. The Battle of Britain in August and September 1940 that pitted the British and German air forces against one another for control of the air space over southern England is another classic example of an access-denial effort against an expeditionary force. China's development of an access-denial capacity thus fits within the long stream of military history.

That being said, each example of an access-denial challenge has its own aspects of tactics and technology that commanders and military planners must master and shape for their purposes. China's access-denial strategy, based on the latest developments of the sensor and missile revolution, has unique features that are now subject to intense scrutiny.

Chapter 3 examined how the Pentagon's Office of Net Assessment became aware in the early 1990s that an adversary could potentially attack U.S. forces at their forward bases around the perimeter of Eurasia. The 1970s Soviet "reconnaissance-strike complex" concept discussed in chapters 3 and 4 was an earlier generation of this threat.[3]

The Persian Gulf War in 1991 was the first large-scale demonstration of the damage a wide-ranging intelligence and command network linked to precision-guided munitions (the envisioned components of the Soviet reconnaissance-strike complex) could inflict on adversary command and control, air, and land forces. After that, analysts at ONA and elsewhere began to contemplate the threat a modern reconnaissance-strike battle network could pose for forward-deployed and expeditionary U.S. naval and airpower. Three decades later, what began as a thought experiment at a Pentagon think-tank is now a real-world problem for U.S. military commanders and planners in the western Pacific.

JOAC Lays Out the Problem, but Not the Answer

Soon after he became chairman of the Joints Chiefs of Staff in 2011, General Dempsey ordered the Joint Staff and other military experts to examine the anti-access issue, define its elements, and devise solutions that involved all four services. The Joint Operational Access Concept (JOAC) that resulted was issued under Dempsey's signature in January 2012.[4] The monograph fashioned a top-level, capstone perspective on the access-denial challenge to show that the problem was not a concern just for the Navy and Air Force, and to reassure the defense bureaucracy that all four services would be included in the solutions the department would pursue.

JOAC's authors performed a notable public service by honestly describing the challenges U.S. military forces would increasingly face merely obtaining access to war zones, let alone prevailing against adversaries. Even more notable was their blunt candor concerning the risks and barriers U.S. policymakers and military planners would face attempting to fashion practical solutions to access challenges, especially those posed by peer competitors such as China. JOAC described the military problem well, but its authors were not sanguine about an easy solution.

JOAC asserted that *cross-domain synergy*—"the complementary vice merely additive employment of capabilities in different domains [land, sea, air, space, and cyber] such that each enhances the effectiveness and compensates for the vulnerabilities of the others"—should be the central operating tenet for U.S. and allied forces attempting to prevail against adversary access-denial capabilities.[5] An example of cross-domain synergy would be employing submarine-launched cruise missiles to suppress enemy air defenses as a prelude to an air campaign. Another would be the use of cyber weapons to disrupt an adversary's space-based reconnaissance and command network. JOAC also called for U.S. and coalition forces to achieve cross-domain synergy at lower organizational levels to enable U.S. forces to generate the speedy decisions and actions necessary to exploit fleeting local vulnerabilities in adversary forces and systems. Faster decision-making and exploitation of opportunities would more likely occur if lower-echelon commanders were empowered to act independently and had the cross-domain tools envisioned by the concept.[6]

JOAC's description of the high-end challenges to theater access matched the description of China's military modernization discussed in chapter 4. The document's list of looming access barriers included precision-guided and long-range cruise and ballistic missiles; long-range and integrated surveillance and targeting networks; antisatellite weapons that threaten U.S. space systems; and a submarine fleet capable of defending sea lanes that U.S. forces would use to transit to an operational theater.[7] As we have seen, these are all principal investments of the PLA.

One of JOAC's purposes was to guide the development of joint warfighting doctrine for overcoming access barriers. JOAC offered a list of precepts for future authors of doctrine and war plans involving access-denial challenges. Unfortunately, most of these precepts were either facile, impractical, or counterproductive. Among the precepts were "maximize surprise," "disrupt enemy reconnaissance and surveillance efforts," "prepare the operational area in advance," "exploit advantages in one or more domains to disrupt enemy anti-access/area-denial capabilities in others," and "create pockets of local domain superiority."[8] These were hardly original ideas.

JOAC's other suggestions to "maneuver directly against key operational objectives from strategic distance," "attack enemy anti-access/area-denial defenses in depth," and "attack the enemy's space and cyber capabilities" may either be beyond the capabilities of U.S. and allied forces or may create unfavorable escalation risks, points discussed in more depth below.

In JOAC's concluding portions the Joint Staff authors soberly laid out the steep challenge facing both policymakers and military planners as they contemplated the implications of China's military modernization. JOAC listed thirty operational capabilities U.S. military forces should possess if they expected to succeed in a high-end access-denial battle. The list included capabilities such as the following:

1. The ability to perform effective command and control in a degraded and/or austere communications environment.
2. The ability to locate, target, and suppress or neutralize hostile anti-access and area-denial capabilities in complex terrain with the necessary range, precision, responsiveness and reversible and permanent effects while limiting collateral damage.
3. The ability to conduct and support operational maneuver over strategic distances along multiple axes of advance by air and sea.
4. The ability to mask the approach of joint maneuver elements to enable those forces to penetrate sophisticated anti-access systems and close within striking range with acceptable risk.[9]

Many of these required capabilities are operations few if any U.S. or allied commanders have ever had to execute, at least outside of scripted training events. The United States has not faced large-scale opposed access to the global commons since 1945. Today's commanders and their staffs thus face the disorienting task of having to discard long-standing assumptions and procedures related to strategic maneuver, engagement ranges, logistics support, and force protection, among many other considerations. U.S. and allied training exercises over the past decade have increasingly included access-denial barriers in their design, challenging commanders to improvise solutions to these situations as elements of the exercises. But as chapter 3 pointed out, discarding long-standing ways of doing things has not been a notable characteristic of U.S. military culture for many decades.

JOAC's authors performed their highest public service when they listed ten risks that if not addressed could compromise the joint-access concept—and presumably the viability of access operations by U.S. and coalition forces.[10] Among their frequently discussed points was the possibility that U.S. and allied forces would fail to achieve sufficient cross-domain synergy, the key tenet of the concept. This failure could occur because of an adversary's success at degrading the coalition's command and control network, thus preventing the effective integration of domain capabilities. China's cyber warfare and counterspace capabilities are notable concerns in this regard. Failure could similarly occur because the systems in the various domains are unable to integrate their operations or because operational demands make it too complicated to do so.

Although JOAC called for cross-domain synergy to occur at low organizational levels to speed up actions and take advantage of fleeting opportunities, lower-echelon commanders and staffs may be untrained, ill-equipped, insufficiently connected, or lack the authority to achieve the cross-domain synergy JOAC's authors intended.

Perhaps even more critical, JOAC's authors posited that U.S. and allied forces may simply lack the systems and capabilities to implement some of the concept's required precepts and tasks. In addition, policymakers may conclude that it is too expensive to acquire these systems and capabilities. For example, the concept calls for attacking an adversary's systems and networks at depth. U.S. and coalition forces may not be able to acquire at a reasonable cost the capabilities needed to find and target mobile and stealthy adversary platforms operating from deep continental positions. Similarly, planners may find it impractical to logistically support the concept at strategic distances through contested lines of communication.

Finally, and perhaps most crucially, JOAC's authors suggested that policymakers may not want to execute some of the concept's essential features. Deep strikes against enemy systems and networks could greatly increase escalation risks in ways unfavorable to U.S. interests. For example, policymakers may hesitate to bombard the homeland of an adversary armed with intercontinental-range nuclear forces. Attacks on an adversary's space and computer systems would likely lead to retaliation against U.S. systems, an escalation that could impair U.S. forces more than those of the adversary. These concerns are discussed below.

JOAC's formal title—*Joint Operational Access Concept, Version 1.0*— emphasized its "first draft" nature, likely no accident for General Dempsey and the authors. It was a reminder of how little work had been done by the U.S. military on the access problem, how much more needed to be done, and, by implication, how late the Defense Department arrived at the issue. Dempsey deserves credit for putting his signature on a document that candidly discussed how ill-prepared and ill-equipped his forces were for the high-end access challenge they faced in the western Pacific and elsewhere. The first step for fixing a problem is admitting that it exists. JOAC did that. JOAC was also intended to move the immense and largely inert defense bureaucracy to adapt before an access crisis strikes. On that point, JOAC was much less successful.

How Air-Sea Battle Fell behind Reality

Well before General Dempsey had the Joint Staff draft JOAC, ensuring by its nature that all four services would have a role in dealing with the access-denial problem, Air Force and Navy staff planners had quietly been at work on the Air-Sea Battle concept. The Defense Department's 2010 *Quadrennial Defense Review* made explicit mention of the Air-Sea Battle concept and called on the department to implement its tenets.[11]

Even before it could receive the formal blessing of the department's top officials, Air-Sea Battle sparked a backlash from critics. The secretive nature of the planning, explained as necessary for operational security, raised suspicions. Advocates for the ground forces saw the Army and Marine Corps, still at war in Iraq and Afghanistan, threatened with having their future budgets gutted to pay for the exotic technology Air-Sea Battle would likely require. Further, many strategists were skeptical about a concept that openly relied on large-scale bombardment of a nuclear-armed peer competitor like China. These critics foresaw a boondoggle of spending that would enrich certain defense contractors but result in weapons and capabilities that could never be used.

In February 2012, Gen. Norton Schwartz, then chief of staff of the Air Force, and Adm. Jonathan Greenert, then CNO, responded to this criticism with an essay published in the journal *American Interest.* Hoping to silence Air-Sea Battle's critics, Schwartz and Greenert described the military problem the concept was designed to address and explained some of its operational methods.[12]

According to Schwartz and Greenert, access denial was becoming a pervasive problem, and not just a one-off situation in the western Pacific. They asserted that ad hoc solutions designed for specific episodes would not be adequate in the future. Instead, the Defense Department needed a permanent and wide-ranging organization, both at the Pentagon and at field commands, to ensure comprehensive interservice integration. The concept was not a power and budget grab by the Air Force and Navy, they insisted, but merely sensible planning and coordination to cope with an increasingly omnipresent problem; it was the very kind of prudent action Defense Department officials should be taking.

After making that reasonable case, Schwartz and Greenert went on to explain how Air-Sea Battle would work in combat. Instead of rebutting skeptics, however, the two officers raised doubts about the concept's practicality.

Air-Sea Battle was in essence about protecting U.S. and allied warships and bases from adversary missiles. In their *American Interest* article, Schwartz and Greenert described three lines of effort designed to thwart precision missile attacks: (1) *disruption* of adversary reconnaissance and command networks; (2) *destruction* of adversary missile-launching platforms such as submarines, aircraft, and ships to reduce the missile threat to allied forces; and (3) *defeat* of adversary missiles before they impact allied targets. A networked and integrated joint force able to operate at great depth would be required to execute these three lines of effort.

Disrupting an adversary's reconnaissance and command network—in other words, disrupting that adversary's ability to locate and target opponents—involves a variety of passive and active measures, some of which are as old as warfare itself. Ancient passive measures still used today include camouflage, hiding out of sight, and employing decoys. Over the past century, combatants have disrupted enemy surveillance by shutting down their radios and radar and employing deception such as fake transmitters. More recent forms of disruption include electronic attacks on adversary sensors and thwarting sensors such as radar through stealthy designs and materials.

More controversial would be kinetic attacks on China's reconnaissance satellite constellations and cyber attacks on the PLA's communication and computer networks. The PLA has strived to emulate the U.S. military's ability to operate under "conditions of informatization." As commanders on both sides know, such a capability, while greatly enhancing command efficiency, also increases vulnerability to command disruption.

Chapter 3 discussed how highly dependent U.S. military forces have become on space and computerized global communication systems, especially expeditionary forces that would be "playing an away game" in the western Pacific. At the same time, China has already acquired a high level of expertise both with space and counterspace operations and with cyber warfare.

China might benefit from war in the space and cyber domains because of the greater reliance by U.S. military forces on space and computer capabilities and the relative difficulty the United States would face in the Indo-Pacific theater establishing alternatives to this reliance. China's position as the continental power improves its position in this regard. As a large continental power in a hypothetical conflict against U.S. expeditionary forces, China will have a much easier time operating a land-based manned and unmanned aircraft reconnaissance network to supplement and, if necessary, substitute for a space-based intelligence and communications system. In a hypothetical war over space-based networks, China will have an easier time fielding substitutes, at least for military operations over China's Near Seas, than will the United States. Thus, for technical and geographic reasons, the United States may find it imprudent to disrupt China's reconnaissance and command networks if doing so invites Chinese retaliation on U.S. networks, which the United States will have a much more difficult time replacing or working without.

Schwartz and Greenert's second line of effort contemplates destroying adversary platforms such as submarines, aircraft, and ships to reduce the missile threat to allied forces. As discussed in chapters 3 and 4, China's land-attack and antiship missile forces make it too dangerous for U.S. short-range tactical airpower—which constitutes the bulk of U.S. striking power—to get close enough to suppress China's land-based aircraft and missile forces. China's airpower will operate from scores of air bases, most of them hardened against air attack and heavily defended by a sophisticated air defense system. China's land-based antiship missiles will operate from mobile transporter-erector-launchers able to exploit the complex terrain to hide from U.S. sensors.

With its heavy reliance on short-range tactical airpower, the United States has the wrong mix of forces to execute Schwartz and Greenert's second line of effort. The 1991 Persian Gulf War indicated the rough order of magnitude of such a campaign, namely tens of thousands of individual bomb aim points.[13] To attack this target set, the United States would have only a handful of B-2 bombers (the only stealthy aircraft with the range to operate inside China's air defense system) and Navy Tomahawk cruise missiles numbering in the hundreds rather than the thousands. Air-Sea Battle's second line of effort—"Killing the archer before he shoots the arrow"—is thus a tough proposition for the current inventory of U.S. forces.

That leaves Schwartz and Greenert's third line of effort: defeating adversary missiles before they impact their targets. Chapter 4 examined the steep challenge faced by U.S. air bases and naval task forces attempting to defend against saturation missile attacks. The current technology favors offensive missiles over passive and active defensive measures. The falling relative cost of guided munitions over the next decade will greatly expand the number of incoming missiles with which defenders must cope. Falling relative missile costs will similarly reduce the value of passive defenses. With cheap but precise missiles available, rationing will be less necessary; attackers will simply strike with more missiles and against more suspected, even if unconfirmed, adversary targets.

The same technological progress will improve sensor fidelity and reduce sensor costs, resulting in their ubiquity on and around the battlefield. The increasing ubiquity and fidelity of sensors will make passive defenses such as deception, dispersion, and camouflage less useful.

Advancing technology should logically also benefit defenders, but active defenses, such as missile interceptors, will continue to be much more costly than offensive missiles, making a race between attackers and defenders a contest defenders will lose. Emerging technologies such as solid-state lasers hold out the hope of swinging the military balance back to defenses. But these technologies are still under development, and the services do not yet have timetables for procuring and deploying them as weapon systems in the field.[14] For the rest of this decade, U.S. and allied military planners will have to assume that offensive systems and forces will have both technical and cost advantages over defenders.

The Air-Sea Battle concept was an uncompetitive response to China's access-denial strategy because it focused expensive U.S. and coalition military resources at China's strengths rather than its vulnerabilities. All three of Air-Sea Battle's lines of effort had flaws that impaired their practicality in wartime. In 2015, the Air-Sea Battle Office at the Pentagon was renamed the Joint Concept for Access and Maneuver in the Global Commons, or JAM-GC, Office.[15] In the months and years afterward, discussion of Air-Sea Battle and its concepts faded away.

Why a Blockade Is Not an Easy Answer

At the beginning of some future crisis with China—one that does not begin with kinetic combat—U.S. policymakers are likely to respond first with noncombat, nonkinetic actions. Examples of such responses include consultations with allies, diplomatic protests, economic and financial sanctions, and legal sanctions against individual Chinese leaders. Much higher on the escalation list is an economic blockade, enforced by employing military and other security forces to curtail maritime and air commerce with China. A blockade would be an act of war under international law, but it would not, at least at first, require widespread employment of weapons and destruction.

A blockade would also seem to be an effective way to obtain leverage over China's leaders. It would target China's trade-dependent economy, which appears to be tantalizingly vulnerable and ripe for exploitation. A maritime blockade would seem to offer a way of creating leverage without having to bomb China and risk the grim possibility of escalation against a formidable nuclear weapon state. China's economy depends on seaborne commerce, both for raw material imports and for finished goods exports. A distant blockade implemented at the Strait of Malacca, the Indonesia archipelago, and the First and Second Island Chains would take advantage of these permanent geographical features to China's detriment. U.S. and coalition surface forces enforcing the blockade at these geographic chokepoints would be at the outer range of China's land-based air and missile power. Closer to China's shore, the United States could use its advantage in submarines to tighten the blockade. A blockade would not require kinetic and cyber attacks on China's homeland, space assets, and other command network, which would avoid the escalation risks inherent in these courses of action.

A blockade thus appears to be a less risky approach than opting for kinetic attacks on China's military forces or its homeland. It would capitalize on geographical advantages and could avoid some of China's shorter-range air and missile power. It attacks a particular vulnerability in the Chinese economy. Perhaps most important, it is a slow and incremental approach, allowing policymakers on both sides to avoid dangerous escalation and to find a way to resolve a conflict without losing face.

Despite these apparent advantages, a blockade of Chinese commerce is not a practical option. A blockade would suffer from two major weaknesses. First, it would inflict almost as much economic damage on U.S. allies and neutral countries as it would on China. A U.S. blockade would be highly unpopular across the world, and likely politically unsustainable for long. Second, the huge volume of commerce and shipping involved is almost certainly beyond the capacity of the U.S. military to manage in an orderly way, making the implementation of a blockade impractical.

A military blockade against China would make the United States an aggressor against the global economy because its damaging economic effects would be felt everywhere. This would especially be the case should the United States be forced to act in response to a nonkinetic Chinese first move, such as a blockade of Taiwan. The risk for U.S. policymakers directing a blockade of China in response is that much of the rest of the world would view the resulting economic calamity as a disproportionate response to the original Chinese offense. It is questionable whether the United States would be able to politically sustain a blockade for the time required to compel a change in Chinese policy, especially when some of the greatest unintended damage would fall on U.S. allies in Asia, Europe, and Latin America.

Economic damage inside the United States and China would also be severe. Because China is an authoritarian country with strict censorship and a large internal security apparatus, it is reasonable to presume that the CCP would stand a better chance of outlasting the domestic and global political backlash from the blockade's consequences than would U.S. and allied governments. This is even more likely to be the case in view of the high level of nationalist feeling inside China compared with that in the United States and the memory of foreign economic exploitation still alive in the Chinese population. A prolonged and economically devastating blockade would almost certainly not favor the United States.

A U.S. blockade would also damage the U.S. diplomatic position, especially with key relationships around Eurasia. In response to a seaborne blockade, China would attempt to reroute trade through Russia and Central Asia. The blockade would boost geopolitical ties between China and Russia and greatly increase Russia's overall geopolitical and economic role, a result not in America's interest. More of Europe's trade with China would go through Russia as well, which could cause Europe to strategically drift away from the United States. In essence, a distant blockade would separate the United States from Eurasian affairs, increase the power of U.S. adversaries there, and inadvertently push away Eurasian allies.

Next, the U.S. military is neither equipped nor organized to execute a distant blockade at the Second Island Chain and beyond. Enforcing a distant blockade would be an immense task. More than 80,000 ships of over 300 gross tons transit the Strait of Malacca every year, a rate of over 219 ships every day.[16] U.S. submarines cannot simply lie off China's ports and sink all incoming merchant ships. Such "unrestricted submarine warfare" and the resultant casualties to third-nation civilians would be even less politically sustainable today than it was for Germany in the twentieth century. Cargo bound for China would be mixed on container ships with cargo bound for many other countries in the region.[17] Cargo in any merchant ship could be bound for numerous ports, and a particular cargo may be sold and assigned to a port of call while the ship is still in transit. The U.S. military would thus have the task of boarding and searching thousands of container ships at a variety of distant points in the Indian and Pacific Oceans, finding cargo bound for China, and somehow diverting that cargo while minimizing disruption to the rest of the global economy.

This task would require the Navy, Marine Corps, and Army to mobilize hundreds of platoon-sized Visit, Board, Search, Seizure (VBSS) teams and support them at sea for a potentially open-ended duration. Staffing two hundred platoon-size VBSS teams on an ongoing rotational basis, for example, could require the Marine Corps and Army to commit at least ten regiment- or brigade-sized units to the task. An additional large combat support organization would be required.

The Navy operates forty-four amphibious ships of all types, no more than one-third of which are operationally deployed at any one time.[18] The amphibious ships are well suited for blockade enforcement because they have troop berthing quarters, helicopter space, small boat facilities, and command suites. Leased commercial ships, on the other hand, even if available in the numbers required, generally do not have these features and would likely be unsuited for prolonged VBSS operations, which would require billeting troops for months at sea and supporting helicopter and small boat detachments.

Other Navy ships, such as the fleet of Littoral Combat Ships, could supplement the forty-four amphibious ships. But that addition would still be trivial considering that scores of ships would have to be boarded and searched every day. Even if supplemented with improvised support, the Navy's amphibious fleet would lack the capacity to sort through the thousands of commercial ships sailing in and out of the western Pacific. In sum, the distant blockade strategy is almost certainly beyond the capacity of the Navy to execute and would leave the United States with no reserve amphibious combat power for other contingencies.

Nor should U.S. planners count on enforcement support from countries in the Indian and Pacific Oceans. The economic effects of the blockade will render the U.S. policy generally unpopular there, among both allies and neutral countries.

Limiting the blockade to just the crude oil trade and the large tankers that transport crude oil from the Middle East and Africa also would not work. China could respond to such an oil blockade by seizing outright the maritime territory it already claims in the East and South China Seas and then using its access-denial forces to defend these seizures from counterattack and, likely, to block commercial transit by the U.S. and allied countries. As mentioned in chapter 1, the Chinese government estimates that these two seas hold enough crude oil to supply China's future needs for many decades. Recapturing the seas and restoring freedom of navigation to the western Pacific would require robust military forces and the willingness to attack China, the very outcome the blockade was meant to prevent.

There would be additional political and geostrategic consequences to an indefinite distant blockade of China. The blockade would be vulnerable to irregular warfare methods and propaganda exploitation. VBSS operations would be blamed for the delays in the arrival of cargo to third-party countries, which would certainly increase hostility toward the United States. U.S. boarding parties would eventually encounter armed resistance, with videos of such encounters quickly appearing in global media, damaging America's diplomatic position.

Finally, U.S. policymakers should not expect that a blockade would impair the PLA or its ability to sustain military operations. China, especially considering its authoritarian government, would be able to redirect sufficient resources from the civilian economy to the PLA to supply its operations.[19]

Although at first glance an appealing option, a blockade on China would encounter immense logistical, economic, and political barriers. Its greatest drawbacks for the United States would be political; a distant blockade would inflict pain on U.S. allies and alienate the United States from global public opinion. A blockade would compel the United States to engage in an opened-ended political-military struggle that would spark resistance and insurgency, this time at sea. As U.S. policymakers have witnessed repeatedly over recent decades, such conflicts have not gone well.

The Pentagon Finally Faces the China Threat—
While Changing as Little as Possible

The 2018 *National Defense Strategy* (NDS), issued under the guidance and signature of Secretary of Defense James Mattis, was a breakthrough for the Department of Defense. The NDS declared that two revisionist powers, China and Russia, would henceforth be the main planning focus of the department:

> The central challenge to U.S. prosperity and security is the *reemergence of long-term, strategic competition* [emphasis in original] by what the National Security Strategy classifies as revisionist powers. It is increasingly clear that China and Russia want to shape a world consistent with their authoritarian model—gaining veto authority over other nations' economic, diplomatic, and security decisions.
>
> China is leveraging military modernization, influence operations, and predatory economics to coerce neighboring countries to reorder the Indo-Pacific region to their advantage. As China continues its economic and military ascendance, asserting power through an all-of-nation long-term strategy, it will continue to pursue a military modernization program that seeks Indo-Pacific regional hegemony in the near-term and displacement of the United States to achieve global preeminence in the future. The most far-reaching objective of this defense strategy is to set the military relationship between our two countries on a path of transparency and non-aggression.[20]

The NDS clearly stated the new focus of U.S. defense strategy: "Interstate strategic competition, not terrorism, is now the primary concern in U.S. national security."[21] The U.S. government had finally named China as the nation's top strategy threat. The NDS directed the Defense Department to make preparing for the Chinese threat the top priority for its planning staffs and the military services.

Most of the Pentagon's vast bureaucracy seemed to welcome such clear guidance, especially when the object of the guidance, the PLA, was a conventional military opponent such as the military services and the department's planning staffs were accustomed to.

The NDS's direction to focus on China and interstate threats, a clear departure from the attention on irregular warfare and the Middle East of the last two decades, invited the military services to boldly rethink their operational concepts, retool their procurement plans, and reshape their organizations and their training programs. Instead, institutional inertia and conservatism largely smothered the mandate.

There were exceptions to this inertia, but overall, the response of the Pentagon's staffs and military services to the 2018 NDS was to change the legacy operational concepts and procurement programs as little as possible. Initially, at least, they merely repurposed the existing legacy programs and policies—programs and policies enacted in a different era for different problems and under different assumptions. That meek response has fallen short of what is required to respond to the PLA's aggressive modernization program and the CCP's accelerating assertiveness.

The Pentagon Bungles the Next-Generation Bomber, Then Scrambles to Adjust

In testimony to the House Armed Services Committee in July 2006, Gen. T. Michael Moseley, then the chief of staff of the Air Force, explained that the Air Force was developing plans for the Next Generation Bomber (NGB), a long-range heavy bomber scheduled to be in service by 2018. The NGB would replace the aging Cold War–era B-52s and B-1Bs, which, except for twenty-one B-2 stealth bombers, constituted the Air Force's bomber inventory.[22]

Sixteen years later, the composition of the Air Force's bomber inventory is unchanged albeit smaller after the service retired seventeen worn-out B-1Bs in early 2021.[23] A decade of effort was wasted because top leaders in the Pentagon during the first decade of this century bungled the modernization of the bomber force. As a result, U.S. military commanders are entering the 2020s, likely to be the most perilous decade in the U.S.-China military competition, without a military asset crucial for maintaining conventional deterrence in the Indo-Pacific region.

The Air Force's B-2 Spirit stealth bomber, the nation's only long-range aircraft capable of surviving and achieving missions inside a sophisticated air defense system such as those fielded by China and Russia, was developed during the 1980s as the Cold War was in its final stage and arrived in service in the 1990s, after the Cold War concluded. The Air Force's original plan was to acquire 132 B-2s to replace its nonstealthy B-52s and B-1s, which would struggle to survive against modern air defenses. But with the Cold War over and policymakers in the Clinton administration and Congress not anticipating another challenge from a peer military competitor, the defense budget in 1997 permanently cut the B-2 purchase to just 21 aircraft.[24] Although made a quarter century ago, this fateful decision had consequences that U.S. military commanders suffer from today. If these commanders had the planned force of 132 B-2s available to them, sustaining conventional deterrence in the Indo-Pacific versus the PLA would be a much simpler task. The B-2s would have the capacity to attack thousands of aim points a day at long range, and do so through challenging enemy air defenses. Chinese policymakers and commanders would doubt their ability to successfully employ the PLA on, say, a military assault on Taiwan against such opposition.

In 2005, with the Air Force still in need of a new bomber to replace the aging B-52s and B-1s, designers began working on requirements and specifications for the NGB, penciling in 2018 as the aircraft's hoped-for entry into service. At this point, designers and requirements writers in the Air Force and the Pentagon began loading ever more elaborate features and capabilities onto the aircraft's planned specifications. One such specification gave the bomber the capability to target and launch air-to-air missiles in self-defense, an expensive feature previous bombers did not have.

Designers also added exotic target location sensors—some of which were likely unproven technology—and other features, and the new bomber's cost and technology risks grew geometrically. In 2009, Secretary of Defense Robert Gates terminated the NGB program. General Schwartz agreed that there were "rational reasons" for doing so.[25]

Why did Air Force planners and designers allow the NGB program's design features to reach the point where Gates and senior Air Force leaders realized the program had become untenable? The likely answer is that weapon program managers know that large programs such as a new bomber occur very rarely, perhaps only a few times in a century. With such opportunities so rare, designers feel compelled to load as many features as possible into the design. Unfortunately for the NGB, the spiraling costs clashed with the simultaneous onset of the 2008 financial crisis, the subsequent need for defense spending austerity, and grinding guerilla wars in Iraq and Afghanistan that occupied the attention of policymakers like Gates at the expense of more distant threats such as a modernizing PLA. In other circumstances, the NGB program might have survived. But not in 2009.

Even so, a year later Gates approved the development of new long-range strike capabilities, including restarting the development of a new Air Force bomber.[26] This new initiative would eventually become the B-21 Raider program. The Air Force, chastened by its misjudgments on the NGB, managed the new bomber program far differently, resulting in a much better outcome. Nevertheless, the first squadrons of B-21s will not be ready for combat until the mid-to-late 2020s. The wasted decade may have grievous consequences for the security of the Indo-Pacific region.

Over the past ten years weapon developers at the Pentagon have worked on other methods of long-range strike. Perhaps the most important and successful of these is a joint Air Force–Navy missile program, the Joint Air-to-Surface Standoff Missile (JASSM). The missile has completed testing, is now in full production, and is sold to international partners such as Australia and Poland. The now-standard extended-range production model has a range greater than 926 kilometers (500 nautical miles), a 1,000-pound warhead, is stealthy, has jam-proof precision targeting sensors, and costs about $1.1 million per missile.[27]

Air Force and Navy bombers and fighter-attack aircraft would employ JASSMs at the beginning of a conflict against high-value targets such as enemy command posts, air defense radar and missile sites, air base facilities, warships docked in port, weapon bunkers, and bridges. With the JASSM's long range, U.S. and allied aircraft will typically be able launch at these targets from beyond the range of an adversary's air defense systems. Once JASSMs and other effects have weakened the adversary's air defenses, U.S. and allied aircraft can approach closer to enemy targets, employing shorter-range and less expensive air-to-surface weapons in larger numbers. The Air Force is planning to acquire up to ten thousand JASSMs, perhaps recognizing the important role the missile would play in a potential conflict against the PLA.[28]

Realizing that Chinese antiship cruise missiles such as the YJ-12 outranged their U.S. counterparts, in 2008 Pacific Fleet officers issued an urgent request to the Defense Advanced Research Projects Agency (DARPA) to develop a new long-range antiship cruise missile. DARPA worked with the Air Force, the Navy, and Lockheed-Martin to modify the JASSM for the antiship mission, thus avoiding the costs and delays of designing a completely new missile.[29] The resulting Long Range Anti-Ship Missile (LRASM) has been tested and is now in production at the same assembly plant that manufactures the JASSM. The Air Force plans to buy up to four hundred LRASMs to be launched from its bomber and fighter-attack aircraft.[30] The stealthy LRASM is designed to find a specific ship in a moving ship formation at sea, avoid enemy missile defenses, and succeed even in a heavily contested electronic warfare and jamming situation.[31] The LRASM provides an important capability for holding at risk PLAN warships during a possible conflict in the western Pacific or elsewhere.

Even with the arrival of JASSMs and LRASMs and their long-range capabilities, the largest proportion of the Air Force's strike capacity still resides in its shorter-range tactical aircraft. Air Force planners have scrambled over the past decade to develop ways to make their short-range fighter aircraft more effective, even as they know that their air bases along the First Island Chain are under grave threat from the PLA's missiles and airpower.

Over the past few years Air Force tacticians and planners have developed the Agile Combat Employment (ACE) warfighting concept. The goal of ACE is to find additional nontraditional airfields from which small detachments of aircraft and support crews could operate for limited periods. Air Force planners envision an agile "hub and spoke" system in which detachments from a main hub base, such as the Kadena Air Base on Okinawa and Andersen Air Base on Guam, would move to austere expeditionary runways elsewhere in the region and continue air operations from these locations. ACE would force an adversary like the PLA to monitor far more potential targets for its air base suppression campaign and perhaps would stretch the PLA's ability to suppress Air Force operations in the region beyond the PLA's missile-launching capacity.[32]

Gen. Charles Q. Brown Jr., at that time the commander of Pacific Air Forces, summed up the ACE concept: "In order to operate, all you need is a runway, a ramp, fuel bladder, a trailer full of munitions, a pallet of MREs [food rations], and some multifunctional Airmen. We should be able to operate from anywhere, any location in the world."[33] To prepare for employing ACE during a prospective future conflict in the western Pacific, Air Force planners studied "every single piece of concrete" across the Indo-Pacific as a possible expeditionary air base and produced a list of locations capable of hosting detachments of Air Force fighter-attack and cargo aircraft.[34]

The decision of Air Force commanders to pursue ACE as the best means of surviving and continuing air operations in the face of prospective salvos of PLA land-attack missiles reveals several conclusions. First, U.S. airpower planners have likely concluded that expending ever more resources on hardening the existing six Air Force bases in the western Pacific—more concrete bunkers, concrete aircraft shelters, and underground facilities—is a losing strategy. It will continue to be cheaper for the PLA to add more missiles than it will be for the Air Force to pour more concrete at the six known air bases. The United States would lose the "concrete versus missiles" race.

Second, adding to air and missile defenses around the hub Air Force bases is also not a sustainable solution. As discussed earlier, offensive missiles and their launch platforms are much less expensive than the targets and the defensive systems attempting to protect them. This syndrome applies to the missile defense of fixed air bases as much as it applies to the Navy's efforts to protect its aircraft carrier strike groups from anti-ship missile attack (it also applies to the PLA attempting to defend its warships and bases). Adding defensive missiles when the attacker can add offensive missiles at perhaps one-tenth the marginal cost is a losing proposition. A 2011 RAND Corporation report examined these defensive options and concluded that although these measures would require the PLA to expend more missiles to achieve its goals, missile defenses and hardening are unlikely to keep the bases in action if China is determined to suppress them.[35]

That leaves "distributed operations," the dispersion of forces into small yet coordinated units spread widely across the theater of operations, as the only remaining option. The result is the ACE concept for the Air Force, with the other services developing analogous versions (discussed later).

ACE is the only sustainable option yet identified, but will it work, especially against an opponent like the PLA, which enjoys the support of a massive and modern military-industrial manufacturing and supply base? Military air operations require a large and sustained flow of fuel, ordnance, spare parts, and supplies to support the personnel running the operation. Air forces have long preferred large, fixed bases with the facilities to support these logistics-intensive tasks. Expeditionary bases would likely be difficult to supply and therefore are unlikely to sustain many combat sorties. Remotely located expeditionary bases may be outside the coverage of air and missile defenses and, if hastily established, could be vulnerable to ground attack by special operations direct action teams. Finally, they are unlikely to have any hardened facilities, and once discovered will be highly vulnerable to missile attack.

Planners of ACE-type distributed operations note that the plan is to operate at the "spoke" sites temporarily, perhaps for mere days or even hours before moving elsewhere. This procedure would enhance survival, but it would come at the cost of sustained, high-tempo combat sortie generation. Planners could preposition supplies at prospective spoke sites, but doing so would reveal these locations to PLA target planners, at least partially voiding an important feature of the ACE concept.

Finally, although distributed operations such as ACE are the best of the choices facing planners attempting to keep U.S. short-range fighter aircraft in the western Pacific relevant, ACE and other distributed operations concepts still face a PLA that is building out a ubiquitous and all-seeing sensor network and ever-growing inventories of smart, deadly, and inexpensive offensive missiles. The Air Force will not be able to conceal the location and composition of its distributed aircraft detachments from the PLA's synthetic aperture radar satellite constellations and armed unmanned reconnaissance aircraft patrols. The PLA's rapid-response hypersonic missiles will be a grave threat to even fleeting hub-and-spoke air operations. It is becoming increasingly difficult for the "hiders" to win the "hider versus finder" competition.

This does not mean that United States should abandon its forward bases in the Indo-Pacific. Maintaining the forward presence of U.S. military forces sends a political message to both America's partners and China that the United States is sustaining its security commitment to the region. As important, the presence of these forces, even though they will be vulnerable to Chinese missile attack, establishes "first strike deterrence." Should PLA commanders decide to remove the threat posed by U.S. forces at forward bases, China would have to escalate the war by attacking more countries, presumably bringing them into the conflict against China. The prospect of adding additional enemies could deter China's leaders from aggressive action in the first place.

ACE is a creative attempt by Air Force planners to respond to the threat the PLA's missiles pose to U.S. bases in the Indo-Pacific region. These planners are doing the best they can with the forces they have and the situation they are responsible for. The problems these commanders are coping with are the consequences of decisions, such as truncating the B-2 acquisition and the mismanagement of the Next Generation Bomber, that policymakers made years and even decades ago. Despite its shortcomings, the ACE concept should play an important role in a larger strategy design for the Indo-Pacific theater.

The Navy Wants an Arms Race It Cannot Win

China's expanding sensor and missile capabilities have been especially damaging to the U.S. Navy's traditional force structure and operational concepts. This damage has extended to the Marine Corps, which relies on the Navy's amphibious ships to accomplish its maritime-related missions. The PLA missile threat has forced a reckoning among analysts over the service's future. This reckoning reached a climax at the end of the Trump administration when dueling plans for the Navy's future fleet design fought for acceptance inside the Pentagon and in Congress. In the end, the credibility of all the plans was questioned amid concerns that Navy planners still have not fully accepted the implication of the current military-technical revolution.

Until U.S. forces acquire the capacity to suppress the PLA's land-based "antinavy," the Navy's surface ships must rely on their ability to defend themselves from missiles. However, the PLA now has the ability to use its various strike aircraft to launch perhaps two hundred or more high-speed antiship cruise missiles from several axes at approaching U.S. naval strike groups. Even if ship defenses knocked down 95 percent of the attacking missiles (the historical rate is much lower), the few that penetrated the defenses would have a shocking effect. And after fending off one such attack, the strike group would likely have few if any remaining defensive missiles to resist a follow-up attack.

Navy scientists hope that solid-state lasers will swing the arms race away from missiles and back to missile defenses. But such weapons will require new ship designs to provide the necessary electrical power and many more years of research and development before an operational and integrated system is ready for the fleet.[36] Until then, the advantage of the antinavy forces will widen; China's antiship missiles will continue to gain in range and sensor sophistication while ship defense systems capable of defeating a saturation antiship missile attack struggle to emerge from the laboratory.

Naval analysts have increasingly concluded over the past decade that the Navy's aircraft carriers cannot play the role they became accustomed to playing in World War II, especially against opponents well-armed with state-of-the-art antiship missiles.[37] Some planners have hoped that the arrival of unmanned carrier strike aircraft will extend the carriers' reach, making them once again relevant. But as chapter 3 explained, the fact that aircraft carriers are limited to hosting small tactical aircraft places an upper limit on their radius of action. In the 2010s the Navy began introducing F-35C fighter-attack aircraft to its carrier air wings. The long-troubled F-35 program did finally deliver a highly capable stealth aircraft to the Air Force, Navy, and Marine Corps. The F-35's ability to avoid enemy air defenses, its advanced abilities to detect and attack targets, and its capabilities to share data across networked platforms are revolutionary competitive advantages. But the Navy's F-35C has a maximum combat radius of about 1,100 kilometers, roughly matching the combat radius of the F/A-18 E/F it will join on Navy carrier flight decks.[38] These combat radii will not be adequate to keep the aircraft carriers out of range of land-based threats to warships that Chinese military forces have already developed and fielded.

In 2013, the Navy successfully tested the X-47B experimental unmanned combat aircraft. The goal of the X-47B program was to demonstrate that an unmanned jet could launch from an aircraft carrier, autonomously perform various missions, and then return and land on the carrier. The X-47B held out the promise of greatly extending the range of the carrier air wing. Without an onboard human crew and built around a single engine, the X-47B would have a much longer operational range than the F/A-18 E/F and the F-35C. That year the Navy also successfully launched and landed the robotic aircraft on the aircraft carrier USS *George H. W. Bush*, demonstrating that an unmanned carrier-based jet is feasible.[39]

Many observers hoped the X-47B concept would make the carrier air wing relevant again against land-based adversaries with long-range antiship capabilities. But the X-47B would require either a constant and secure satellite-based communication connection with an offboard Navy flight crew—a technique the Air Force has employed in global operations for many years with its unmanned MQ-9 Reaper combat aircraft—or highly sophisticated onboard software to take it through enemy air defenses, attack the correct target, and then return it to the aircraft carrier.

Facing these development challenges, the Navy decided to limit the unmanned aircraft's main role to airborne refueling of manned F/A-18 E/F, F-35C, and other manned aircraft. Redesigned and named the MQ-25A Stingray, the unmanned tanker aircraft is expected to arrive in service in 2025.[40] The Stingray will improve the range of the Navy's carrier air wings, but it will not solve the range problem the Navy's aircraft carriers face versus China's long-range land-based antiship forces. Even with the Stingray refueler extending the range of the aircraft carriers' manned strike aircraft, the carriers' strike radius will remain too short compared to the ranges of the land-based aircraft and missiles that threaten carrier strike groups.

As doubts about aircraft carriers' future continued to grow, naval analysts began revisiting the idea of "arsenal ships"—surface ships with the primary mission of launching long-range land-attack and antiship missiles in large numbers. In the 1990s, CNO Adm. Jeremy M. Boorda promoted the concept of a large, single-purpose surface ship that was envisioned to carry up to five hundred long-range missiles. The arsenal ship concept was abandoned when analysts concluded that the ship would concentrate too much of its capability in a single target and would reveal its position to enemy sensors before it could complete its mission and escape a counterattack.[41]

Although the Navy rejected Boorda's concept, it did endorse the idea in a modified form. After the Cold War, the Navy converted four of its Trident-class ballistic missile submarines into cruise missile carriers, each armed with 154 Tomahawk missiles. This gesture toward the arsenal ship concept resulted from an accident in history (the reduction in strategic nuclear forces after the Cold War) and was too expensive to expand into a capability that would match the sustained strike capacity of a carrier air wing. Due to their age, the Navy will soon retire the four converted cruise missile submarines.

Although arsenal ships were deemed impractical to compensate for aircraft carriers' shortcomings, surface missile ships seemed to offer another alternative. Research supported by ONA argued in 2013 that surface missile ships could deliver firepower more cheaply than aircraft carriers.[42]

Previous research had concluded that if an air campaign required striking only a relatively small number of targets, land-attack missiles such as the Tomahawk would be cheaper than the large fixed-capital costs associated with an aircraft carrier and its strike aircraft.[43] If the air campaign was long and required striking hundreds or thousands of aim points, however, aircraft dropping laser- or satellite-guided bombs would be the cheaper option. Indeed, that describes many of the most notable air campaigns the Navy has conducted since World War II and the type of campaign U.S. naval strike aviation has prepared for. It should be little surprise that the Navy's power projection doctrine matched the analysis of what is most cost effective, at least based on past air campaigns.

But ONA's new and contradictory conclusions from 2013 were based on more realistic assumptions about future air campaigns. By these assumptions, heavily defended air space (like China's) will force aircraft to employ stand-off missiles like JASSMs, which match the Tomahawk in cost, instead of cheap bombs. When the cost of aircraft shot down is added, even if only a few, the cost efficiency of the carrier air wing disappears, according to this analysis. In addition, advocates of missile ships will point to the benefits of dispersing the land-attack missiles over many smaller surface ships. This would reduce risk and increase target coverage, especially when compared with the potential loss concentrated in one or a few large aircraft carriers.

The Navy's culture was slow to adjust to these ideas. In December 2016, at the end of the Obama administration, the Navy sent a report to Congress that planned for a fleet of 355 combat and logistic support ("battle force") ships. This 355-ship Navy was an aspirational goal; the Navy had only 275 battle force ships in 2016, and the report did not specify a deadline for achieving the 355-ship goal. Nevertheless, Congress made the 355-ship goal a legislative policy in December 2017.[44]

The composition of the 355-ship Navy fully affirmed the long-standing legacy force design of the Navy. The plan called for 12 aircraft carriers, 104 cruisers and destroyers to protect those carriers, and 38 amphibious ships to support the Marine Corps. The design made no concessions to the PLA antiship missile threat and made no noticeable adjustments to significantly increase the Navy's long-range strike capabilities. The aircraft carrier and amphibious groups remained the central focus of the Navy's operational concept. The assumptions and concepts behind the 2016 Navy force design matched those from 1986 and 1966.

But within a few years the plan for a 355-ship Navy was sinking. By 2019, top Navy officials had begun to endorse "distributed lethality"—the concept of more small missile ships and fewer carriers. In early 2019 top Navy officials attempted to write a budget that would fund new technology initiatives such as unmanned systems, lasers, and new classes of smaller warships that would more widely distribute the Navy's assets and firepower. In April 2019 the Navy proposed retiring the USS *Harry Truman*, with a goal of saving $3.4 billion on the carrier's scheduled overhaul and redirecting those funds to the new emerging technologies. An uproar on Capitol Hill followed, and within hours the White House issued a decision countermanding the Navy's plan.[45]

The *Harry Truman* episode revealed a Navy leadership finally willing to restructure the Navy away from its most vulnerable and expensive legacy platforms toward a more distributed fleet architecture comprising smaller manned and unmanned ships. The quick collapse of the *Truman* gambit showed that they were unprepared for the resulting political backlash. Navy leaders concluded that they needed to start from the beginning on a new and comprehensive fleet design better suited for the threat posed by the PLA's missiles, something the 355-ship plan from 2016 had not done.

The Navy began work in 2019 on another new force design that was eventually called the Integrated Naval Force Structure Assessment (INFSA). The results of the effort, completed in early 2020, were never delivered to Congress or released to the public. Navy officials did say that the INFSA was designed to support the 2018 *National Defense Strategy* and its call for the Pentagon to focus its preparations on peer-level threats from China and Russia. The INFSA called for a fleet of around 390 manned and 45 unmanned or optionally manned ships. No further details about the composition of the fleet or the features and specifications of the proposed ships in the design were released.[46]

Secretary of Defense Mark Esper did not agree with the assumptions the Navy used in preparing the INFSA and in the spring of 2020 rejected the plan and its conclusions. He scrapped the document and ordered his deputy, David Norquist, and the staff in the Office of the Secretary of Defense (OSD) to come up with a new force design for the Navy, which was called the Future Naval Force Study (FNFS). By the summer of 2020 the Navy had largely lost control of the design of its future fleet, which was now in the hands of civilian analysts inside the OSD aided by an outside think-tank.[47]

Like the INFSA, the FNFS was not delivered to Congress or released to the public. The study reportedly called for up to 358 battle force ships (compared to 296 battle force ships in the Navy in 2020) and more than 500 ships of all types when unmanned ships and a new class of small corvettes were added.

But even the mysterious FNFS was not the final word on the Navy's future from the Trump administration. President Trump fired Esper in the administration's chaotic closing weeks, ending the defense secretary's effort to present a naval force structure plan to Congress. On December 9, 2020, the outgoing White House staff publicly released a proposed Navy force structure that set wide numeric ranges for various classes of current and hypothetical ships. The plan called for a fleet of up to 446 manned and 242 unmanned or optionally manned ships, for a total fleet size of up to 688 ships.[48]

In June 2021 the Biden administration released its preliminary Navy force structure plan. Like the December 2020 document from the Trump administration, the June 2021 shipbuilding plan listed only broad ranges of quantities for various ship types, with no numbers specified for either final force level goals or specific numbers of ship to be acquired by year in the decades ahead. The Biden fleet plan appeared conceptually similar to the Trump proposal, only smaller; the Biden plan called for about 15 percent fewer manned ships and about half the number of unmanned ships, summing to an overall fleet about 25 percent smaller than the final Trump proposal.[49]

In September 2021, the Congressional Budget Office (CBO) issued a report that estimated the procurement costs of the Biden administration's Fiscal Year 2022 Navy force structure plan. According to the report, the

Navy's ship procurement budget would have to average $25.3 billion to $32.7 billion per year (adjusted for inflation) each year for three decades to build the proposed fleet. That annual procurement sum is 10 percent to 43 percent higher than the Navy's average shipbuilding budget over the past five years. Direct ship operation and sustainment costs naturally would also increase with the much larger fleet, although the CBO could not calculate that expense given the proposal's lack of detail.[50]

All five Navy force structure proposals—the 355-ship plan from 2016, the INFSA, the FNFS, the December 2020 plan, and the June 2021 plan—have several features in common. None of the five plans seriously reckoned with a thickening and integrated PLA sensor and missile battle network that is specifically designed to destroy the surface warships each plan proposed building in prodigious numbers. None of the plans explained a concept of operations that would offset or overcome the PLA's missile superiority in the western Pacific, other than to sail ever greater numbers of surface ships into the PLA's missile engagement zones in the hope of somehow achieving a good result. None of the plans seemed to take seriously the possibility that Congress would resist the massive increases in shipbuilding and sustainment budgets the plans would require. The plans did not explain how the Navy would recruit, train, and retain the large increase in sailors and personnel each of the plans would require. Many of the ships proposed in the plans, such as a new corvette and a light amphibious warship, are merely notional concepts, not finished designs; given the Navy's recent difficulties receiving new ship classes from contractors in working order and on time, it is difficult to see these new concepts being present in the fleet until the 2030s. Finally, the plans did not seriously explain how the U.S. naval shipbuilding industrial base, far smaller now than it was at the end of the Cold War, could possibly build the fleets they proposed in a timely way and then maintain them in the decades ahead.

The last decade has seen top leaders in the Navy and the Pentagon slowly beginning to reckon with the implications of China's growing sensor and missile battle network. Their response has been a series of naval force structure plans that seem based on the idea of countering massed and deadly million-dollar PLA antiship missiles with vulnerable warships costing hundreds of millions or billions of dollars. Advocates of a large U.S. naval buildup have been lured into a naval arms race against a competitor that possesses the largest shipbuilding enterprise in the world, far exceeding the U.S. shipbuilding capacity.[51] What remains missing is a realistic way forward for U.S. and allied naval power. It will be up to top policymakers above the Navy to design a way for U.S. and allied maritime power to support a comprehensive military strategy for the Indo-Pacific region, something that is also missing.

The Marine Corps' Radical New Concept

Shortly after he became the commandant of the U.S. Marine Corps in 2019, Gen. David Berger became the first of the service chiefs to propose a dramatic restructuring of his service in response to the military-technical revolution. He issued blunt planning guidance to his service based on his experience as the commander of Marine forces in the Pacific and the commander of combat development for the Marine Corps.[52] That experience, Berger said, "has helped shape my conclusion that modest and incremental improvements to our existing force structure and legacy capabilities would be insufficient to overcome evolving threat capabilities. . . . We must acknowledge the impacts of proliferated precision long-range fires, mines, and other smart weapons, and seek innovative ways to overcome these threat capabilities."[53]

General Berger directed the Marine Corps to implement revolutionary changes to its force structure. Instead of being a force designed for either large-scale amphibious assaults or sustained land campaigns, the Corps would fashion itself to deploy in small units along the First Island Chain. These units, armed with antiship missiles, would "stand in" deep inside China's missile engagement zones. From there they would "attrite [attack] adversary forces, enable joint force access requirements, complicate targeting and consume adversary ISR resources, and prevent fait accompli scenarios."[54] In Berger's view, this refashioned Marine Corps would no longer need any tanks, five of its active and reserve infantry battalions, most of its cannon artillery, eight of its helicopter squadrons, and more than a third of its planned force of F-35B fighter-attack aircraft, all of which he ordered the service to shed. In their place the Marine Corps would acquire truck-mounted long-range antiship missiles and more reconnaissance capacity, especially unmanned aircraft.[55]

This directive was a dramatic disruption of the Marine Corps culture to create a force responsive to China's battle networks. Berger stated that the legacy Marine Corps he had inherited was obsolete for the current and future threat environment. The new concept followed the 2018 *National Defense Strategy*'s command for the services to focus their preparations on the peer-level threats from China and Russia. Having recently commanded Marine Corps forces in the Pacific and concluded that the PLA was the "pacing threat," Berger made blunting a PLA fait accompli action along the First Island Chain his service's top planning priority.

Berger admitted that there were some significant shortcomings in his concept that he and his service would need to fix. Among some observations in his force design directive, Berger noted the following:

- Range and operational reach matters in the Indo-Pacific Area of Responsibility.
- The hider-versus-finder competition is real. Losing this competition has enormous and potentially catastrophic consequences.
- Mobility inside the WEZ [the enemy's weapons engagement zone] is a competitive advantage and an operational imperative.
- Logistics (sustainability) is both a critical requirement and [a] critical vulnerability.[56]

Could Berger's new concept work, given these requirements? Berger himself admitted, "I am not confident that we have identified the additional structure required to provide the tactical maneuver and logistical sustainment needed to execute [the concepts] in contested littoral environments against our pacing threat." He also noted that the Marine Corps still needed to "develop military deception, camouflage, cover, concealment, and obscurant capabilities to defeat [the enemy's] terminal phase attack and challenge broad area surveillance." He tasked his subordinates to continue designing, testing, and experimenting to devise solutions to these problems.[57]

The PLA missile threat clearly made the Marine Corps' previous operational concepts and force design obsolete. Berger noted that "our forces currently forward deployed lack the requisite capabilities to deter our adversaries and persist in a contested space to facilitate sea denial."[58] Things needed to change, and Berger ordered those changes.

But will Berger's operational concept make a significant difference, considering the sensor and missile firepower advantages the PLA will enjoy over the First Island Chain and beyond? The PLA's space-based surveillance systems plus its manned and unmanned air, surface, and subsurface reconnaissance platforms will be able to provide PLA commanders operating from nearby continental positions with thorough and continuous observations of known and suspected Marine Corps missile positions. This PLA sensor network, linked to nearby land-attack and antiship missile launch platforms, will make it nearly impossible for Marine Corps missile units to move safely either on the small islands they would occupy or from one island to another.

Without the ability to move or resupply after missile launching begins, Marine Corps missile units would have to fight the war from the positions they occupied when hostilities commenced. Near-continuous observation by the PLA would make it difficult to hide ground-based missile units, which consist of numerous vehicles for transporting the missiles plus command, communications, and support equipment. If a potential host country along the First Island Chain—for example, the Philippines—had not already allowed Marine Corps missile units to set up on desired locations before the start of hostilities, it is unlikely the Marines could get to these positions afterward. The PLA's continental position would give it an advantage with the large-scale employment of armed unmanned systems and decoys, which the PLA could use to induce Marine Corps missile units to launch and reveal their positions. And with the Marines unable to resupply their static positions with additional missiles, the PLA's advantage in missile supplies would dominate after a few days of combat.

Some have suggested hiding the Marine Corps missile units in standard twenty-foot shipping containers. But PLA sensors would still be able to observe the "pattern of life" associated with missile units, which includes

A Soviet Tu-22M Backfire bomber with the Kh-22 Kitchen antiship cruise missile in 1983. In the 1970s and 1980s this was the U.S. Navy's first brush with the modern land-based "reconnaissance-strike complex." *Defense Imagery, photographer unknown*

A Chinese Su-27 Flanker fighter-bomber on a training exercise over Anshan Airfield, China, in 2007. In 2020 the PLA operated 634 Flanker variants. That number continues to grow, bringing China's airpower deep into the western Pacific Ocean. *U.S. Defense Department/SSgt. D. Myles Cullen, USAF, March 24, 2007*

The USS *Theodore Roosevelt* Carrier Strike Group transiting in formation with the USS *Makin Island* Amphibious Ready Group in the South China Sea in 2021. The ability of these strike groups to fend off a barrage of supersonic cruise missiles has yet to be tested. *U.S. Navy/MC3 Terence Deleon Guerrero, April 8, 2021*

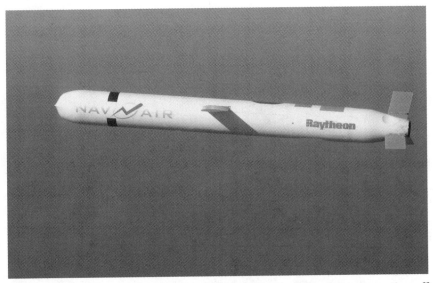

A Navy Tactical Tomahawk Block IV land-attack missile undergoing testing off California in 2002. The Tomahawk has one of the longest ranges among U.S. tactical missiles, but it is not long enough for the Indo-Pacific theater when launched from surface ships. *U.S. Navy/Released*

A Long-Range Anti-Ship Missile (LRASM) on a test flight in 2018 after launching from a B-1B bomber. This smart, stealthy missile will be a key weapon for countering China's growing maritime power. *Lockheed Martin, May 23, 2018*

A B-1B Lancer, B-2A Spirit, and B-52H Stratofortress fly near Barksdale Air Force Base, Louisiana, on February 2, 2017. In a war against China, U.S. commanders will rely on the shrunken inventories of these aging aircraft until the B-21 Raider arrives in service late in the 2020s. *U.S. Air Force/Sagar Pathak*

Artist's rendering of a B-21 Raider bomber on a test flight at Edwards Air Force Base, California. The Air Force plans to acquire at least one hundred of the advanced and stealthy B-21s by the mid-2030s, a force that could ensure deterrence in the Indo-Pacific for decades. *U.S. Air Force graphic courtesy Northrop Grumman*

An antiship Naval Strike Missile launches from a remotely operated truck-mounted launcher during a test in California in November 2020. The Marine Corps is reorganizing to form small teams equipped with weapons like this to be deployed along the First Island Chain. *U.S. Navy*

The U.S. Department of Defense tests a hypersonic glide body for the Army's Long-Range Hypersonic Weapon program during a launch from the Pacific Missile Range Facility, Kauai, Hawaii, on March 19, 2020. The range of this proposed Army hypersonic weapon will be inadequate against the PLA in the Indo-Pacific theater. *U.S. Navy*

A Navy F-35C on a test flight near Patuxent River, Maryland, in 2012. The stealthy aircraft has advanced sensors and networking, but its range is too short to keep its aircraft carrier base at a safe distance from China's antiship missiles. *U.S. Navy photo courtesy Lockheed Martin/Released*

MQ-25 Stingray unmanned aircraft at a Boeing company facility in St. Louis, Missouri, in 2019. The U.S. Navy's first unmanned jet will be an airborne refueler, not a strike aircraft, leaving the Navy's aircraft carrier range problem unsolved. *Eric Shindelbower, February 21, 2019*

Artist's rendering of the USS *Constellation* (FFG-62), first of the U.S. Navy's new class of frigates. Operating with missile-armed unmanned surface vessels, these frigates could be a low-cost, low-risk naval force in deterring China in the Near Seas. *Courtesy Fincantieri*

The experimental unmanned surface ships *Ranger* and *Nomad* under way off California on July 3, 2021. The Navy plans to convert commercial supply vessels like these into missile ships for its Large Unmanned Surface Vessel (LUSV) program. *U.S. Navy*

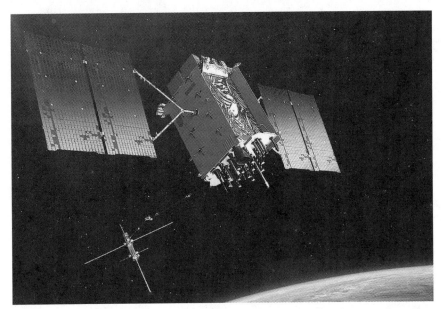

Artist's rendering of an Air Force Global Positioning System (GPS) Block III satellite in orbit around the earth. Large, expensive, and vulnerable satellites such as these are obsolete and are being replaced with more survivable constellations composed of scores of small, networked satellites. *U.S. Space Force*

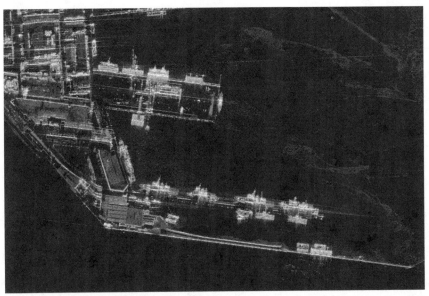

A section of China's Huangdao port imaged from one of Capella Space's small synthetic-aperture radar satellites in low earth orbit. Capella's satellites provide images like this to analysts in near real-time, day and night, through cloud cover, with a resolution of fifty centimeters. *Courtesy Capella Space*

security, maintenance, and other daily support routines. The PLA's intelligence gathering would be simplified on the mostly small islands where Marine Corps missile units would have to operate along the First Island Chain. Missile units attempting to hide among civilian shipping containers and in civilian guise would be committing "perfidy," potentially a war crime. The PLA could respond by attacking any group of shipping containers it suspected, with ruinous results for civilian commerce.

In his force design directive, Berger observed, "The individual/force element which shoots first has a decisive advantage."[59] With refined sensor networks now increasingly granting finders dominance over hiders, commanders on both sides will be under immense pressure to fire their missiles first during a crisis, before their missile units can be destroyed by the other side's missile volleys. As in August 1914, commanders on both sides will urge their policymaker superiors to authorize the first missile volleys, to inflict what damage their forces can rather than be destroyed in place having accomplished little. Berger's observation confirmed this dangerously destabilizing fact.

Berger's concept is better than what came before, but the PLA's sensor and missile dominance in the western Pacific make the concept problematic, with Berger himself noting shortcomings that likely cannot be fixed soon.

But despite these deficiencies, Berger's new Marine Corps will have an important role as a component in a larger deterrence force design in the Indo-Pacific region, a subject chapters 6 and 8 will discuss.

Needed: A Competitive Strategy for the Indo-Pacific Region

Elsewhere inside the Pentagon, other staffs went to work on important modernization projects. Many of the most notable projects focused on intelligence analysis and data sharing, the goal being to get accurate target information quickly to the weapons best in position to attack a target. Examples include the Defense Department's growing budget for artificial intelligence (AI) research, which is also a research priority for the PLA. Both sides hope that AI will enable their intelligence analysts to find threatening enemy forces and targets quickly and accurately from the vast seas of data their satellite constellations, unmanned systems, and signal intelligence sensors will continuously collect. AI will have other roles for military operations such as more efficiently organizing and delivering supplies to military units in the field and better predicting maintenance issues.

Joint All-Domain Command and Control (JADC2) is a concept: the creation of a vast data network that would ultimately link all sensors that are looking for enemy military units with all "shooters," or weapon platforms, that could attack them. The goal of JADC2 is to achieve information and decision-making superiority over an adversary during military operations. AI would be critical to enable the accurate processing of the vast data stream a JADC2 system would generate and then employ that data to formulate rapid and accurate decisions for weapons connected to the network. Under its grandest ambitions, JADC2 would link the sensors and shooters operating in all domains (space, air, cyber, maritime, and land) in a theater of operations.[60]

Promoters of the military applications of emerging technologies such as AI; vast, secure, and jam-proof data networks such as JADC2; enabling communication technologies such as fifth- and sixth-generation wireless networks; and quantum computing believe that success on future battlefields will require gathering, processing, analyzing, and acting on information more rapidly and accurately than an adversary can. Given the lethality and falling relative costs of offensive weapons, they are undoubtedly right. Combatants armed with large numbers of these precise and deadly weapons will be able to inflict devastation on opponents if they can collect the information about where to strike and then quickly act on that information.

Information dominance will be necessary for success against a competitive opponent like China. But information dominance by itself will not be sufficient. The United States and its allies will also require adequate quantities of munitions and launch platforms that are relevant for the geography of the Indo-Pacific region.

U.S. and allied policymakers still lack a deeper understanding of what strategic outcomes they are trying to achieve in the Indo-Pacific region and what roles military forces can contribute to those outcomes. They require a better understanding of what the PLA will be able to achieve and what those capabilities imply for how U.S. and allied policymakers should design their military forces in response. Perhaps most important, U.S. policymakers still need to reckon with the competitive advantages China brings to the rivalry in the Indo-Pacific and the costs to the United States if its own policymakers do not fashion a strategic response that accounts for China's advantages. The United States and its allies do have some advantages, and China has vulnerabilities. The U.S. response over the last decade has not sufficiently taken these facets of the competition into account.

Each U.S. military service over the past decade has implemented relatively minor adjustments in response to the PLA while protecting its legacy programs against significant disruption. The Air Force's main adjustment has been the "agile combat employment" shell game, which seeks to retain a role in the Indo-Pacific for the service's dominant fighter aircraft culture. The Navy's adjustment has been to convince Congress to fund a naval arms race against the world's largest and most cost-efficient shipbuilder while retaining the aircraft carrier strike group at the center of its force design. The Marine Corps is boldly restructuring itself around small missile teams attempting to hide on the First Island Chain, a concept the Marine Corps Commandant admits he built on unverified assumptions. The Army's Long-Range Hypersonic Weapon is that service's contribution to needed long-range strike capabilities. But the proposed missile's range of up to 1,400 miles (about 2,200 kilometers) is too short to be relevant against China when based on U.S. territories on the Second Island Chain, which likely will be the only basing option.[61] The new missiles are estimated to cost more than $40 million each, a high price to pay to strike a single aim point.[62] And even when launched from a mobile launcher the missile would face the same challenges inherent in surviving PLA missile attacks as those faced by the Air Force's air bases, the Navy's carrier strike groups, and the Marine Corps' missile teams. In the absence of comprehensive and sustained supervision from top-level policymakers, the U.S. military services are putting preservation of their legacy cultures above bold ideas and adjustments that will enable them to meet the PLA threat. The result has been uncoordinated ideas rather than an effective and competitive response.

As the remainder of this book will explain, many of the concepts the services are developing will have useful roles in a broader comprehensive strategy for deterring prospective Chinese aggression in the Indo-Pacific region. But the comprehensive strategy later chapters will describe employs these concepts for different purposes than service planners currently contemplate.

The United States has focused valuable resources at China's strengths rather than its vulnerabilities and weaknesses. This disjointed response has not reckoned with the fact that as the expeditionary power, U.S. power projection forces will be more expensive than China's anti-access forces. A military strategy premised on a high-tech battle of attrition will not favor the expeditionary force, especially when it goes against a continental rival with nearly equal technology and lower costs. Strategies that are directed at China's best enduring advantages are not likely to succeed.

Finally, the U.S. response lacks a theory of success. What is the specific connection between the response's recommended actions and its desired results? Ultimately, conflict is about persuading adversaries to settle disputes on favorable terms that will endure. For military action to achieve lasting success, it must connect to this idea. Have policymakers and military planners made a connection between their plans and successful war termination? Commencing military action without a clear end state and without a theory of how the proposed action will achieve that end state is a recipe for frustration.

These criticisms illustrate a larger problem. Strategists coping with the security challenges in the Indo-Pacific should step back and view the problem from first principles. They should undertake a thorough approach to strategy formulation, one that makes a comprehensive assessment of all the players, declares what the strategy must achieve, devises a theory of success, and then crafts competitive and effective policies and programs for achieving the desired outcomes. The remainder of this book will lay out this prescription.

6

Designing a Competitive Military Strategy for the Indo-Pacific

The U.S. strategy for the Indo-Pacific region has been premised on a universally accepted conclusion that U.S. military power can thwart any overt military aggression. Once China's leaders and PLA commanders no longer agree with that conclusion, deterrence will break down and the United States will need a new strategy. Policymakers in Washington and the Indo-Pacific region will need better strategy options than those currently contemplated if they are to preserve stability, guide China's behavior in a direction favorable to U.S. interests, and prevent a destabilizing regional security competition from breaking out.

Finding a better strategy begins with finding a good strategy formulation process. And that begins with defining what a strategy is. Richard Rumelt, a veteran strategy consultant and professor emeritus at the University of California at Los Angeles, defined a strategy as "a coherent set of analyses, concepts, policies, arguments, and actions that respond to a high-stakes challenge."[1] A strategy is not simply a set of goals or aspirations for an organization, essential as those are. A successful strategy must also include a realistic set of programs, policies, and resources designed to achieve the organization's goals in a competitive context.

For example, the 2017 *National Security Strategy* of the United States describes goals and aspirations. But its title is a misnomer. It is not a strategy, because it contains little discussion of how the U.S. government will organize its resources to achieve these goals and aspirations (previous versions issued by other U.S. presidents were no better in this regard).[2] Stating goals is relatively easy. Designing realistic ways to achieve the goals, marshalling the necessary resources, and convincing an organization to implement the design effectively are much harder tasks.

The output of a strategy process could be a set of documents describing the organization's new program and policies, and the supporting resources that will support the new program. But this work product is incomplete and is unlikely to result in success even if brilliantly crafted. Completion will occur when the organization's culture accepts the strategy process and enthusiastically implements the results. To increase the odds of success, the organization should seek not just a strategy—which inevitably will become stale—but a strategy process that becomes a permanent feature of its routine operations and culture. A strategy process includes implementation, evaluation, critique, and guidance for the next strategy iteration. The goal of this process is continuous adaptation and improvement.

Most organizations face challengers, which make strategy design and execution even more difficult. Organizations in the business world face competitors seeking a bigger market share at the organization's expense. Businesses also face potentially hazardous changes to the economic and legal environments. Military forces face enemies on the battlefield. All organizations face resource constraints. Strategy design in competitive situations thus requires leaders and planners to find advantages in the operating environment, discover their organization's comparative strengths, and determine the vulnerabilities of their competitors. A competitive strategy will include these factors in its design while also building in hedges for the risks the organization must face. With these additional complications, it is no wonder that so many business ventures fail and that other large and immensely endowed organizations such as the Department of Defense struggle to achieve their goals, evidence that they have failed to design competitive strategies.

Why Bother with Strategy?

A strategy helps an organization adjust to changes in the world in which it must operate. Changes can come through the slow accumulation of social or economic trends, the shifting preferences of clients, or the disruptive arrival of innovative or better-resourced competitors. A formal strategy process is only one method by which organizations attempt to cope with change. Many rely on the intuition of the organization's top leaders or simply muddle through, making small adjustments to deal with immediate problems. These techniques may appear to work for a time. But without a systematic method for thoroughly evaluating its changing environment, an organization risks finding itself set adrift by change.

Implementing a new strategy means making changes to an organization's processes, to the duties and status of the organization's managers, and even to the organization's culture. Making changes almost always creates winner and losers, not to mention disorientation when employees are required to do their jobs differently or are even cast aside. A meaningful strategy process must lead to disruption, something organizations naturally resist.

An effective strategy process thus must battle against the organization's strong preference for inertia. Resistance can be cultural or bureaucratic. Small or young organizations are typically led by a founder who, if the organization has survived its childhood, has gained the respect of the organization's stakeholders and has created a unique culture that serves to reinforce loyalty and cohesion among employees and clients. The organization will likely see its culture as being a valuable attribute and will resist a strategy process that could bring on introspection and change. Charismatic founders may similarly resist a process that would expose their judgment to scrutiny or supplant their authority.

For larger organizations such as military establishments, resistance to a formal strategy process will come from bureaucratic interests protecting their status, programs, and budgets. Elements within, say, the Defense Department that are threatened by change will find powerful allies in Congress and in large defense contractors, who are likely to conclude there is lower risk to them in perpetuating existing programs and structures than betting on hypothetical programs that may require adjustment to disruptive change. Adaptive change may occur despite these obstacles, but it may occur too slowly to keep up with new threats in the operating environment. Nevertheless, a thorough strategy process remains the best hope for adjusting to a changing world.

Strategy Begins with Assessment

An effective strategy process has four steps: assessment, design, execution, and evaluation. This section discusses these steps in the context of searching for a competitive strategy for the Indo-Pacific region.

Strategy should begin with an assessment of the players in the competition and the environment in which they will compete. The assessment phase collects the baseline data and analyses on clients, competitors, partners, and the operating environment that will inform the remainder of the strategy process.

Assessments should begin with customers and clients, past, present, and future. For businesses, this is an obvious place to begin, for there can be no business without understanding who the business' potential customers are, what they will want from the business, and how the business can reach them.

U.S. military organizations like the Department of Defense and the Indo-Pacific Command have clients too. Most obvious is the chain of command above, leading to the president. The service chiefs and senior officials in the Pentagon understand very well that Congress is another critically important stakeholder. Military commanders and planners should also remember that the public, too, will judge their plans and how well they are implemented, making the voting, taxpaying public perhaps the most important client of all.

History provides numerous examples of military commanders and planners who failed to understand their customers and fashion solutions suited to their needs and constraints. On the eve of World War I, war planners on all sides were focused entirely on the technical aspects of mobilization, the rapid assembly of mass combat formations along their frontiers, and the urgency of striking first to gain the initiative and disrupt enemy preparations. Ignored completely was the idea that the military instrument and military planning should support statecraft, foreign policy, or even negotiations during a crisis. When such a crisis erupted in the summer of 1914, attempts by political leaders to settle the dispute were ignored by military planners, whose focus on mobilization and obtaining the first-move advantage trumped all other considerations. The result was disaster.[3]

Top-level U.S. commanders and military planners must answer first to their chains of command, leading up to the president; but they must also cope with the requirements and limits of their two other clients: Congress and the public. To do otherwise similarly flirts with disaster. The requirements and limits of all three clients should figure into strategy. This seems an obvious point, and yet policymakers routinely ignore it. Even after public opinion had soured on the manpower-intensive and casualty-ridden stabilization strategy used in Iraq, policymakers in 2009 pressed for the same unpopular strategy for Afghanistan, charting out an operational time line they should have known would exceed the support of all three clients.[4] With minimal political support remaining for the strategy, the United States wound down its campaign in Afghanistan in 2021 in failure.

For the competition with China, the United States needs a strategy that will sustain broad appeal and will thus endure across political administrations. It must be a strategy that sustains U.S. public support for an open-ended period. This implies a strategy that maintains stability with a low risk of combat, has a reasonable financial cost, and supports commonly accepted American values such as conforming to accepted norms and protecting the weak from bullying. Sustained American public support will also require partners in the Indo-Pacific region to make a substantial effort in their own defense.

Once the baseline data and analyses of clients, competitors, partners, and the operating environment are in hand, assessment next requires a deep study of the competition with the goal of understanding its current and future interests, capacities, strategies, strengths, and vulnerabilities. There are countless examples of organizations that failed because they did not understand their competition. Nearly every week brings a story of some major business that did not understand or did not take seriously the cumulative effects of a competitor's continuous improvements or the disruption caused by the emergence of an innovator in the marketplace.

Examples similarly abound in military history. British officers planning the defense of Singapore in 1941 largely dismissed the idea that an adversary could attack in force down the Malay Peninsula. When a Japanese army used this very approach in 1942 and forced Singapore's surrender, the result was the worst disaster in British military history. More recently, many U.S. policymakers and planners underestimated the risk of insurgency in both Iraq and Afghanistan, even though the U.S. government had supported a successful insurgency in Afghanistan in the late 1980s.

The assessment phase must also consider the interests, strategies, and attributes of the organization's partners. For businesses, partners include suppliers, financiers, distributors, product allies, and employees. The partners of national security strategists and military planners include other agencies in the government, foreign state allies, nonstate partners, and contractors. The interests and attributes of their partners should be a central consideration for U.S. national security planners. Whether the task is irregular warfare in the Middle East and Central Asia or establishing a modern security architecture in the Indo-Pacific, America's partners will be both essential for success and among the most troublesome planning factors.

Assessment should include research on the future operating environment, particularly trends and potential disruptions that could bear on strategy design. The U.S. National Intelligence Council's quadrennial *Global Trends* series is one example of an attempt to comprehensively discern relevant and potentially disruptive economic, technological, and social trends that may occur over the next two decades.[5] In the mid-1990s, several assessments of security trends correctly anticipated the falling costs and broadening dissemination of microprocessor-based military technology, which resulted in the military-technical revolution that is now so threatening to U.S. military forces and doctrine.

The final and most crucial assessment is the organization's appraisal of its own strengths, vulnerabilities, capacities, and interests. This self-assessment should result in a realistic description of the *means* available to the organization, an essential input in the strategy design process. Objective self-assessment is asking a lot from members inside an organization, who are themselves engaged in a competition with their peers for status and advancement. Under such circumstances, the organization's members who are participating in the strategy process (ideally, its line managers and staff) are unlikely to openly discuss their units' weaknesses and shortcomings. Many organizations employ outside consultants to perform internal assessments that the organization's own staff cannot be counted on to do itself.

Once again, history offers innumerable examples of organizations that failed because they did not recognize their own limitations. The German army's war plans for the Western Front in 1914 and for the invasion of the Soviet Union in 1941, for example, badly overestimated the ability of the army's supply services to deliver adequate supplies to massed mobile formations operating far beyond forward railheads. The result in both cases was disaster when the offensive capacity of forward units withered at climactic moments. U.S. and allied policymakers responsible for strategy in Afghanistan relied on NATO's assurance that it could create large, effective, and resilient Afghan security forces. The resulting failure to do so had disastrous consequences for NATO's campaign.

Assessment is mainly research. But poorly performed research will cripple the rest of the strategy process. The information that is gathered and analyzed will only be as good as the researchers doing the work. Assessment involves forecasting, always a hazardous venture and one almost guaranteed to involve blind spots and embarrassing errors of exclusion and distortion. Or it may result in an indigestible mountain of data. Finally, and perhaps most frequently, the assessment phase may include a bias that consciously or unconsciously predetermines the results of the entire strategy process.

Given the resources required to perform a thorough assessment and the potential for error and misdirection, one may wonder whether the effort is worth the expense. Quite simply, however, effective strategy design is not possible without a systematic examination of the competitive world in which the organization must function. That examination is the purpose of the assessment phase.

Designing a Competitive Strategy

Having achieved an understanding of the operating environment and assessed the needs of clients, the strengths and weaknesses of competitors, and the resources and constraints of their organization, strategy designers are equipped to proceed to the next steps.

Ideally, the facts and analysis produced during the assessment phase would have formed a clear picture about the future operating environment. But that will never be the case—facts and analysis will always be insufficient. Strategists will always need to make assumptions to complete the picture. Assumptions are unavoidable in any strategy process, but they also introduce risk and the possibility of error. It is thus best to make assumptions explicit and to subject them to open critique. Assessments plus assumptions equal the strategist's vision of the future operating environment. With that vision, the strategist has a basis to formulate realistic goals and, later, the programs and policies to achieve those goals.

Organizations pursue goals (or at least they should) to solve specific problems. So before enumerating goals, an organization should understand and clearly state the core problems it needs to solve. In *Good Strategy/Bad Strategy: The Difference and Why It Matters*, Richard Rumelt listed "failure to face the problem" as a key indicator of bad strategy.[6]

Rumelt called on strategists to dig under the surface to find the true underlying problem. For national security strategists and military planners, the problem is usually deeper than just figuring out how to inflict damage on an adversary's military forces. Ending a war on favorable terms requires compelling an adversary—both its leaders and its foot soldiers—to accept conditions they would likely have rejected at the start of the conflict. In this sense, the true objective is not a city, a hilltop, or the destruction of a tank regiment or a fleet but rather changing the calculations occurring inside the adversary's mind. Armed coercion may be only one aspect of reaching this true underlying objective.

Rumelt also warned against choosing impractical or unattainable objectives.[7] It is pointless for business or government policymakers to expend scarce resources on goals that are clearly beyond reach. In the realm of military strategy, policymakers must consider the costs required to achieve the desired ends.

This seemingly obvious proposition becomes murky in execution. Strategy accrues costs in both the short run and the long run. Attempting to minimize one often leads to increasing the other. Early in World War II, for example, Allied leaders agreed on a policy of unconditional surrender of the Axis powers. Removing the possibility of a negotiated settlement greatly increased the short-run cost of the war, since a policy of unconditional surrender would require the near-complete destruction of Axis military forces. The idea, however, was to minimize long-run costs even at the price of increasing them in the short run. In making this decision, the Allied leaders were seeking to avoid a negotiated armistice such as the one that ended World War I. That truce, which left Germany's military potential intact, added to the long-run costs for the Allies when an embittered but still capable Germany restored its military capacity. In the 1991 Persian Gulf War, the United States and its coalition partners opted to minimize their short-run costs by signing a ceasefire with Iraq, leaving it to their successors to manage the long-term costs and consequences, which ended up being considerable. When deciding on the *ends* of a national security strategy, policymakers will have to envision a sustainable end state, the costs and practicality of achieving that end state, and the ongoing costs of maintaining that end state.

The strategist's next step is to spell out the *ways*—the policies, programs, concepts, organizational changes, deployment of resources, and other measures—that will employ the organization's *means* (identified during the assessment phase) to achieve the strategy's *ends*.

But before beginning a detailed enumeration of the strategy's ways, the strategist must clearly describe the strategy's *theory of success*. A theory of success should describe in a simple and convincing manner why, in the context of the assessment and assumptions, the means applied by the strategy's ways will achieve the desired ends. The theory of success is the logic underpinning the strategy.

After the May 1863 Confederate victory at Chancellorsville, Confederate leaders met to discuss their war strategy. Gen. Robert E. Lee argued for an invasion of the North. His theory of success supporting this course of action was that a convincing Confederate victory deep inside Northern territory would provide a psychological shock to Northern policymakers that would compel them to negotiate a settlement. For Lee, continuing to play defense in Virginia, even if it conserved Southern resources, lacked a theory of success because it did not hold out the hope of changing the calculations of the North's policymakers, the condition that was ultimately required to end the war on terms favorable to the South.

U.S. Cold War policy was based on two documents: George Kennan's July 1947 *Foreign Affairs* article titled "The Sources of Soviet Conduct" and *NSC 68: United States Objectives and Programs for National Security*, written by the State Department's Policy Planning staff and signed by President Harry Truman in April 1950.[8] Both envisioned open-ended resistance of Soviet expansionist pressure. Both also contained a theory of success that reassured readers that this resistance would not have to last into perpetuity. Kennan asserted that "the United States has it in its power to increase enormously the strains under which Soviet policy must operate, to force upon the Kremlin a far greater degree of moderation and circumspection than it has had to observe in recent years, and in this way to promote tendencies which must eventually find their outlet in either the breakup or the gradual mellowing of Soviet power."[9] Likewise, *NSC 68* stated, "The only sure victory lies in the frustration of the Kremlin design by the steady development of the moral and material strength of the free world and its projection into the Soviet world in such a way as to bring about an internal change in the Soviet system."[10] For both plans, the theory of success was containing Soviet expansion and sustaining Western strength until the Soviet Union's weaknesses led to its "mellowing" or internal change. The assumptions underlying this theory of success would occur, but only after four decades of perseverance.

Specifying the strategy's ways leads to the drafting of organizational changes, budgets, programs, and incentives for the organization's operational units. With resources always limited, policymakers will have to make decisions on priorities, sequencing, and synchronization, both internally and with outside partners. In late December 1941, a few weeks after the United States entered World War II, President Franklin Roosevelt and Prime Minister Winston Churchill agreed that the defeat of Germany should be the alliance's top priority and should receive adequate resources to achieve a predetermined sequence. Within the European campaign, wresting control of the sea lines of communication in the Atlantic Ocean from Germany's submarine forces was a required first priority, to be followed by a strategic air campaign against Germany's military-industrial capacity and transportation infrastructure. These two campaigns were capital- and technology-intensive and required high levels of crew training and experience. They also had to succeed before the Allies could complete the destruction of Germany's armed forces on the European continent. The Allies' virtual absence of capacity in these areas at the start of the war delayed the war's conclusion by at least two years and thus added greatly to the war's total costs.

Risk is an inescapable feature of strategy. Resources are always limited. Policymakers must therefore determine which of their objectives will get the first call on resources, leaving those with lower priorities underfunded and exposed to risk. For example, U.S. defense policymakers must periodically choose between keeping the current force ready for combat by expending limited resources on equipment maintenance and realistic training or instead preparing for future adversaries by spending more now on research and weapons for the future. Making that choice requires assessing whether current threats or future threats are more problematic.

In many cases, policymakers will conclude they have sufficient knowledge to assess the risks they must choose among and then make rational choices within the context of their objectives. During the early decades of the Cold War the top defense priority for U.S. policymakers and planners was preventing nuclear war with the Soviet Union while also resisting

Soviet expansion. Defense plans, research budgets, and procurement focused on this goal, which resulted in large sums spent on Air Force and Navy strategic nuclear programs and systems. Such deterrence prevented nuclear war, so one can conclude that this strategy worked. However, the Soviet Union observed and later adjusted its own strategy, employing proxy and irregular warfare to sustain its competition with the West in ways that bypassed the focus of the U.S. defense program.

U.S. military forces entered Vietnam in the 1960s without a warfighting doctrine, organization, or the training necessary to succeed against that irregular warfare challenge. This U.S. risk exposure occurred because U.S. defense policymakers, arguably rationally, focused more attention at that time on preventing nuclear war and other major war challenges than on devising programs and policies for thwarting irregular adversaries. Pentagon planners achieved their first priority, deterring nuclear war and avoiding Soviet nuclear blackmail. But U.S. ground forces' ability to conduct irregular warfare became the risky vulnerability. This is a reminder that strategy is almost always a *competitive* contest involving thinking adversaries.

Risk management should be an explicit feature of strategy design. Strategists and policymakers should understand where they are increasing their risks, even if hedging against those risks may not be possible. If known risks later develop into problems, the policymakers will at least have a head start on mitigation, having pondered the risk already.

Finally, the strategy process ends—and begins again—with an evaluation of the strategy's performance. This should lead to a new assessment phase and a renewal of the strategy process.

For most organizations, the simple strategy outline discussed in this chapter is insufficient. All strategy models suffer from inescapable frailties. Leaders must attempt to assimilate a daunting amount of detail about the world in which they function. That mountain of data, no matter how voluminous, will still likely overlook many critical considerations. Strategies are about the future, which requires forecasts and assumptions, many of which will be wrong. Finally, strategy implies change, which all organizations are bound to resist in some way.

What is the alternative to a good strategy process? An organization that "muddles through" is almost guaranteed to collide with changed circumstances for which it will not be prepared. In the Indo-Pacific region, muddling through and institutional resistance to new ideas and the changes they imply have left the United States unprepared for the rapidly evolving security situation there. The United States needs a competitive strategy for the region—and that will come only from a better strategy process.

The Strategy Process Applied to China, Starting with Some Tough Assumptions

Let us now apply this strategy framework to the challenge the United States and its allies face in the Indo-Pacific. Chapters 1 through 5 provided, at least in summary form, an assessment from which to design a strategy. The next step is to use this assessment to formulate assumptions that will underlie a strategy. U.S. policymakers underestimated the speed of China's military modernization. They also underestimated the aggressiveness of Xi Jinping's foreign policy and Xi's willingness to take risks. Based on those experiences, current and future U.S. policymakers would be wise to consider what would have been "worst case" assumptions a decade ago.

1. *To protect its growing interests and hedge future uncertainty, China will continue its buildup of air, naval, missile, and military space capabilities with the goal of establishing control over its maritime and air lines of communication, beginning with those in East Asia and then extending across the western Pacific and into the Indian Ocean.* China's security interests, within the region and beyond it, will continue to expand. Regardless of how China's economy evolves in the years ahead, it will still retain a high dependence on exports markets and imports of raw materials. China's commercial deals with Russia and Central Asian countries indicate its attempts to reduce its dependence on the sea lines of communication across the Indian Ocean, through the Strait of Malacca, and through the Near Seas. But even if these attempts are successful, China will still retain a high exposure to seaborne trade, a disturbing risk from Beijing's perspective.

2. *Over the next decade the PLA will match the U.S. military in technical quality and will substantially outnumber U.S. forces in the Indo-Pacific theater.* Even as China's economic growth rate slows in the decades ahead, it will still possess the financial capacity to increase military spending. The growth of China's military expenditures will likely exceed the growth rate of its economy. Given China's expanding global interests and their own personal insecurities, China's leaders will maintain their drive to field a modern and competitive military force by 2035, if not earlier. The failure of China's political warfare campaign will cause further reliance on military coercion. The size of China's economy will permit the continued rapid buildup of the PLA without imposing on China the same level of burden that eventually felled the Soviet Union.

3. *The security competition in the Indo-Pacific region will be open-ended.* The last chapter of this book will discuss some important trends that will favor the United States and its allies compared with China during the rest of this century. That said, U.S. policymakers and planners should not count on a fortuitous deus ex machina, such as a financial crisis inside China or turmoil inside the CCP, to spontaneously resolve the grave security problem the United States and its allies face in the Indo-Pacific region and beyond.

4. *America's current security partners in the region may not remain "on its side" through the open-ended security competition with China.* A few countries may agree to bandwagon with China, either seduced by China's growing economic and military strength or coerced by it. This could lead to significant geographic, political, and diplomatic gaps in the security architecture the United States and its remaining allies would like to build. U.S. military planners may not be able to deploy military forces to important terrain in the region, which would leave gaps for the PLA to exploit and complicate U.S. and allied military planning.

5. *China has weaknesses and vulnerabilities that the United States and its allies in the region can use to influence China's behavior.* This chapter will discuss these weaknesses and vulnerabilities in more detail. The purpose of studying these is to generate leverage that can influence China's behavior during an open-ended peacetime competition. Should

conflict occur, the United States and its allies would seek to use these weaknesses and vulnerabilities to increase China's costs and attempt to settle the conflict on favorable terms.

6. *China's leaders will not always respond to incentives.* U.S. policymakers and planners should develop a strategy that enhances and sustains conventional deterrence in the Indo-Pacific. Deterrence theory assumes a player has the ability to influence the opponent's behavior and decisions. But even if U.S. planners believe they have implemented a good strategy for influencing the behavior of China's leaders, deterrence could still fail for a variety of reasons, including misperceptions and countervailing incentives that dominate the decisions of these leaders. In this case, U.S. and allied leaders will need to generate the methods and resources to protect their interests regardless of China's decision-making process.

Given the assessment described in chapters 1 through 5 and the assumptions listed above, what is the looming military problem facing U.S. and allied policymakers and planners? The problem is that conventional deterrence is breaking down. The risk is growing that China's political leaders and military commanders will convince themselves that the PLA will have feasible military options to solve China's security problems as these leaders see them. If this happens, conventional deterrence will have ended, and the risk of war will jump.

The "strategic end state," or goal, of a new military strategy for the Indo-Pacific naturally follows from this statement of the problem. The end state is to sustain and reinforce conventional military deterrence in the region by sustaining and reinforcing the belief in the minds of China's decision-makers that military aggression or coercion are not effective options. Achieving that end state will mean that the United States and its allies have protected the sovereignty of China's neighbors in the region and sustained free access to the region's commons, the same conditions that have existed there for the past seven decades. Specifically, effective conventional military deterrence will mean that China's leaders will not be tempted to employ the PLA's growing capabilities to, for example, blockade or coerce Taiwan, or attempt to seize the Senkaku Islands, or block commercial ships or warships from transiting international waters in the Near Seas as allowed by international law.

Setting a goal or end state of sustaining conventional military deterrence against possible Chinese aggression seems an obvious, even trite, conclusion from a comprehensive strategy process. But as we saw in chapter 2 and elsewhere, many analysts do not accept this goal as feasible or worth the cost or risk.[11] Among those who *do* wish to reinforce deterrence, there is wide disagreement about what form that deterrence should take and how to achieve it. In all cases, achieving sustained deterrence will become increasingly difficult as the PLA's capabilities expand and transform.

The United States and its allies *can* sustain conventional military deterrence against a peer competitor like China over an indefinite period and at a reasonable cost. The remainder of this book will explain how. But doing so will require efficiently matching allied strengths against China's vulnerabilities while preventing China from doing the same to them. Understanding and correctly identifying each side's "centers of gravity" are crucial to solving this problem.

Find the Adversary's Vulnerabilities and Protect Your Own

Effective deterrence rests on finding China's weaknesses and vulnerabilities. U.S. and allied policymakers and planners can exploit those weaknesses and vulnerabilities to create leverage that can influence China's peacetime behavior in favorable ways. Should conflict occur, policymakers and planners would attempt to use these elements of leverage against China's vulnerabilities to resolve the conflict on favorable terms.

Planners should begin by finding China's centers of gravity—key assets or outcomes that would most effectively persuade China's decision-makers that aggression will not succeed. *JP 5-0: Joint Planning*, the Defense Department's top-level military planning document, defines a center of gravity as "the source of power or strength that enables a military force to achieve its objective and is what an opposing force can orient its actions against that will lead to enemy failure."[12]

Examples of centers of gravity at the strategic level include a particular military force such as a warship fleet, an alliance, political or military leaders, a set of critical capabilities or functions, and national will. Centers of gravity exist in an adversarial and competitive context and derive from the relationship between opponents in the contest. All sides in a contest have centers of gravity; a policymaker or commander should thus expect opponents to be searching for vulnerable centers of gravity as targets for their actions as well.

There are numerous centers of gravity that could influence the behavior and decision-making of China's leaders in a peacetime competition or in a crisis. For example, if China's leaders fear internal instability, riots, civil war, and terrorism, then the CCP's internal security forces could be an important center-of-gravity target. Likewise, if China's leaders fear a blockade or other maritime disruption, or Taiwan's independence and a lack of PLA capacity to deal with Taiwan, then the PLAN would be an important center-of-gravity target. Chinese strategic assets such as missile forces, telecommunications infrastructure, counterspace forces, and pipelines might also be center-of-gravity targets for U.S. military planners. U.S. and allied planners can sustain and strengthen deterrence if they can convince China's leaders that U.S. and allied forces will have the ability to hold these types of targets at risk, regardless of whatever actions the PLA might make at the start of a conflict.

Joint Planning reminded its readers that adversaries are likely to vigorously defend their important center-of-gravity targets, and it may thus be impractical to attack them directly. Likewise, a commander may have to expose vulnerable or critical centers of gravity such as ground troops or warships to reach the enemy's center-of-gravity targets, bringing into question the risks and costs of such an approach.[13]

China's military planners have undoubtedly assembled their own list of vulnerable U.S. and allied centers of gravity. U.S. and allied tactical airpower located on the handful of air bases in the region and aircraft carrier strike groups in the western Pacific would be center-of-gravity targets if it was clear that these assets were the main component of U.S. plans. U.S. bomber aircraft, normally based in the center of the United States, would be more difficult for the PLA to reach but would be a critical center-of-gravity target for PLA planners. Perhaps the most important center-of-gravity target for PLA planners would be the national will of the United States and its allies. Chinese planners might seek to demoralize Americans by inflicting large-scale casualties on U.S. forces in the Indo-Pacific. U.S. policymakers and planners could inadvertently facilitate this outcome if they based large numbers of military personnel at vulnerable forward bases in the region.

In sum, center-of-gravity analysis searches for the most important and most vulnerable assets and results that will affect the opponent's military capabilities, incentives, and decision-making. Each side should expect its centers of gravity to come under attack. And both sides will plan for how to attack the enemy's centers of gravity while protecting their own.

The Search for Sustainable Deterrence

The growth of the PLA and the rapid change in the military balance in the Indo-Pacific region has analysts on all sides closely examining more detailed aspects of the military balance and what these details might mean for decision-makers considering military options to achieve policy outcomes.

The first preference for U.S. and allied policymakers and military commanders is to maintain "deterrence by denial" in the region, the condition that has existed there but is now ebbing away. Deterrence by denial exists when the defender (here, the United States and its security partners) has the convincing military capacity to defeat an adversary's aggression. Deterrence by denial centers on convincing (to all sides) military control over the outcome. When deterrence by denial is succeeding, prospective aggressors agree they do not possess feasible military options.[14]

But as this book has explained, China's leaders may believe that they will obtain feasible military options, perhaps in this decade. The rapid growth in spending on China's military power suggests that CCP leaders believe they can reach this goal, especially as the PLA obtains the capability to strike more U.S. and allied center-of-gravity targets.

U.S. and allied decision-makers need a theory of success that will reinforce the decaying state of deterrence by denial in the region. The theory of success in this case is to maintain the doubt in the minds of China's leaders that a military fait accompli–type attack or other military coercion could succeed, because U.S. and allied military power would defeat it.

U.S. and allied planners will reinforce deterrence by denial in the Indo-Pacific when they get China's decision-makers to believe three things. First, prospective Chinese war plans will require the PLA to engage U.S. military forces early in the conflict, ensuring that U.S. military forces will be combatants. U.S. and allied military planners should design operational concepts that will make it unavoidable for China to attack U.S. military positions and personnel, preferably with the first shots of the conflict. These U.S. forces at the forward edge of the conflict zone should be too small to constitute a center of gravity but large enough to interdict prospective PLA forces in combat, such that PLA planners could not ignore them.

U.S. military planners have employed this notion of a "trip wire" guaranteeing U.S. involvement in the past. During the Cold War, the U.S. military garrison in West Berlin was isolated deep behind the NATO–Warsaw Pact front line farther to the west. Had the Soviet and Warsaw Pact armies attacked Berlin, there was no hope of saving the U.S. brigade there. But the Berlin Brigade's doom would have guaranteed a military conflict between the United States and the Soviet Union, a dangerous prospect that presumably deterred the Soviets from aggression against Berlin.[15]

Second, the U.S. and allied operational concept should compel China to attack the military forces and territory of other countries in the region, resulting in horizontal escalation and additional opponents that China will have to fight. This will increase China's costs and risks, perhaps enough to convince China's leaders to abstain from aggression.

Third, the United States and its allies should invest in forces that the PLA will have difficulty interdicting but that will be capable of countering the PLA's attacking forces. Effective deterrence by denial is based on the defender's ability to convincingly control the military outcome. A U.S. and allied battle network built around persistent and survivable sensor arrays and connected to long-range strike capabilities based outside the PLA's reach would meet this condition. This long-range strike battle network would be the main element of the coalition's military power against the PLA.

These are the concepts, or *ways*, that the United States and its partners would best reinforce deterrence by denial in the Indo-Pacific. Under the operational concept just described, the PLA would have to attack U.S. and allied forces to achieve its fait accompli, but it would also be unable to thwart the U.S. long-range battle network beyond its reach. The desired outcome is for China's leaders to understand that their prospective offensive plans would result in a conflict whose outcome they could not control. Generating this belief among China's leaders would fulfill the strategy's theory of success—deterrence by denial.

In the event that the United States and its allies cannot sustain conventional deterrence by denial, policymakers would then have to consider the less preferred deterrence-by-punishment approach. Deterrence by punishment seeks to deter an aggressor through the threat to inflict unacceptable costs. Examples of such punishment are the threat of nuclear retaliation against the Soviet Union during the Cold War and the threat of financial and economic embargos against China should the PLA attempt to coerce or seize Taiwan.[16] The problem from the defender's perspective is that the aggressor retains options and choices, namely over how much pain the aggressor is willing to sustain as it proceeds with the aggression.[17] Historical examples such as North Vietnam's leaders during the U.S.-Vietnam War and Japan's leaders at the end of World War II have established that some adversaries will withstand horrific levels of punishments before submitting to an opponent, and sometimes not even then.

Even so, U.S. and allied policymakers and planners should prepare options for a deterrence-by-punishment approach against China. The first step of this preparation is identifying the assets and conditions China's leaders value most highly and then determining how the coalition can hold those assets and conditions at risk.

In an essay in the October–November 2012 issue of *Survival*, Michael Pillsbury discussed sixteen potential areas of strategic vulnerability for China's leaders.[18] Pillsbury, a senior fellow at the Hudson Institute and a former top planner for China and Asian issues at the Department of Defense, also called for stepped-up research on China's strategic decision-making process similar to the research on the Soviets' decision-making conducted during the Cold War. Pillsbury's "sixteen fears" can be grouped into seven broad categories:

1. Fear of internal instability, riots, civil war, and terrorism
2. Fear of a blockade or other maritime disruption
3. Fear of Taiwan independence or a lack of PLA capacity to deal with Taiwan
4. Fear of a land invasion; of the military capacity of regional neighbors such as India, Russia, Japan, and Vietnam; and of China's territorial dismemberment
5. Fear of bombardment from long-range bombers or aircraft carriers
6. Fear of attacks on important strategic assets such China's missile forces, its antisatellite capability, its computer and telecommunications network, and its energy pipelines
7. Fear of escalation and loss of control.

Planners can match Pillsbury's list with a center-of-gravity analysis to develop a list of potential assets and targets that could dissuade and deter aggression by China's leaders. An example that would connect with the first item on Pillsbury's list would include attacks on China's internal security forces, with a goal of weakening the CCP's control over the Chinese population.[19] Other examples linking to Pillsbury's list include important infrastructure systems, China's ports and shipping capacity, and iconic symbols such as China's space program facilities. An additional set of targets could include the personal assets of some of China's leaders. The United States and NATO successfully employed this technique during the Kosovo air campaign in 1999 to create internal friction among Serbia's leaders, which compelled Serbian leader Slobodan Milosevic to end that conflict.[20]

A deterrence-by-punishment approach would be risky. Coalition planners would not know in advance the pain tolerance of China's leaders, which, depending on the stakes involved, could be very high. The approach would almost certainly require extensive bombing of China's mainland, a great risk (see chapter 7). Finally, widening the war in this manner would undoubtedly lead down unexpected paths, with uncertain and dangerous consequences.

For these reasons, policymakers and planners will prefer to possess the capabilities for conventional deterrence by denial, which will focus military operations against adversary military capabilities and which, when effective, will deny the adversary any choices in the military outcome. As the next chapters will explain, the United States and its allies can achieve this capability. Doing so, however, will require a better strategy than the one currently in place and overcoming institutional resistance to needed reforms.

Impose Costs, Conserve Resources, Play the Long Game

U.S. and allied policymakers and strategists will need a strategy their countries can sustain over a long, open-ended contest. The strategy will have to be efficient, fashioned to conserve resources while also sustaining convincing deterrence. Finally, the strategy will have to sustain broad public support over potentially many decades. This implies a strategy that does not place a heavy burden on citizens' finances, freedoms, or way of life.

As concerns rise over how to cope with China's increasing military capacity and assertiveness, analysts and planners are revisiting U.S. strategy during the Cold War. Much of their attention focuses on how Andrew Marshall's Office of Net Assessment assisted a succession of U.S. defense secretaries in formulating competitive strategies aimed at managing the long-term competition with the Soviet Union.[21]

Between 1973 and 1990 Marshall's office, joined by many other military planners, fashioned approaches that attempted to match U.S. comparative advantages against Soviet weaknesses, hoping either to divert Soviet resources away from threatening capabilities or to weaken the Soviet Union's overall military capacity. Notable examples included U.S. bomber and cruise missile programs from the late 1970s, which aimed to divert Soviet military spending into air defenses; the aggressive U.S. maritime strategy from the mid-1980s, which sought to draw Soviet naval power away from allied sea lines of communication; and, perhaps most famously, the Strategic Defense Initiative, which threatened to negate the huge Soviet investment in intercontinental ballistic missiles. By one estimate, the U.S. investment in bombers and cruise missiles during the Cold War forced the Soviet Union to spend $120 billion on defenses against the U.S.

bomber threat, resources that the USSR could otherwise have invested in expanding its offensive capacity.[22]

Since the Soviet Union did subsequently collapse, it is appealing to conclude that the U.S. competitive strategy approach made a major contribution to that result. Indeed, Marshal Sergei Akhromeyev, chief of the Soviet General Staff at the end of the Cold War, later concluded, "The Soviet Union could not continue the confrontation with the United States and NATO after 1985. The economic resources for such a policy had been practically exhausted."[23]

Unfortunately, and as previous chapters have explained, it is China, and not the United States, that is successfully executing a cost-imposing strategy. The Defense Department's annual reports on China's military power state that China has the most active missile development programs in the world. The PLA now fields state-of-the-art offensive ballistic and cruise missiles that in almost all cases exceed the performance and capabilities of U.S. and Western-produced models. Just as the Soviet Union had to forty years ago, the United States has responded by spending more on defending U.S. assets than on offensive capabilities that would hold Chinese interests at risk and compel China to allocate greater resources on its own defense.

Examples of U.S. defensive responses—and thus China imposing costs on the United States—include continued procurement of air-defense destroyers to protect U.S. aircraft carrier strike groups; continued development of new defensive missiles, radars, and combat systems for these destroyers; the Army's spending on theater ballistic missile defenses, now installed in Japan, South Korea, and Guam; the Air Force's Agile Combat Employment tactic for dispersing its short-range fighter aircraft; and finally, and most egregiously, the succession of ever-grander Navy shipbuilding plans, proposed to keep pace with China's warship construction but without regard to China's much lower shipbuilding costs and its deadly and comprehensive antiship battle network.

A decade after China's military modernization finally became the top concern at the Pentagon, the United States still lacks a long-term and sustainable strategy for maintaining conventional military deterrence against China in the Indo-Pacific region. U.S. responses thus far have been defensive, reacting to China's offensive and cost-imposing initiatives. The PLA has achieved its goal of developing and fielding the world's best land-attack and antiship cruise and ballistic missiles. This reveals that PLA planners have identified the U.S. and allied centers of gravity they intend to strike and which they believe will conclude a conflict on terms favorable to them. By contrast, U.S. investments in offensive capabilities have been limited, do not reflect a focus on important center-of-gravity concepts, and are not imposing significant defensive costs on China, leaving the PLA with more resources to further expand its offensive capacity.

China has seized the initiative with its military modernization program and is breaking down conventional military deterrence in the Indo-Pacific. This chapter described a strategy process U.S. and allied planners can use to assess the strategic situation, formulate needed assumptions, set realistic goals, and uncover competitive advantages. As important, the United States and its partners will need a strategy they can sustain financially and politically for perhaps decades. They lack such a strategy even as the strategic situation in the Indo-Pacific continues to worsen. The remaining chapters of this book will discuss some tough but necessary reforms that will produce better concepts and capabilities, and a better strategy for the region.

7

Thwarting a Chinese Fait Accompli

Job One for Aerospace Power

The Indo-Pacific region is often thought of as primarily a maritime theater for military operations. We have seen, however, that the falling costs of missiles and targeting sensors, and China's rapid production of both, will make survival increasingly untenable for massed ground combat formations, air bases, and surface warships. When the submarine threat is added, the ability of surface naval forces on either side—including aircraft carriers—to survive and achieve useful results west of the Second Island Chain likewise becomes questionable.

Thus, future warfare in the region, at least in the initial stages, will likely consist of transient patrolling and raiding in the Near Seas rather than a persistent presence and control. Patrolling and raiding will best be done by long-range aircraft, which can attack and then retreat out of the range of the adversary's battle network better than naval and ground forces can. In a theater dominated by long-range precision missiles, retreating after a raid will be critical for survival and ultimate success.

Long-range airpower dominance will thus be the key to success in the Indo-Pacific theater. Unfortunately, the structure of U.S. forces in the region has drifted far from this concept. But building a force of long-range stealthy strike aircraft and other long-range strike capabilities is necessary if the United States is to persuade China's decision-makers that establishing Chinese military hegemony in the region will not be feasible.

U.S. military planners need to redesign military forces in the region to cope with China's military modernization with several goals in mind. First is the capability to convincingly deny the PLA the ability to achieve exclusive military control over the Near Seas. Second is the ability for U.S. and allied forces to hold at risk, with conventional strike operations, assets valued by China's leaders to dissuade them from coercive strategies. Third, U.S. defense planners should design and acquire military forces that will give U.S. and allied decision-makers more flexibility over the timing and employment of military power. Achieving this flexibility would reduce the dangerous "use it or lose it" instability that the current force structure, centered on short-range forward-deployed forces, has created.

The United States needs the ability to employ conventional airpower with consequential effect anywhere in the region during wartime if it is to accomplish these tasks. Unfortunately, U.S. policymakers neglected the modernization of long-range strike capabilities during the first decades of this century, endangering the ability of their military commanders to accomplish essential missions. The U.S. airpower force structure, with its excessive weighting to short-range platforms, is unsuited for the Indo-Pacific. The main U.S. air bases in the region are too vulnerable to Chinese missile attack, and the vast preponderance of U.S. airpower has insufficient range to be effective.

Taiwan could be the most likely flashpoint for military conflict between the PLA and U.S. and partner military forces. The Taiwan flashpoint also illustrates the advantages the PLA will enjoy as the nearby continental power and the weaknesses U.S. and allied military commanders will suffer from due to a shortage of bases, a force structure too heavily weighted to short-range platforms, and the dangers presented by the current military-technical revolution. Fortunately, there are solutions to the Taiwan military problem if U.S. policymakers and defense officials can overcome the institutional and cultural barriers standing in their way.

Taiwan: China's Military Priority, America's Hard Case

The introduction noted the concern of some former and current U.S. officials and senior military commanders regarding a possible PLA fait accompli assault on Taiwan. If PLA military action against Taiwan is indeed just over the horizon, there are several trends that might explain why. Most of these trends point to a window of opportunity for China that is briefly open and will close again later this decade.

The first trend is the rapid modernization of China's navy (discussed in chapter 4). According to the Defense Department, the PLAN's Eastern and Southern Fleets, composed largely of modern warships, could mobilize as many as fifty-one large and medium amphibious ships along with ninety-nine surface combatants and thirty-four submarines to protect the amphibious assault force during a landing operation across the Taiwan Strait. The PLAN armada would vastly outnumber Taiwan's naval forces.[1]

Second, Taiwan's defense forces are undergoing a major reorientation in their force structure and battle doctrine. The new "overall defense concept" largely abandons Taiwan's classic defense model based on conventional forces such as fighter aircraft, tanks, and ocean-going warships. Taiwan's military forces under the new concept would instead be built around small, dispersed units armed with mobile and portable antiaircraft, antiarmor, and antiship missiles. This unconventional "asymmetric," almost guerilla-like, force could better hide from the PLA's sensors and missiles, survive and fight without centralized command and control, and continue to ambush PLA invaders until their invasion collapses.[2] The overall defense concept is an improvement over the previous concept, which was based on prestigious but vulnerable items such as F-16 fighter jets and the Taiwanese navy's frigates. It will take years for the changeover to be complete, however, and during this period Taiwan's defenses could be disorganized and exposed.

Third, U.S. military forces in the region are similarly attempting to catch up to the threat posed by the PLA's modernization. But as with Taiwan's forces, it will take years to overcome the previous lack of attention to the problem (discussed in chapter 5). This lag period of reorientation and modernization is another aspect of the briefly open window the PLA may enjoy this decade.

A decision by the CCP's leaders to resort to military force to dominate Taiwan would be more evidence of the failure of their political warfare campaign. The citizens of Taiwan certainly noted China's de facto abrogation of the "one country, two systems" status of Hong Kong, which involved the mass imprisonment of Hong Kong's democracy leaders, the imposition of a police state to end Hong Kong's civil society, and the imposition of effective direct rule from Beijing. There is thus no prospect of a negotiated settlement between China and Taiwan.[3] With no prospect for negotiations and a period of turmoil as U.S. and Taiwanese defense forces scramble to catch up with the PLA's advances, China's leaders may perceive a fleeting opportunity to strike before those modernization programs mature.

Chapter 2 discussed the chaotic and Hobbesian consequences that would likely ensue in the Indo-Pacific region should a PLA military conquest of Taiwan succeed. Deterring a PLA attack on Taiwan has thus become perhaps the most pressing issue for U.S. and allied policymakers and planners.

What is the present state of deterrence? Since deterrence exists inside the mind of the potential aggressor, no one except China's top leaders can definitively answer that question. Outside analysts have widely differing views. But the mere existence of widespread doubt about Taiwan's ability to survive an onslaught is itself highly troubling evidence that deterrence in the western Pacific is breaking down.

Rather than an outright attack, Chinese policymakers may opt to begin with a maritime and air quarantine of Taiwan instead. Under this scenario, China's coast guard, navy, and air force would impose an inspection regime against merchant ships and aircraft destined for Taiwan to search for weapons bound for Taiwan's military and security forces. The Chinese government would explain its legal justification for this quarantine as follows: It is universally accepted that Taiwan is a part of China, and the Chinese government is justified in extending its sovereignty over its own territory. The first step in exercising this sovereignty is preventing potentially rebellious armed groups from receiving any more armaments.[4]

From China's perspective, there are several arguments supporting quarantine as the initial approach. First, some foreign observers may agree with China's claim to sovereignty, which would delegitimize both Taiwan's self-defense and intervention by outside powers like the United States.[5] Second, should the United States and perhaps other allies such as Japan and Australia attempt to force a relief convoy through the PLA's quarantine line, China would hope these countries would appear to be the aggressors, unlawfully interfering in China's internal affairs. PLA commanders would like to see the scenario play out in this way because U.S. military commanders would have to gather and concentrate at least some of their forces to escort the relief convoy. Those forces would constitute the vulnerable center-of-gravity target that PLA strategists seek.

China's leaders would initiate the quarantine when they were confident the PLA would be victorious after the inevitable remaining steps of the scenario play out. Those remaining steps would likely entail the activation of the PLA's "active defense" doctrine, which employs offensive action and surprise at the operational and tactical levels to achieve China's defensive goals at the strategic level.[6] The remaining steps of the scenario under active defense would include attacking the relief convoy, attacking and suppressing Taiwan's command-and-control and counter-invasion military forces, and then amphibious and air-mobile landings of PLA ground forces on Taiwan. Finally, PLA air and naval forces would display readiness to attack U.S. forward bases along the First and Second Island Chains to deter any further outside intervention.

Despite its massive numerical superiority over the defenders, an amphibious assault on Taiwan would be complicated and hazardous for the PLA. There are very few periods during the year when the weather and seas around Taiwan are calm enough for military amphibious beach landings. Further, Taiwan has very few beaches and shorelines suitable for landing soldiers and equipment, which eases the task for the island's defenders. The PLA no doubt has considered an attack using transport helicopters and cargo aircraft instead of beach landings. But the PLA has a modest inventory of military transport aircraft, especially the heavy-lift models required to sustain an assault force with the many thousands of tons of provisions it would require for a Taiwan pacification campaign. The PLA could compel civilian airliners into service, but keeping seized Taiwanese airports operating in the face of counterattacks and indirect-fire weapons would be a challenge. Thus, the PLA will require the large capacity of seaborne shipping to deliver over beaches and through captured ports the quantity of supplies its invasion and occupation force will require.[7]

Even considering the difficulties the PLA would face, some analysts believe that Taiwanese resistance would not last long. Simply put, the PLA's massive advantage in firepower and its ability to deter outside intervention by U.S. and allied forces would be highly intimidating and demoralizing to Taiwan's soldiers and citizens. It does not help that morale in Taiwan, among both soldiers and the civilian population, is so poor.[8] Taiwan's military equipment, especially for its ground forces, is old and outdated, with most of its combat vehicles dating back to the 1960s.[9]

Neither Taiwan's soldiers nor its civilians have much confidence in their ability to resist a PLA attack. Army leaders in Taiwan do not believe their forces can maintain resistance past two weeks.[10] Taiwan's new overall defense concept, based on the distributed operations of small units and building societal resilience, aims to change this gloomy forecast. But the transformation from the old system to the new one will take many years, and a PLA invasion may be just a few years away.

What can the United States and its allies do about the crisis building over Taiwan? In their report for the Council on Foreign Relations, Blackwill and Zelikow emphasized U.S.-led regional diplomacy and preparation focused on engaging Japan and Taiwan itself. They discussed the threat of the devastating economic and financial consequences of a PLA attack on Taiwan, which they hope would deter China's leaders. They also discussed the need for U.S. and Japanese policymakers and military commanders to prepare responses for the quarantine scenario and to prepare their societies for possible mobilization in response to a prospective Taiwan crisis.[11]

Diplomacy and financial threats are necessary but insufficient elements of convincing deterrence. The most convincing deterrent to China's leaders determined to conquer Taiwan would be conventional military deterrence by denial; namely, visible allied military capabilities that all would understand would defeat a PLA invasion or blockade force. And that means the capability to quickly destroy the PLAN's amphibious ships, escorting surface combatants, and other cargo ships supporting the invasion. If the United States and its allies could convincingly demonstrate this capability regardless of the PLA's plans, deterrence by denial would be in place.

Former senior U.S. defense officials have recently discussed the need for this very capability. Robert Work, a former U.S. deputy secretary of defense, and Michèle Flournoy, a former U.S. undersecretary of defense for policy, have both explained why U.S. military forces need the capacity to sink several hundred Chinese warships within the first few days of a conflict if the United States and its allies are to sustain convincing deterrence.[12] If China's leaders and PLA commanders believed the United States and its allies had this capability and could execute such a counter-navy campaign with low costs, they would likely be deterred from an assault on Taiwan.

What options are available to U.S. military commanders in view of the PLA's buildup of "anti-access" sensors and missiles? One military option that very few analysts believe remains available is the action the United States took during the 1996 Taiwan Strait crisis, when President Bill Clinton ordered two aircraft carrier strike groups to sail toward Taiwan in response to PLA missile tests aimed at intimidating Taiwan's population. The PLA's massive buildup of sensors and antiship missiles since then has been specifically designed to thwart another use of that response. Another U.S. Navy response could center on the employment of its excellent submarines. However, the Navy would be able to sail only a small number of submarines into the confined seas around Taiwan, where they would have to contend with the PLA's underwater sensor arrays and a PLAN quiet diesel-electric submarine force that would greatly outnumber them. U.S. and allied planners would not be able to count on submarines by themselves to quickly sink the hundreds of ships that the Work and Flournoy deterrence formula calls for.

That would leave the Air Force, and specifically its long-range bomber force, to accomplish the mission. As the next sections will explore, aircraft are excellent killers of ships, a historical trend that technology will sustain into the future.

Aircraft Are the Nemeses of Warships

On July 21, 1921, Brig. Gen. Billy Mitchell, USA, led a group of bombers from the embryonic Air Corps against the former SMS *Ostfriesland*, a captured and decommissioned German battleship, and sank it.[13] Many observers at the time considered the demonstration a meaningless stunt since the battleship was not maneuvering and had no crew to fire its weapons in defense.

By the end of World War II in 1945, there was no longer any doubt that aircraft had become warships' nemesis. The pattern was set early in the war. In May 1941, the German super-battleship *Bismarck* was damaged in the North Atlantic by torpedoes launched from aircraft from the British aircraft carrier *Ark Royal*. Unable to maneuver, the *Bismarck* was chased down and sunk by Royal Navy battleships. Royal Air Force Lancaster bombers sank *Bismarck*'s sister ship *Tirpitz* in November 1944. In December 1941, Japanese aircraft from aircraft carriers sank or damaged eighteen warships at Pearl Harbor. A few days later, Japanese land-based aircraft sank the British warships *Prince of Wales* and *Repulse* off the coast of Malaya. In May and June 1941, U.S. Navy aircraft defeated two Japanese invasion convoys in the Coral Sea and near Midway Island, sank five aircraft carriers and numerous other ships, and turned the tide of the Pacific war.[14] Achieving air superiority henceforth became a requirement before any military operation on the surface, whether land or maritime, could safely proceed.

In February 1947, a joint Army and Navy commission published the results of its study of Japanese naval losses during World War II. U.S. and Allied military forces had sunk 656 Japanese warships. Of these, land- and aircraft carrier–based aircraft sank 303 warships, or 46 percent of Japan's warship losses (142 of the sinkings involved land-based aircraft); submarines sank 217 Japanese warships; all other causes, including Allied surface ships, were far behind in the count.[15] Aircraft had become the dominant threat to surface ships.

In 1982, land-based aircraft engaged surface ships in another duel, this time off the Falkland Islands near Argentina. British planners greatly underestimated their foe. They expected to lose no more than two or three ships in the conflict. Instead, the Argentine air force, despite possessing just five Exocet antiship missiles, sank six British ships and badly damaged another ten, almost all with manually aimed "dumb" bombs. Argentine air attacks sank or damaged twelve of the twenty-three British air defense and escort destroyers and frigates, and air attacks on British amphibious ships near the end of the conflict killed fifty-one British soldiers in one day. Had Argentine bomb fuses been more reliable (many failed to detonate), and had the air force had, say, twenty Exocets rather than just five, British warship losses would have been even higher, with possibly disastrous results for the British campaign.[16]

During the Cold War, the U.S. Air Force, in cooperation with the Navy, began training its bomber crews for ocean surveillance, mine-laying, and maritime strike missions against the Soviet navy. By 1983, Air Force B-52 bombers armed with Harpoon ASCMs were flying patrol missions out of Maine and Guam. The Air Force made plans to send 10 B-52s armed with up to 120 Harpoon missiles against a large Soviet surface naval force. The B-52s would approach the Soviet fleet from several directions at low altitude to avoid detection and overwhelm the fleet's defenses with a saturation missile attack. The bombers would then return to base for another mission.[17] Chapter 3 discussed how the Soviet Backfire bomber force planned to attack the U.S. Navy in the same way.

There are simple reasons why aircraft are so effective against even the most heavily defended surface warships. Long-range patrol and bomber aircraft have the range, speed, and sensors to patrol and hold at risk large areas of the ocean on a single mission. These large aircraft can carry substantial amounts of fuel and weapons. The surface ships they are hunting are by contrast slow and unable to hide at sea. During the Cold War and before, surface warship groups would attempt to evade detection by shutting down all electronic emissions such as radars and radios. This tactic would be useless today against the constellations of synthetic aperture satellites that are providing near real-time imaging of even small objects on the surface day and night and through all weather. Finally, aircraft, especially large bombers, can overwhelm the defenses of surface fleets with large volleys of guided munitions.

Aircraft demonstrated their dominance over warships in 1941 and set a trend that will continue well into the future. Some U.S. strategists responded to the rapid growth of China's navy with a call to greatly expand the U.S. fleet (chapter 5 described some of these plans), but history and emerging technology both point to aircraft, especially long-range bombers, as the best approach for countering warships. That will particularly be the case in the Indo-Pacific.

Why Bombers Will Rule the Pacific

The last section discussed why aircraft trump warships; on an ocean, the range, speed, and firepower of aircraft, especially bombers, make them dominant over the surface below. They will be particularly ascendent over the Indo-Pacific theater with its vast stretches of open ocean, long distances between bases and countries, and great volumes of airspace to patrol. Short-range weapons and slow-moving platforms that are effective in a more confined theater such as Europe cannot command such an enormous area. And by logical extension, these features will accentuate the advantages of systems that do possess speed, range, payload, and endurance. That describes long-range bombers and their helpers.

An equally important argument for the primacy of long-range bombers in the Indo-Pacific theater is that U.S. commanders are unlikely to have many other decisive options available. China's advantageous continental position and the PLA's operational concept based on large numbers of land-attack and antiship missiles will deny the use of short-range tactical airpower located on aircraft carriers and air bases near China to U.S. commanders. These commanders might have Marine Corps missile teams attempting to hide along the First Island Chain and submarines lurking near Taiwan and in the Near Seas, but these forces will struggle to survive against the PLA's sensor networks and numerically superior submarines and missiles. And even if they could survive, they would lack the munition stocks to wage a campaign involving potentially thousands of targets.

Once again, that leaves the U.S. long-range bomber force as the only alternative. Here we can see the potentially fateful consequence of the misguided decision in the 1990s to terminate the B-2 stealth bomber program after acquiring just 21 aircraft. Had Congress purchased the 132 aircraft envisioned for the program, there would be little doubt today concerning conventional military deterrence against the PLA in the Indo-Pacific theater.

The original planned inventory of 132 B-2 bombers flying 35 aircraft per day during a campaign would have been able to strike up to 560 aim points on ship targets per day with precise and heavy antiship weapons (16 LRASMs per aircraft), with little the PLAN could do in defense. As noted earlier, former senior U.S. defense officials Robert Work and Michèle Flournoy asserted that a U.S. capacity to sink 300 PLAN warships in 72 hours would provide convincing conventional military deterrence. The planned B-2 force would have achieved this standard. The B-2's very small radar cross section allows it to safely fly closer to adversary air defense than nonstealthy aircraft can approach.[18] This feature allows the B-2, and later this decade the B-21, to carry a large load of inexpensive, short-range, but highly accurate precision-guided bombs.[19]

Unfortunately, the Air Force does not have a short-range, inexpensive, and self-guiding munition appropriate for attacking underway surface ships. The bomber force must rely solely on the very capable but relatively expensive LRASM for this task. Equally unfortunate is the Air Force's current plan to acquire just 400 LRASMs while it acquires 10,000 JASSMs, from which the LRASM is derived. The Air Force could do much for deterrence by denial if it shifted planned production of, say, 2,000 JASSMs to LRASMs instead. The Air Force will need many more than 400 LRASMs to wage an effective campaign against the PLAN and its auxiliaries.

The Air Force should begin fielding squadrons of the new B-21 Raider long-range bomber during the second half of the 2020s. The B-21 will be even stealthier than the B-2, with more advanced sensors and networking capabilities, and should be cheaper and easier to maintain, resulting in more aircraft available daily for combat missions.[20] The B-21's weapons payload size remains a secret, although it is likely to be roughly similar to the B-2's.[21]

Unfortunately, the arrival of that capacity is still years away. The first B-21s might be ready for combat around 2026, with the Air Force receiving one hundred aircraft into service by perhaps 2032.[22] The delivery of the full production force of B-21s will patch the hole left by the termination of the B-2 program in the 1990s. The B-21 will be able to execute the counter-maritime mission describe above, along with similarly demanding missions against well-defended targets, and do so with even more confidence in success than the B-2.

Meanwhile, there will be a dangerous gap between now and the arrival of the B-21s, which China's leaders may seek to exploit. The issue for U.S. and allied military planners during the early and mid-2020s is how to employ the current bomber force to maintain conventional military deterrence, particularly during a prospective crisis over Taiwan.

During this dangerous period, U.S. commanders in the Indo-Pacific will likely have no more than fifty bombers of all types available for combat. This would include perhaps only ten or fewer stealthy B-2s. B-2s and B-52s reserved for the strategic nuclear deterrence mission would further reduce these numbers. The reason for this reduced number is the previous lack of investment in bombers, the advanced age of the bombers in service, and a lack of funding for maintaining these old aircraft.[23]

Could this reduced force achieve the deterrence mission against the PLAN that Work and Flournoy described? Over the next few years, U.S. commanders in the Indo-Pacific might have only five B-2s available for all missions during a conflict, including attacks on PLAN ships in the Taiwan Strait. Nonstealthy B-1s and B-52s armed with LRASMs could attempt attacks on PLAN ships in the strait. But they would have to fly as close as 370 kilometers from their targets, putting them at risk of interception by PLA fighter patrols and long-range surface-to-air missiles.

The small bomber force U.S. commanders will have during the first half of the 2020s will still have the capacity to launch hundreds of missiles per day (a B-52 can carry twenty missiles, a B-1, twenty-four).[24] But this assumes that the crews of these bombers can effectively employ low-level radar-evasion tactics, electronic warfare support, and decoys to evade the PLA's air defenses, which will be formidable during a prospective Taiwan invasion scenario. Uncertainty regarding the ability of the B-1s and B-52s to succeed during a Taiwan scenario undermines deterrence by denial and thus increases the risk of Chinese aggression.

Another concern is the prospect of PLA disruption of U.S. and allied command networks through direct attacks on command centers and electronic jamming of communication networks. U.S. military forces plan to cope with potential disruptions to centralized command systems by delegating authority to dispersed lower-echelon units and encouraging initiative by lower-ranking officers guided by broadly framed mission orders.[25] The U.S. bomber force is well suited to this "mission command" approach. Mission orders could direct bomber crews to employ their initiative to attack maritime targets of opportunity in, say, the Taiwan Strait, which in a Taiwan invasion scenario they could assume to be hostile. The bombers could receive targeting data from supporting reconnaissance assets over the extremely high frequency portion of the electromagnetic spectrum, which is impervious to jamming (explained further below).[26]

The U.S. bomber force is a quintessential center-of-gravity target for PLA planners. They might well believe that successfully attacking the bombers' five home bases in the central United States would effectively knock the United States out of the war, since the United States would then have little left to fight with. U.S. commanders responsible for defending North America are concerned about surprise cruise missile attacks on the continental United States and are attempting to improve defenses against this possibility.[27]

Dispersing the bomber force among more bases would complicate a PLA effort to destroy the force on the ground. As discussed in the chapter 5, the Air Force's Agile Combat Employment concept faces many problems inside the densest portions of the PLA's missile engagement zones. But ACE could be very effective for protecting the bomber force during a conflict with China. A bomber's much greater operating radius opens a much greater number of airfields for potential use. For example, detachments of two to four bombers could deploy to forward locations in Alaska, Hawaii, Australia, Diego Garcia in the Indian Ocean, and elsewhere and be six to ten hours from targets in the Near Seas. Bombers flying from scores of potential locations in the continental United States would be thirteen hours from their targets and could recover at bases on the edge of the region or beyond. The PLA will have very few weapons to attack these locations and would in any case target only a small number of aircraft at each dispersal base.

The Air Force and its partners would have to organize a logistics and sustainment enterprise to support a global ACE concept for the bomber force in wartime. During the Cold War against the Soviet Union, the Air Force had such a global enterprise supporting the Strategic Air Command. With this legacy, the Air Force should have the ability to reconstruct this capacity for a modern context.

The Bombers Will Need Helpers

The Air Force's bombers—and other strike platforms, for that matter—will require support to achieve their goals. Even with their long-range flight capabilities, bombers will require refueling by tanker aircraft to reach targets across the long expanses of the Indo-Pacific theater. The Air Force is currently modernizing its large inventory of tanker aircraft, an effort that will extend through the 2030s.

Information, always important for combat success, will be even more important in the future. China, the United States, and other military powers understand this and are racing to develop vast networks of sensors, secure and jam-proof high-speed communications capabilities, artificial intelligence software to find relevant data and conclusions, and cyber tools for attacking opponents' computer networks and defending their own networks. The combatant that can most quickly and accurately find the enemy's forces and get attack orders to weapons in a position to strike will have an immense advantage. This explains the large sums the Chinese and U.S. governments are spending on AI software, quantum computing, secure and rapid communication networking, electronic warfare, and cyber network attack and defense.

The space domain and satellite constellations will be prime center-of-gravity objectives. The military forces of many countries use space-based satellite constellations for intelligence, surveillance, and reconnaissance (ISR); communications; navigation; and weather forecasting. Space became a contested military domain in the 1960s when the United States and the Soviet Union developed and tested weapons capable of destroying satellites in low earth orbit (LEO). Since then, China, Russia, and other countries have tested additional methods of disrupting satellites, including directing lasers and other forms of energy at satellites' sensors ("dazzling") and jamming the telemetry between satellites and ground stations on the surface.[28]

Military-related satellite constellations were never completely safe from attack even in the early decades of the Space Age, but satellites in the highest geosynchronous orbit (GEO) during this era were considered beyond the reach of ground-based weapons. An informal agreement between the United States and the Soviet Union to abstain from threats against GEO satellites, where both sides maintained their strategic nuclear command-and-control assets, reinforced the sanctuary in GEO.

During the Cold War era it was expensive to launch payloads into space, and launch opportunities were rare. The high cost, combined with the relative safety of space and the state of satellite technology, encouraged military satellite developers to design and launch large models packed with as many features as feasible. Through the Cold War and for almost two decades after, military satellite constellations comprised small numbers of large and expensive satellites, creating a concurrent incentive to attack these exceptionally important assets.

The PLA's successful test of a surface-to-space interceptor that destroyed an obsolete Chinese weather satellite in January 2007 was a watershed event. The strike created a large debris field that is still in orbit. In May 2013, the PLA conducted a nonimpact antisatellite missile test, this time with its interceptor reaching a height of more than 30,000 kilometers, or GEO altitude. This demonstration proved the PLA's ability to attack adversaries' space systems on all orbits.[29]

The Chinese tests, along with Russian antisatellite developments, made it clear that building military satellite constellations around a few large and exquisite satellites was no longer a tenable strategy. The coincidental arrival of two trends over the past decade has given military space system designers options to mitigate many of the antispace threats. First is the sharp decline in the cost of launching payloads into space. Private-sector entrants such as Space Exploration Technologies (SpaceX) have developed reusable orbital boosters that have greatly lowered the cost of space access.[30] Second is the arrival of small imaging satellites, some as small as a loaf of bread, such as those produced by private-sector companies such as Planet Labs.[31] Capella Space, another private-sector company, has established a constellation of small synthetic aperture radar satellites that provide frequent and highly detailed imaging of the surface, day and night in all weather conditions.[32] Both companies, along with other private-sector space-imaging companies, sell their imaging services to the Department of Defense.

Countering an adversary's military space capabilities will become much more difficult as competitors launch new satellite constellations with these characteristics. Space competitors such as the United States and China now have the technology to build imaging, communication, and navigation satellite constellations composed of scores or hundreds of small but capable satellites, connected in networks. These satellite networks will share their data and will enjoy the protective benefits of wide distribution and redundancy. Imaging, communication, and navigation capabilities will exist on many constellation sets owned and operated both by governments and by private-sector players. With declining launch costs and growing numbers of launch locations, including rapidly established expeditionary launch sites, military and private-sector space players will be able to quickly reconstitute satellite capabilities when necessary.

The Defense Department's Space Development Agency plans to redesign its reconnaissance and communication satellite networks along these principles, taking advantage of the rapidly declining costs of launch services and the small but capable satellites themselves. Large arrays composed of numerous satellites communicating through laser relays will go far in thwarting counter-satellite threats. In addition, placing these satellite constellations in orbits one thousand kilometers above the earth or higher will challenge the effectiveness of surface-based directed-energy antisatellite dazzlers.[33]

These new features of space operations will make it more difficult for both the United States and China to deny the use of space to each other's military forces. Air Force bombers should continue to benefit from space imaging, communications, and navigation resources during a potential conflict in the Indo-Pacific region as U.S. Space Force commanders and designers install the satellite constellations just described.

The bomber force will receive assistance from additional helpers. One such helper is the long-range RQ-180 unmanned high-altitude reconnaissance aircraft. The RQ-180 is still formally a secret Air Force program, although aviation journals have been discussing it for a decade. The aircraft is highly stealthy with a very low radar cross section and is designed to persist for long missions inside otherwise defended airspace. The RQ-180 has transoceanic range and can fly missions lasting as long as twenty-four hours. In addition to imagery and targeting, commanders could use the RQ-180 for electronic warfare against an adversary's communications or to relay data to and from strike aircraft and to other command nodes. According to published reports, an Air Force unit is actively flying RQ-180s on operational missions.[34] In a Taiwan crisis, reconnaissance aircraft like the RQ-180 would patrol the battle area and provide target information to the U.S. bomber force, which could then attack the targets with JASSMs, LRASMs, and other munitions.

U.S. and allied submarines could also provide target information to the bombers and other weapon platforms. In a prospective battle for Taiwan, Chinese and coalition submarines would patrol the waters around the island and the East China Sea. These submarines could locate and attack surface ships with torpedoes, although doing so might reveal their position and put them at risk of a counterattack. U.S. submarines could launch limited numbers of long-range Tomahawk cruise missiles at fixed targets on land or, with targeting support from aircraft, at surface ships, but also at the risk of revealing the submarine's location. The PLAN's quiet diesel-electric submarines, operating from nearby home ports, will outnumber U.S. and allied submarines in a Taiwan scenario and will also benefit from support from the PLA's sensor networks, aircraft, and unmanned reconnaissance vehicles.

U.S. and allied commanders might better use their submarines for reconnaissance and target identification, thus preserving their stealthiness and lowering their risk of destruction. Submarines could identify PLAN ship targets in the Taiwan Strait and elsewhere and relay that information to the bomber force, supplementing the data provided by satellites and reconnaissance aircraft such as the RQ-180.

In sum, the U.S. and allied battle network of sensors, communication resources, and "shooters" such as the bombers could provide a robust capability to thwart a prospective PLA invasion of Taiwan. That will certainly be the case by 2030 when the B-21 Raider is available in substantial numbers. During the remainder of the 2020s, however, the depleted and technologically challenged U.S. bomber force might be unable to prevail against the PLA fighting so close to its home bases. The outcome may depend on the rules of engagement policymakers issue to U.S. commanders fighting the battle and the munitions available to U.S. crews—topics discussed in the next section.

Attacking China's Territory: Too Dangerous or a Compelling Necessity?

In their Taiwan crisis report to the Council on Foreign Relations, Robert Blackwill and Philip Zelikow strongly advised against U.S. and allied military plans that included strikes against mainland China as basic components of the initial allied response. They offered this advice in the context of a PLA air and maritime quarantine of Taiwan meant to demonstrate China's sovereignty over the island.[35] Because the PLA would likely enjoy military superiority around Taiwan, they suggested a response that relied more on political, economic, and financial damage to China than on military consequences, employing the deterrence-by-punishment approach discussed in chapter 6.

Blackwill and Zelikow preferred an allied strategy that would compel the PLA to shoot first at a prospective allied relief convoy. In that event, U.S. and allied military forces would limit their response to the PLA forces active around Taiwan and avoid strikes on the Chinese mainland unless China struck the United States or its allies. Their strategy would compel China to make the choice to escalate, and thus make China culpable for the war and its consequences.[36]

If the PLA attacked only the civilian convoy and its naval escorts, the United States, Japan, and other allies could employ their large inventories of tactical airpower from nearby bases on Okinawa, Japan, Guam, Palau, and elsewhere. Large numbers of stealthy F-22 air superiority aircraft and F-35 strike aircraft over Taiwan could cripple the PLA's war plan. But allied planners should not count on China to refrain from attacking these bases. It would be unthinkable for PLA commanders to allow the allies to retain their tactical airpower assets, especially when the PLA has prepared for years to remove them from the conflict through attacks on their bases.

Would PLA strikes on Okinawa, the Japanese homeland, and Guam then justify U.S. and allied bomber and long-range cruise missile attacks on PLA military assets on China's mainland? Blackwill and Zelikow affirmed that the United States should retain that option should escalation proceed to "general war." But in their view, the United States and its allies should strive to avoid such escalation and certainly should not initiate it. They stressed the importance of limiting the overall damage such a war could produce. They also asserted that the allies' best deterrent assets are political, economic, and financial; early allied escalation to "general war" might squander these assets.[37]

But would it be possible for U.S. and allied military commanders to win a battle around Taiwan without striking PLA bases on the mainland? If the PLA were to attack Taiwan, the mainland would very likely incur battle damage from Taiwanese aircraft and missile bombardment. Suppressing Taiwan's airpower and land-attack missile capacity will thus be major goals for the PLA's offensive. But the Taiwan defenders are almost certain to inflict at least some bomb and missile damage on mainland PLA naval bases, air bases, missile bases, command posts, warehouses, and assembly areas. The policy issue for U.S. leaders is whether U.S. military forces should add to the strikes the Taiwanese force would make against mainland targets.

From the perspective of military efficiency, attacking adversary bases is imperative. Military forces are complex systems with weaknesses on which opponents should apply pressure. For example, the most difficult place to defeat a combat aircraft is in the air, where the aircraft is performing its designed functions and using its designed capabilities. The aircraft is much more vulnerable on the ground, where it is not doing what it was designed to do, which explains why air bases are priority targets in military campaigns. Other vulnerable points of the "aircraft system" are the aircraft's necessary supports: pilots, maintenance personnel, spare parts, fuel, munitions storage, and command networks. Perhaps the best of all targets in the aircraft system, at least in a long campaign, is the aircraft factory; damaging or destroying the factory destroys the aircraft before they even exist. The same systems logic applies to surface warships, submarines, and ground forces. A decisive allied military campaign would seem to require a campaign to defeat the PLA's combat systems in their entirety.

But aside from attacking the systems' components, there may be targets on the Chinese mainland that U.S. policymakers might feel compelled to attack. For example, should the PLA's counterspace forces, either direct-ascent surface-to-space satellite intercept missiles or ground-based anti-satellite laser dazzlers, attack U.S. imaging and communication satellites, U.S. policymakers and commanders might feel compelled to counterattack against those PLA counterspace forces on the surface inside China. The same logic and urgency might apply to PLA surface-to-air missile units located near China's coast that fired at U.S. aircraft flying near Taiwan.

China has spent considerable resources on protecting its command-and-control structure, its logistics assets, its missile forces, and some of its naval assets in bunkers and technologically advanced underground facilities.[38] The United States will need large, stealthy bombers to carry the types of bombs needed to attack these targets. Indeed, retaining the ability to hold such targets at risk may be one of the most important components of a credible deterrence strategy. Chinese leaders might act with more restraint against an adversary able to hold the high-value assets in these bunkers at risk.

A key objective of an American and allied military campaign against China would be regaining and maintaining control of the sea and air lines of communication in international waters, and air space in the western Pacific. In the past, this has primarily been a task for naval forces charged with defeating the opposing navy and then establishing control over the seas. However, the PLA's ability to dominate the Near Seas with its land-based missiles and airpower places U.S. policymakers and commanders in an unfamiliar position. Superior naval power is not enough to establish sea control over the Near Seas and the western Pacific out to three thousand kilometers from China's coast. China's land-based missile and air power will have to be suppressed as well. And doing that will require attacking targets on the Chinese mainland.

The United States will need new technology and tactics to suppress China's land-based antinavy missiles and airpower. The problem for U.S. military planners is that those missiles and airpower components are largely dispersed, mobile, and designed to be hidden or sheltered in hardened or underground facilities. China's DF-21D antiship ballistic missile, for example, is based on a medium-range missile that is moved about and launched from a transporter-erector-launcher. Most of China's land-based antiship and land-attack cruise missiles are also mounted on TELs. China's maritime strike airpower, which includes both bombers and fighter-attack aircraft, is located at scores of air bases, most of which are hardened against attack.[39]

Once they enter the Air Force's inventory, B-21 bombers will be able to loiter and search for ground targets in defended air space, one method of addressing this problem. But that is an expensive approach, and the economics will not favor the United States. It will be cheaper for China to produce more missiles and TELs than it will be for the United States to produce more bombers. In this finder versus hider competition, the United States will need a cheaper strategy.

In the 1990s, the Air Force developed the Low Cost Autonomous Attack System (LOCAAS), a program it successfully tested but later terminated. LOCAAS was a small (about one meter long), jet-powered UAV designed to search autonomously for specific targets on the ground and then attack them. LOCAAS missiles would be launched from aircraft outside an adversary's air defense system, then fly to a predetermined patrol area and begin searching the ground for specific targets, such as TELs, using a precise laser-radar (LIDAR) sensor similar to the sensors on self-driving cars. Once a LOCAAS located a target, it would dive on it and destroy it. If a LOCAAS exhausted its fuel before finding a suitable target, it would self-destruct by crashing into water or an empty field. A group of four LOCAAS missiles could search up to a hundred square kilometers before exhausting their fuel.[40]

LOCAAS was designed to equip U.S. military forces with the capability to safely search for important mobile targets inside an adversary's air defense system. U.S. forces would launch hundreds of LOCAAS missiles at a time into suspected TEL operating areas and either destroy them or force them to shelter where they could not launch their missiles. The concept called for producing more than ten thousand of the small UAVs, with a marginal per unit cost of about $70,000.[41] At that price, the United States would likely be on the winning side of a production competition, compared with the cost of additional Chinese cruise and ballistic missiles on TELs or passive and active air defenses.

LOCAAS's autonomous decision-making was deemed an essential feature. Designers assumed that electronic warfare, jamming, and adversary attacks on the U.S. military communication system would prevent the many LOCAAS units flying in combat from maintaining connections to operators "in the loop" at a rear command post. Thus, LOCAAS was designed to make its own attack decisions. In the early 2000s, when the program was terminated, such lethal autonomy for robots was apparently a cultural barrier U.S. defense officials were unwilling to cross.[42] Even when LIDAR achieved higher target identification accuracy than humans in an aircraft cockpit could make, cultural and political sensitivities concerning a robot's lethal decision-making led to LOCAAS's cancellation.

However, the fact remains that the United States and its allies will not be able to safely operate their warships in the Near Seas—thus reestablishing freedom of navigation—until China's land-based antinavy forces are suppressed. Even after U.S. and allied airpower and submarines succeed in defeating the PLAN (itself a challenging task) the United States and its partners will need something like LOCAAS as an affordable and competitive answer to China's mobile missile forces and dispersed and protected airpower.

The original 1990s version of LOCAAS, although a conceptual breakthrough, lacked the performance qualities necessary to be effective in the vast Pacific theater. Its range was only around one hundred kilometers, with a loiter-search time limited to just thirty minutes.[43]

U.S. military forces possess existing technologies they can quickly repurpose as autonomous search-and-attack weapons and thus higher-performance successors to LOCAAS. For example, the Air Force has already acquired more than a thousand Miniature Air-Launched Decoy (MALD) missiles. MALD's mission is to fly ahead of strike aircraft and appear to be a dangerous threat to the adversary's air defense system. When successful, a MALD missile will induce the adversary to reveal the locations of air defense radars, surface-to-air missile launchers, and air defense aircraft to friendly strike aircraft. These aircraft can either avoid these threats or attack them first. Each MALD is about 3 meters long and weighs just 135 kilograms. A small jet engine powers the MALD at a high subsonic speed with a range of about 900 kilometers. MALD-J, the latest variant purchased by the Air Force and Navy, includes an electromagnetic jammer. In 2013, the Air Force purchased a production batch of MALD-Js for about $408,500 per missile.[44]

The Air Force could refashion MALD or a similar small, inexpensive, and expendable missile into an autonomous search-and-attack weapon. Like LOCAAS, the MALD attack variant would have LIDAR, plus imaging infrared and millimeter-wave radar sensors for precise identification of specified targets day and night and through clouds. The MALD attack variant would fly at a much higher altitude than LOCAAS and thus could search a much larger area of the ground, up to 3,000 square kilometers per missile compared with 25 square kilometers for the original LOCAAS. It is realistic for a B-2 or B-21 bomber to carry up to 100 MALD attack missiles, which combined could search up to 300,000 square kilometers of terrain for antiship missiles on TELs. Many missile TELs cannot travel off roads or are restricted to mostly solid, flat surfaces, which would reduce the required search area.[45]

Under this concept, a few B-2 and B-21 bombers could deploy many hundreds of MALD attack variants that would search for missile TELs, attack and destroy those they found, and suppress the launch capability of the remainder. Although temporary, the mere threat of this U.S. autonomous search-and-strike capability would degrade the PLA's land-based antinavy forces, permitting more operating freedom for allied naval forces.

The United States and its allies will require a capability like this if they are to regain control of the western Pacific. Using inexpensive and autonomous systems based on the LOCAAS concept would be a competitive approach since the United States would be able to increase the capacity of this autonomous search-and-attack program for less than the PLA would have to spend on more missiles, TELs, and their defenses.[46]

There are good reasons why Blackwill and Zelikow strongly recommended against U.S. attacks on China's mainland, at least as a basic element of a U.S. initial response. Years of experience with war games and simulations focusing on Taiwan and other similar scenarios have revealed the hazards of seemingly minor military escalation. In many of these simulations, escalation proceeded up to and beyond the nuclear threshold as decision-makers on both sides sought a tactical military advantage and the point at which the opponent, fearful of further destruction, would give up instead. The lesson from these experiences is to keep the conflict at the lowest possible level, both for humanitarian reasons and to make it easier for the combatants to find "off ramps" to leave the conflict before reputation and prestige pressures become too great.

Even so, attacks from some combatant—Taiwan's defense forces, for example—will likely strike mainland Chinese targets whether U.S. policymakers prefer it or not. What Chinese decision-makers do at that point will also be out of the control of U.S. and allied leaders. The U.S. Air Force's bombers with their global reach are an asset no other prospective combatant possesses. Should the PLA escalate to territorial strikes against tactical air bases on Japan and Guam, the bomber force would provide the United States with more strike capacity against mainland targets than the PLA could send against the United States, Japan, or other allies. U.S. military planners, possessing this "escalation dominance," should ponder how to use this capability to compel the termination of the conflict on favorable terms.

8

Roles for Naval Power in the Sensor and Missile Age

T he start of missile combat in the Near Seas would likely halt maritime commerce in much the of western Pacific Ocean.¹ Commercial
ship owners and crews would not sail through a war zone marked
by intense antiship missile fire, and few insurance companies would cover
shipping losses in the war zone if ship operators could avoid them instead.

For reasons this book has explained, the United States and its allies
will likely lose control of the seas in the western Pacific during the initial
phase of a war with China. The U.S.-led alliance would have to fight against
the PLAN, now the largest combat navy in the world and a fleet operating
close to its home ports. The alliance would also have to battle China's
land-based antinavy forces, composed of long-range antiship ballistic and
cruise missiles, and hundreds of aircraft armed with world-class antiship
cruise missiles, supported by increasingly sophisticated and redundant
reconnaissance and command networks. Defeating the PLAN will not by
itself restore control of the seas and freedom of navigation. Regaining sea
control will also require defeating the PLA's land-based antinavy force or
inducing it to stand down.

This does not mean the PLA will gain sea control for itself. U.S. and
allied submarines and U.S. long-range airpower will challenge the PLAN's

surface ships, which will be equally susceptible to identification from allied sensor networks and vulnerable to antiship missiles and torpedoes. The result is likely to be mutual sea denial, with the western Pacific a deadly maritime war zone for all.[2]

U.S. and allied policymakers have traditionally looked to the Pacific Fleet to retain control of the maritime Indo-Pacific. In the past, the military analysis of this challenge involved the comparison of opposing fleets, with the outcome depending on factors such as seamanship, leadership, ship and weapon technology, allies, tactics, weather, and the fortunes of war. Until recently, there was little question that ships and their crews (including ships that launched aircraft) determined which country would control the seas.

But the military-technical revolution has upset that analysis. With land-based antinavy capabilities reaching far out to sea, sinking the enemy's fleet is only the first step toward establishing control of the sea. Also necessary—and now more difficult—will be the suppression or destruction of the enemy's land-based air and missile power.

The Navy's leaders have been aware of this problem for more than two decades and have attempted to address it with increasing urgency over the past decade. Unfortunately, this generation's military-technical revolution has overwhelmed the Navy's surface forces, including its aircraft carriers, and has made obsolete the Navy's long-standing operational concepts for sea control and power projection. The Navy's traditional operational methods, centered on aircraft carrier and expeditionary strike groups, are no longer tenable against the PLA's battle networks. And despite much research, experimentation, and effort, there are no technical or tactical solutions on the horizon that will make it feasible for the Navy's strike groups to stand, fight, and survive deep inside the PLA's missile engagement zone, as they would have to do given the short range of the Navy's weapons compared with those of the PLA.

This does not mean that the Navy or naval forces are obsolete. As this chapter will explain, U.S. and allied navies will have several critical roles in a long-term competition against China and the PLA. These critical roles will include providing presence and reassurance to allies and partners before conflict occurs and reinforcing deterrence during an open-ended peacetime competition against China. Another critical role will be restoring security, reestablishing sea control, and reclaiming maritime and island territory at the end of a conflict.

But against a major conventional power like China that has invested great sums to exploit the military-technical revolution, U.S. and allied surface naval forces will have a diminished role during the most intense phases of kinetic conflict. The missile threat now limits the traditional combat roles of surface ships and has created grave risks for their improper employment. Policymakers and commanders need to reset their expectations for the roles of naval power during the current military-technical revolution.

The revolution's realities should compel substantial changes in the way naval forces are designed, acquired, and employed. The expense of acquiring and maintaining naval forces will be a substantial element of a long-term competitive strategy against a peer competitor like China. In a competitive strategy, the design of U.S. naval forces should impose costs on China. Further, U.S. and allied policymakers should escape the current trap of having China impose costs on them. This implies a design for naval forces that minimizes expense and is instead a supporting economy-of-force line of effort within the overall defense program.

These are controversial yet unavoidable conclusions. The current military-technical revolution follows a long line of similar revolutions throughout military history that have upended military concepts. The arrival of horse cavalry, the long bow, cannons, the rifled musket, railroads, radios, aircraft, and spacecraft are historical examples. The winners were those who embraced the changes, anticipated their implications, and then adapted their forces and methods to the new reality.[3] Today's winners will be the policymakers and planners who apply the implications of the current military-technical revolution to their military forces and concepts. These implications affect naval forces most of all.

What Can Naval Forces Do Anymore? The Navy's Traditional Missions in a Future Threat Context

The U.S. naval services (the Navy, Marine Corps, and Coast Guard) published their latest public strategy document in December 2020. The document emphasized the roles of maritime power across the entire spectrum of conflict, from providing a visible forward presence of U.S. military power during peacetime to the contributions warships and submarines would make attacking enemy ships and land targets during a war. The document stressed the important role that naval forces—not least the civilian law enforcement Coast Guard—play in setting and defending acceptable norms of behavior, defending freedom of navigation for commerce, building and reassuring alliances with other countries, and deterring aggressive actors from contemplating opportunistic fait accompli seizures of territory or other hostile actions.[4]

What about the role of the naval services during high-intensity combat against peer opponents like the PLA? The naval services' strategy document asserted that the Navy and Marine Corps will fight as elements of a much broader joint force including the Army, Air Force, Space Force, and allies. The document explicitly discussed the support that airpower, including the Air Force's bombers, will play in setting the conditions for success on the surface and against the adversary's naval and land-based forces.[5] The document's discussion of how a successful war at sea will require contributions from all services and success in all domains (space, air, sea, land, and cyber) is a recognition that the current military-technical revolution brought major changes in what naval forces can accomplish by themselves.

Long-range airpower, supplemented by submarines, will of necessity be the main predators of surface warships. Possessing the capability to quickly destroy the PLA's surface fleet will be the best method of thwarting a Chinese fait accompli strike against Taiwan, the Senkakus, or other similar military goals the PLA might wish to achieve. Clearly possessing this counter-maritime capability will reinforce deterrence by denial in the western Pacific and beyond.

What does this imply for the design of U.S. and allied naval forces in the context of the PLA's exploitation of the military-technical revolution? The next section will discuss past and current thinking on this question.

New Navy Designs, Past and Future

In the security competition with China, the United States and its coalition partners will define maritime success, and indeed overall strategic success, as maintaining freedom of navigation throughout the Indo-Pacific region, especially the East and South China Seas, where China's antinavy forces will be most powerful. The design of the U.S. fleet is increasingly unsuited to achieving this objective.

The Navy's high-end guided missile destroyers and cruisers can no longer accomplish the tasks the Navy needs to achieve. Despite being the most technologically advanced multimission surface combatants, they are losing the race against precision antiship missiles, whose capabilities are rising while their costs fall.[6] The priority task for the Navy's destroyers and cruisers is to defend the Navy's aircraft carriers against air and missile attack. When those ships can no longer confidently defend the aircraft carriers against saturation antiship missile raids, as is now the case, the Navy's aircraft carrier strike groups will no longer be useful in China's Near Seas. Indeed, deploying them there would expose an iconic center-of-gravity target to the PLA's battle network—exactly the opposite of what a sound strategy should do.

In response to this long-developing concern, some naval theorists have called for a radical redesign of U.S. naval power to adapt to the military-technical revolution. In 2009, the Pentagon's Office of Net Assessment engaged Wayne Hughes, a retired U.S. Navy captain and a professor of operations research at the Naval Postgraduate School in Monterey, California, to study the looming threat from the PLA's antiship missiles and sensors. Hughes and his colleagues issued a report in 2009 proposing a "New Navy Fighting Machine" that would dramatically reshape the Navy.

Hughes' design stepped away from a Navy organized around the large aircraft carrier strike group. The report recommended cutting the Navy's large nuclear-powered aircraft carrier fleet from eleven to six and instead building a force of smaller carriers hosting short-takeoff, vertical-landing F-35B jets. Similarly, Hughes recommended replacing the Navy's sophisticated and expensive multimission guided missile destroyers with a wide variety of simpler, cheaper, and smaller single-purpose ships.[7] He also recommended adding more submarines along with long-range unmanned aircraft and bombers, just as this book advises doing, asserting that a larger, more diverse fleet would be more resilient in combat.[8]

Under Hughes' plan, the fleet would grow in numbers as smaller and relatively inexpensive single-purpose ships replaced expensive, overengineered hulls. The U.S. shipbuilding industry would benefit because this fleet would require more shipyards than currently operate. Navy procurement would benefit because contractors would have to compete for contracts. As a final benefit, the plan would result in ships easier to maintain, with better training and command opportunities for the Navy's personnel.[9]

But would Hughes' New Navy Fighting Machine improve the ability of the Navy to maintain control over the East and South China Seas during a conflict with China? Hughes did not sound hopeful in that regard. His report recommended "affordable numbers of small, lethal combatants capable of demonstrating a commitment to defend" U.S. allies and partners around the Near Seas. Rather than providing serious military capability, such a force—presumably ships no larger than patrol boats, corvettes, and frigates—would function as a sacrificial trip wire, forcing the PLA to draw American blood and thus risk a large and costly war. Hughes envisioned the same trip-wire function for the vulnerable U.S. air bases on Okinawa, Japan, and South Korea; the combat aircraft there hold PLA forces at risk and, in Hughes' view, would force China into costly horizontal escalation. But Hughes implied that in a prolonged conflict, these bases would have little tactical utility for the U.S. coalition, a conclusion this book has also reached.[10]

In 2013, Robert Rubel, a retired U.S. Navy captain and former dean of the Center for Naval Warfare Studies at the U.S. Naval War College, largely endorsed Hughes' New Navy Fighting Machine concept, noting that China's Near Seas were no longer the place for the Navy's largest capital ships (its aircraft carriers, cruisers, and destroyers).[11] Instead, Rubel agreed with Hughes that the United States should maintain its surface naval presence in the Near Seas with small and inexpensive ships backed by the menace of powerful deterrent forces over the horizon. Until the United States is willing to patrol the Near Seas with expendable trip-wire ships, Rubel argued, the Navy will be increasingly unwilling to risk a presence in these waters, thus eventually ceding these seas to China's control.[12]

Implementing the trip-wire concept requires the presence of credibly menacing military power over the horizon ready to intervene and retaliate after the small ships are attacked. But after the PLA has acquired confidence in its ability to suppress U.S. forward bases and attack U.S.

naval strike groups three thousand kilometers and beyond from China, credible menacing U.S. military power would be limited to its bomber forces and the small number of submarines able to operate in the region.

U.S. naval planners should not presume that these small surface combatants will escape discovery when sailing near China because of their size. As chapter 4 discussed, China's reconnaissance satellite constellations, unmanned surveillance aircraft, submarines, maritime militia, and other intelligence-gathering capabilities will provide PLA commanders with virtually real-time data on surface targets out to the Second Island Chain. With all-weather synthetic aperture radar imaging now capable of resolution of one meter or less, small ships will not escape detection.[13] A 2013 RAND study on naval design noted that "eventually, breakthroughs in sensor technology may make any platform, anywhere, observable and vulnerable."[14] "Eventually" is now. Even the smallest U.S. surface ships can no longer hide from Chinese sensor networks.

The Marine Corps' new operating concept posits that its platoon-sized, missile-armed units will be able to maneuver from island to island on small, unobtrusive coastal transports. But almost nothing on the surface will be unobtrusive to detailed SAR imaging and other PLA surveillance methods. Nor will any allied missile-armed unit be too small or unthreatening to escape a PLA missile attack. The declining cost and improving performance of antiship missiles relative to their targets will make it economical for PLA commanders to attack just about any detected combatant. For example, each of the Navy's new small, "affordable" guided missile frigates will cost more than $1 billion, for which sum the PLA could purchase hundreds of antiship missiles.[15]

The Navy's latest strategy document discussed "distributed operating concepts" based on smaller, more affordable platforms, including small robotic or remotely operated missile ships designed to operate without crews. The goal of this concept is to present the adversary with many more targets to contend with and to greatly expand the missile presence and lethality of U.S. and allied naval forces.[16]

Given the aircraft carrier's severe shortcomings in a China scenario, it is not difficult to make the case for land-attack and antiship missiles distributed over many smaller ships as an alternative. But missile ships have their own weaknesses. The Navy's surface ships and submarines launch Tomahawk cruise missiles from vertical launch cells. This clever system expanded the missile capacity of these ships and allowed commanders to vary the missile load-out of ships depending on the anticipated mission. The downside is that the cells cannot be reloaded at sea; surface ships and submarines must return to port, tie up at a dock, and have technicians and dock cranes reload the expended cells.

This is a substantial contrast to aircraft carrier operations where the Navy's underway replenishment ships resupply carrier strike groups with fuel, munitions, food, spare parts, and other provisions, allowing the carriers to remain in combat for weeks or months. The inability to reload vertical missile cells while under way remains a severe limitation for the missile ship concept.[17] Why the problem has not yet been solved remains a mystery. The logical conclusion is that missile cell reloading at sea faces technical barriers that make the procedure impractical.

The Navy would benefit from a new land-attack cruise missile with a much longer range than the 1,600-kilometer Tomahawk Block IV. At that range, Navy surface missile ships attacking even coastal targets are within the radius of the PLA's missile engagement zone. To threaten targets inland, the missile ships would have to sail for many hours or days deep into the PLA's missile engagement zone. The Navy needs a land-attack cruise missile with at least double or even triple the range of the current Tomahawk to attack important targets inland from China's east coast. However, there is no public evidence that the Navy is developing a longer-ranged successor to the Tomahawk.[18]

The Navy is developing a submarine-launched hypersonic weapon with a conventional warhead. The planned range and performance of the missile are not publicly known, and the missile is not expected to enter service until the late 2020s.[19] Like the Army's proposed theater-range hypersonic missile, the Navy's hypersonic missile is likely to be expensive and available only in small numbers.

"Distributed lethality," the Navy's current design concept, descends from Hughes' 2009 study for the Office of Net Assessment. Distributing the Navy's missiles over a larger number of smaller platforms is certainly an improvement over the legacy naval design. Even so, the redesign will not by itself provide a way for the Navy to maintain control of the East and South China Seas in the face of the PLA's land-based air and missile power. As this book has discussed, establishing deterrence against a determined and well-armed adversary like China will require the U.S.-led alliance to possess the capability to deny the PLA its objectives during high-intensity combat. The Navy's surface ships will not be able to contribute much during this scenario because they would be exposed to the PLA's battle networks.

The Navy and its maritime partners in the Indo-Pacific will, however, have several critical roles to play should high-intensity combat occur. Policymakers will have to adjust their expectations of what naval forces can contribute against the PLA and call for a naval force design that matches these revised expectations.

The Navy's Role in Conventional Deterrence

Chapter 5 reviewed some of the naval forces structure plans prepared during the Obama, Trump, and Biden administrations. These proposals included a December 2016 plan for a 355-ship Navy, the Integrated Naval Force Structure Assessment (INFSA) from late 2019, the Future Naval Force Study of 2020, the Trump White House proposal from December 2021, and the Biden administration's preliminary plan from June 2021.[20] All these plans were developed in response to the growth of the PLAN, and all proposed many, sometimes hundreds, more ships—manned and unmanned—and large increases in the Navy's shipbuilding and maintenance budgets.

These plans seem to have been premised on a theory that massed fleets of naval power, built by a World War II–style shipyard mobilization, can overwhelm the PLA's battle networks. In addition, the planners seem to have believed that many smaller ships will somehow be safer from PLA missile attack either because they will be harder for the PLA's sensors to find or because the number of targets will overwhelm the PLA's command system.

But as this book has discussed, even the most technologically advanced warships are not protected from saturation attacks from inexpensive but deadly precise volleys of antiship missiles. Nor will small ships escape the PLA's sensors; even the smallest of the proposed U.S. warships are up to 200 feet long, while space-based synthetic aperture radar satellites can distinguish objects less than 3 feet long in all weather, day or night. Further, these warships, whether sailing alone or in concentrated formations, would have to sail for days inside the PLA's missile engagement zones to bring their weapons into range against useful PLA targets. This is especially true in a Taiwan conflict scenario.

Policymakers should discard their excessively ambitious naval design plans and their visions of a Navy immediately successful in high-intensity combat against the PLA's battle network and instead call for a naval design that aligns with the tasks naval forces can actually accomplish during the current military-technical revolution.

Which roles and tasks should this reformed naval design focus on? The most important role for allied naval forces is to be a "force in being" that PLA commanders will not be able to ignore or avoid. This force in being would be large enough to threaten, say, a PLA naval force aimed at Taiwan or PLA naval bases along China's coast, but small enough not to constitute a war-losing center-of-gravity target should the PLA damage or destroy it.

Ideally, if China and the PLA have fait accompli designs on Taiwan or elsewhere, the PLA would have to attack the U.S. and allied naval force in being to achieve their goal, thus ensuring armed conflict between China, the United States, and likely others in a U.S.-led alliance. The term "force in being" is most often applied to an inferior force trying to maintain relevance against a superior opponent. This appellation will not wear well for members of the U.S. Navy, which is still the greatest naval force in the world, but the concept is relevant for the situation U.S. and allied naval forces face in China's Near Seas.

If the force-in-being concept is to succeed, policymakers must have the political will to place U.S. and allied missile-armed surface combatants in the PLA's line of fire, where they will be vulnerable to the PLA's missiles. The political will to risk U.S. and allied warships and sailors in this manner leads to the second important role for naval forces: reassuring allies and partners in the Indo-Pacific region that the United States is committed to the promises it has made to them regarding their security and the security of the region. That reassurance will be credible only when the United States maintains forces continuously deployed in the region and constantly on patrol in the most dangerous areas. Like the Berlin Brigade during the Cold War, these forces will not win the war against China, nor should they be designed to do so. Depending on the level of surprise the PLA might be able to achieve, these forces may not even be capable of delaying the PLA's fait accompli campaign for long. But they will succeed as a trip wire when they ensure a wider and mobilized war between China and the United States and its allies. If China's leaders fear that prospect and abstain from attacking, the forward-deployed forces will have achieved deterrence by denial and thereby have kept the peace.

A third important role for naval forces against the PLA will be their contributions to intelligence-gathering, reconnaissance, and target identification. U.S. and allied naval forces should be designed to collect accurate and timely targeting information and to supply these data to the regional and global all-domain intelligence and command networks. The all-domain command network would then transmit target data to long-range strike platforms such as bombers and long-range missile units. Missile-armed surface ships and submarines could of course attack targets themselves, but they will make their best contributions when they provide timely targeting data to the overall battle network without revealing their positions.

Submarines will be particularly useful in this role. The Navy's *Virginia*-class nuclear-powered submarines have an unlimited range, are quiet and difficult to detect, and are heavily armed with guided torpedoes and land-attack Tomahawk missiles. Japan's latest diesel-electric submarines are also world-class platforms. But launching their weapons risks exposing their positions, especially in the Taiwan scenario where they would presumably sail near thick concentrations of PLAN warships, submarines, underwater sensors, and patrol aircraft. Providing targeting data to the all-domain intelligence and command network might be the best use of these assets. Later this decade, the U.S. Navy could acquire large numbers of relatively inexpensive unmanned and autonomous submarines for intelligence gathering and target identification, a capability that would supplement and expand the intelligence gathering performed by manned submarines.[21]

Waiting for the Endgame: The Navy and Marine Corps in War Termination

Chapter 5 discussed how the Marine Corps is refashioning itself for distributed small-unit missile combat along the First Island Chain. Under this new force-planning guidance, the Marine Corps is formally discarding its previously established purpose to provide two Marine expeditionary brigades for a large-scale amphibious assault against a defended shoreline, because the military-technical revolution has made such a maneuver unfeasible. Instead, the Marine Corps is preparing to disrupt the PLA's maneuver in the western Pacific with its newly formed dispersed missile units.[22]

This new concept for the Marine Corps supports the theories argued in this book. Small antiship and antiaircraft missile teams dispersed along the First Island Chain will act as a force in being by compelling the PLA to attack them during a fait accompli military assault. The new concept imposes costs on China because the missile teams are inexpensive while the PLA's response, requiring more sensors, missiles, and staff attention, will likely be expensive. The PLA will have to kill Americans and allies to remove the Marine Corps missile threat, a prospect that should improve deterrence.

These Marine Corps missile units are not likely to survive long, because the PLA's sensors will be able to find them, and they will not be able to maneuver and resupply. At best, they will temporarily disrupt a large and determined PLA assault. Even so, the planned Marine Corps missile presence along the First Island Chain will reassure allies and contribute a significant component to a U.S. and allied force in being in the region.

It would be unfortunate if the adoption of the new Marine Corps concept came at the cost of the service's previous capacity to conduct substantial amphibious assaults. The new guidance states that the Marine Corps is not foreclosing this possibility, although it will no longer be a planning priority.[23]

And indeed, the United States and its allies will still need the capacity to conduct significant "forcible entry operations" during a prospective conflict against the PLA. U.S. and allied planners should expect that the PLA will seize islands and other territory. PLA soldiers may occupy this seized terrain and remain even if the PLA fails to accomplish its overall campaign objectives. In addition, should the U.S. and its allies win the war, policymakers and commanders may see the need to seize key terrain previously occupied by China (e.g., in the South China Sea) to improve the coalition's postwar strategic position and to reestablish effective conventional military deterrence.

Achieving these goals will require a capacity for forcible entry operations, most likely in the form of amphibious assaults. As the Marine Corps guidance acknowledges, these operations will not be feasible while the PLA's battle network is still intact and poses a threat to the Navy amphibious ships that would deliver Marines to an amphibious objective. Assuming the U.S.-led coalition is on a path to achieving supremacy in the warfighting domains (space, cyber, air, maritime, and land), amphibious operations against PLA positions in the Senkakus and the South China Sea, and against potential PLA bridgeheads on Taiwan could become feasible.

By this logic, these operations would occur nearer the end of the conflict. This implies that the Navy's force of large amphibious ships and the Marine Corps units that did not begin the war as missile units on the First Island Chain would have to wait while the space, cyber, air, and other components of the joint force established superiority over the PLA's air, maritime, and missile forces. This process would resemble the Pacific campaigns in World War II, where the sequence of amphibious assaults against Japanese garrisons occurred after U.S. forces established air and maritime supremacy around each amphibious objective's area.

The Marine Corps is thus redesigning itself with the goal of blunting and perhaps thwarting a potential PLA fait accompli strike along the First Island Chain, although that concept will not by itself be a war-winning approach. But while the Marine Corps and the Navy's amphibious forces reshape themselves, they should not discard the large amphibious assault mission. The U.S.-led coalition will need this capability at some point during a conflict against the PLA.

Imposing Costs with a New Fleet Design

Chapter 6 discussed how competitors can use cost-imposing strategies to induce opponents to expend resources on defensive instead of offensive capabilities. Other cost-imposing strategies could include devising inexpensive actions or capabilities that reduce the effectiveness of the opponent's capabilities, or taking actions that force diplomatic, financial, or political costs on the opponent.[24]

The United States should design and acquire a naval force structure that contributes to a wider cost-imposing strategy on China. The overall goal of that cost-imposing strategy should be to sustain and strengthen deterrence by denial against China in the Indo-Pacific region. The cost-imposing elements of the strategy would force the PLA to invest in defensive rather than offensive capabilities, reduce at an efficient price the effectiveness of the PLA's combat systems, and force China's leadership into actions that create diplomatic, political, and financial costs. The desired result is convincing China's leadership that military aggression will be a losing course of action for China. A re-formed U.S. naval program can contribute to this strategy.

The first step for U.S. policymakers, however, is to realize that China is already successfully imposing costs on the United States, especially in the maritime domain. Thus, the first step for devising a re-formed naval design is to stop cooperating with China's successful cost-imposing strategy. Top policymakers should decline a naval arms race against China. They should reject assertions that more warships can somehow overwhelm the PLA's counter-maritime battle network. And they should understand that there are other and better means and methods than maritime power for defeating China's maritime power.

With that step accomplished, policymakers can then focus on what they want U.S. maritime power to contribute to a cost-imposing strategy against China. A U.S. naval presence in the Near Seas composed almost entirely of manned missile frigates and additional unmanned corvette-size missile ships would best meet that need. An example of such a fleet would be ten of the new *Constellation*-class guided missile frigates (FFG-62) and forty large unmanned surface vessels (LUSVs). The Navy is still designing the latter but will likely use existing commercial ships as a model. Each of the new frigates will have thirty-two missile cells that can launch a mixture of land-attack, antiaircraft, antiship, and antisubmarine weapons.[25] The Navy intends the LUSVs to have offensive weapons such as antiship and land-attack missiles, although the quantities per vessel are still unknown.[26] The corvette-size LUSV, at about 1,000–2,000 tons of displacement, is likely to be half the size of the new frigate, so let us assume that each LUSV is equipped with sixteen missile cells.[27] Commanders of the frigates or commanders elsewhere in the region would control the missiles in the LUSVs, which would require offboard sensors or guidance to find targets.[28]

This proposed fleet of frigates and unmanned missile ships would have 960 missile cells spread over 50 small ships, 10 of which would have crews. By comparison, the U.S. Seventh Fleet's surface combatant force, based at Yokosuka, Japan, consists of 3 cruisers and 5 destroyers with a combined 861 missile cells.[29] The frigate-led fleet would place about 2,000 officers and sailors at risk, assuming each of the 10 frigates has a crew of 200. The Seventh Fleet's current force of 8 cruisers and destroyers requires 2,635 officers and sailors.[30]

Thus, the force composed of crewed frigates and unmanned missile ships would be armed with more missiles and put fewer personnel at risk than the Seventh Fleet's current surface combatant force. But beyond this lies an even greater difference. The majority of the missile cells of the frigate-led force would be loaded with offensive land-attack and anti-ship missiles aimed to disrupt a PLA fait accompli assault. The Seventh Fleet's current surface combatants are armed primarily with air defense missiles to protect the fleet's aircraft carrier homeported at Yokosuka. The frigate-led force would switch the fleet's missile composition from defense to offense and thus would impose costs on the PLA rather than the reverse, as is currently the case.

The frigate force's antiship and land-attack missiles would not be enough to win a war against the PLA. But it would constitute a potential threat that the PLA could not ignore and would have to attack during a fait accompli campaign. The PLA would have no difficulty successfully attacking the small ships, especially the LUSVs, but such an attack would kill U.S. sailors, which would almost certainly trigger a larger war. The PLA might try to attack only the LUSVs in the hope that killing "robots" would not trigger a U.S. response. But a goal of the force-in-being theory is to induce the adversary either to take actions that will be seen as aggression or to decline from doing so out of fear of the consequences. The remaining frigates would have up to 320 missiles that could respond to a PLA first strike against the LUSVs.

The proposed U.S. Near Seas surface fleet would be relatively inexpensive. The Navy plans to acquire each new frigate for about $1 billion.[31] The LUSV program is just beginning development, so future unit costs are unknown. If we assume $100 million per LUSV, including weapons, the Navy could acquire the entire fifty-ship force for about $14 billion, a little more than the cost of one *Gerald R. Ford*–class aircraft carrier ($12.1 billion each) or about nine DDG-51 *Arleigh Burke*–class guided missile destroyers ($1.6 billion each).[32]

As discussed elsewhere in this book, the ships in the current Seventh Fleet are no more likely to survive large and determined PLA saturation missile attacks than would the frigate-led force. But a U.S. aircraft carrier strike group is an iconic and prestigious center-of-gravity target, the loss of which, with its more than 7,500 officers and sailors, could crumble the will of U.S. policymakers and the public to continue the war. By contrast, the proposed fleet of frigates and LUSVs, lacking any similar iconic status, would not create the same political risk in the case of its destruction. Its destruction would nevertheless succeed in triggering a war between China and the United States, something China's leaders would have to consider before setting such an attack in motion.

U.S. theater commanders have traditionally called on aircraft carrier strike groups to display U.S. power and reassure regional allies and partners. But in the case of China and the Indo-Pacific region, the credibility of this tradition is waning as more observers understand the vulnerability of aircraft carriers to the PLA's battle networks. Indeed, during a developing crisis U.S. commanders will likely have to rapidly withdraw the aircraft carrier strike groups (such as the aircraft carrier strike group currently based at Yokosuka) beyond the PLA's missile engagement zone to prevent the loss of a political center-of-gravity target. That will hardly reassure U.S. allies.

By contrast, the frigate missile force standing its ground during a crisis would be a reassuring signal to allies. And the Navy could pursue this better option while also avoiding a naval arms race with its much larger and more efficient shipbuilding competitor.

This discussion of missile ships as an alternative to aircraft carrier strike groups applies to reforming just the surface combatant portion of fleet design. U.S. and allied submarine forces (including, in the future, large numbers of unmanned autonomous submarines) will continue to play a critical role in supporting long-range strike operations, the main element of deterrence against China. In addition, the Navy should retain sufficient amphibious warships to support island recapture operations at the end of a conflict.

On the one hand, these are controversial recommendations that go against traditional Navy design concepts. On the other hand, the recommendations endorse the Navy's own current thinking on "distributed lethality" and take those thoughts to their logical conclusions.

Getting to the Navy of the Future

The United States is a maritime power that needs a strong navy to protect its global interests. Preparing for a possible conflict with China in the western Pacific is just one of the Navy's missions, but it is arguably the most important, perhaps second only to strategic nuclear deterrence, in consequences for U.S. interests. Indeed, the Biden administration's Interim National Security Strategic Guidance issued in March 2021 left little doubt that the Indo-Pacific region and the competition with China is the country's top security priority.[33] So although the Navy needs to prepare for missions across the globe, policy guidance to the Navy has directed it to place its preparations for China and the Indo-Pacific at the top of its list of priorities.

Deterring China from attempting fait accompli aggression will require U.S. military forces, especially the Navy, to maintain a forward presence that reassures U.S. allies and partners and holds China's military ambitions at bay. Should the United States withdraw from this responsibility, a pre–World War I–style regional arms race and competition for security would likely result, creating greater risks to U.S. interests.

The military-technical revolution has created a growing mismatch between the Navy's design and its ability to accomplish its fundamental missions in the Indo-Pacific. The decades-long practice of replacing legacy aircraft carriers, destroyers, and amphibious ships with more modern and sophisticated ships of the same type no longer works. Even the newest surface ships have already lost the battle against the increasing capabilities and falling relative costs of adversary land-based missiles and sensors.

Americans have always considered the Pacific a naval theater, and America's military history there is first and foremost a naval history. Almost immediately after the United States acquired Hawaii, Guam, the Philippines, and other possessions after the Spanish-American War, the U.S. Navy, under President Theodore Roosevelt, began planning how to defend—and if necessary retake—the Pacific from Japan.[34] U.S. Indo-Pacific Command, based in Hawaii, has always had a U.S. Navy admiral as its commander. From this cultural perspective, it is understandable that current and future policymakers will think first about the Navy when they have concerns about U.S. security interests in the Indo-Pacific region. Open access to the sea has been a key American interest since the nation was founded, and protecting that access is one of the Navy's core missions.

But the military-technical revolution has upset the long-standing link between naval dominance and the security of sea lines of communication; and the American perception of the Pacific as a naval theater needs to change as a result. The march of technology has reshaped the Indo-Pacific into primarily an aerospace theater of operation. A combatant—the PLA or the United States and its allies—must first establish dominance over the space, cyber, and air domains before any maritime and land-based operations can succeed. And given the reach of the PLA's battle networks, U.S. and allied commanders will have to achieve this dominance at operational and strategic ranges—much farther than the tactical range to which naval forces, even with aircraft carriers, are restricted.

Accepting the notion that the Pacific is now an air and space rather than primarily a naval theater will allow policymakers and planners to recognize new concepts for how to defend U.S. and allied interests in the region. In the Indo-Pacific, long-range air and missile power must be the main element of military power and deterrence, with reformed, small-scale, and distributed naval power a supporting and economy-of-force component. It will be a challenge for decision-makers and military planners to adjust to this concept and take their organizations down new paths. But that is where the current military-technical revolution is leading them.

9

How to Win the Long Marathon in the Indo-Pacific

D esigning and then implementing an effective strategy to address
China's military potential is an especially demanding task for
U.S. policymakers. Almost every dimension of the problem adds
difficulty and complexity to the challenge. China is already a greater rival
than any the United States has faced since it emerged as a global power
more than a century ago.

Comparisons with large military competitions in the recent past reveal
the challenge. World War II required the United States to mobilize for
a global war effort. But once it did so, U.S. production combined with
that of the Allies easily swamped that of the Axis powers. The combined
armaments production in 1943 of the Allied powers (the United States,
Soviet Union, and Great Britain) exceeded that of Germany and Japan by
a ratio of 3.4 to 1.[1] By 1944, success in that war was not in doubt. During the
Cold War, U.S. economic and technical advantages over the Soviet bloc
permitted a military competition that barely strained the United States
but bankrupted the Soviet Union.[2]

In China, by contrast, the United States faces a rival with substantially
equal economic output and potentially comparable military spending,
especially when China's military spending is compared with America's

allocation of defense resources to the Indo-Pacific region. Unlike the Soviet Union, China will be capable of sustaining an arms race with the United States on roughly equal terms. China will face increasing economic challenges as the century proceeds, as this chapter will later discuss, but over the medium term it will be a true military and economic peer with the United States.

As the "home team," China gets more out of its military spending than U.S. expeditionary forces in the Indo-Pacific region do. The effectiveness of U.S. military investments there is diluted both by America's global security responsibilities and because the United States is the "away team" forced to project its military power to a distant region. The United States will be able to add the military potential of its partners in the region to its side of the ledger. But some countries in the region may bandwagon with China rather than joining with the United States. The result is a security challenge that U.S. policymakers have not faced in the modern era.

Second, policymakers responsible for the design of U.S. military forces have been too slow to understand the structure of the military problem in the Indo-Pacific even though analysts in the Pentagon accurately perceived the problem three decades ago. Overconfidence in an assumed lead in U.S. military technology and nearly two decades of small wars have led policymakers to lose sight of China's technological progress and prowess. With the PLA's military strategy now placing much of America's tremendous investment in its naval forces and some of its airpower at risk of becoming irrelevant, U.S. military planners and commanders must cobble together new ways of performing basic missions in a region they previously took for granted.

America's Indo-Pacific allies are valuable assets. But they are also a challenge for U.S. diplomats. In Western Europe during the Cold War, former enemies were able to put the past behind them and coalesce around NATO and the concept of collective security, glued together by the bald Soviet threat. Certainly there were disagreements among NATO's member nations, particularly in the early years, but American diplomats today would surely welcome that relative unity of purpose compared to what they must wrestle with in Asia.

Although China's military modernization is well known in the region, defense spending in frontline places such as Taiwan, the Philippines, and Japan is shockingly small. Fears of U.S. abandonment or entrapment into an American military misadventure still plague many U.S. allies there.[3] With little prospect of any permanent and effective security institutions developing in the region, U.S. diplomats will continue to face uncertainty and ambiguity as partners plead for U.S. protection while simultaneously hedging to keep their options open.

The United States thus faces an open-ended security competition against a true peer opponent. No less than America's standard of living, the future of its relationships around the world, and its status as a great power are in the balance. The United States will bring more allies and partners into the competition than China. But those allies and partners will also pursue their own interests, with their cooperation with U.S. goals contingent and episodic. No security issue will be more consequential for American interests than this one. China policy will be a great challenge for a long time to come.

Americans Are Now Concerned about China

U.S. policymakers managing a long-term security competition will be constrained by the costs and risks the U.S. public will be willing to sustain over the long run. Americans' views of China and the risks it poses have darkened over the past decade, although they largely maintain warm feelings for U.S. allies and partners elsewhere in the Indo-Pacific region. These public attitudes support a U.S. policy of engagement, forward defense, and deterrence against possible Chinese aggression.

A Pew Research poll conducted in 2012 found that only 28 percent of the U.S. public viewed China's military might as a top concern, and only 31 percent of government executive and legislative branch officials perceived China as a major threat.[4] Economic anxiety was still lingering in the United States in the wake of the 2008 global financial crisis, and many in the U.S. public registered more concern about China's economic competitiveness than its military modernization, a topic that received scant media attention at that time.

The U.S. public's perception of China's military power has changed dramatically since 2012. A Pew Research poll published in March 2021 found that 86 percent of the U.S. public perceived China's military power as a somewhat serious or very serious problem for the United States, with 54 percent in the "very serious" category. Forty-eight percent of the U.S. public thought that limiting the power and influence of China should be a "top priority" foreign policy goal. The percentage of the U.S. public that believed this grew sixteen percentage points between 2018 and 2021. Eighty-nine percent of the poll's respondents saw China as either a competitor or an enemy of the United States.[5] Another Pew poll from 2021 found that two-thirds of the U.S. public felt "cold" toward China, a sharp increase since 2018. By contrast, six in ten U.S. poll respondents had "warm" feelings toward Japan, a steady reading since 2018.[6] A poll of the U.S. public conducted in the summer of 2020 showed that respondents thought the United States should take substantial risks to defend Japan, Australia, South Korea, and Taiwan against possible Chinese aggression.[7] U.S. policymakers favoring forward engagement and an efficient cost-imposing military deterrence strategy in the Indo-Pacific should feel confident that Americans will support such an approach.

Can the United States Sustain Deterrence over the Long Run?

As mentioned earlier, U.S. policymakers and the public face the prospect of sustaining deterrence against a true peer competitor for a long and indefinite period. The competition will be dynamic, punctuated by military-technical surprises, changing diplomatic developments, and disruptive political events. U.S. policymakers will have to adjust their methods and means to sustain deterrence under these changing circumstances.

Is it feasible to sustain deterrence against China indefinitely? U.S. policymakers and strategists need to be realistic about trends in the balance of power. If their analyses conclude the trends are unfavorable, they may conclude that time is not on their side. In that case, they might be inclined to conclude a deal over, say, mutually agreeable spheres of influence (likely at the expense of U.S. allies in the Indo-Pacific region).

In 1969, President Richard Nixon and Henry Kissinger, his national security adviser, foresaw a bleak future for the United States in the security competition against the Soviet Union. The Soviet economy appeared to be enjoying a two-decade boom that provided the resources and industrial capacity for massive investments in military capacity, especially strategic systems such as intercontinental ballistic missiles and large ocean-going naval forces, a new development for that traditional land power. The United States, by contrast, was attempting to wind down a costly and inconclusive guerilla war in Vietnam while dealing with an increasingly unstable economy and social disruption. Having concluded that trends and time favored the USSR, Nixon and Kissinger abandoned the fight in Vietnam and sought the best arms control deals with the Soviets they could negotiate. They also made a deal with China, a recent enemy, in an attempt to add pressure on the USSR.[8]

With the advice of Andrew Marshall and his staff at the Office of Net Assessment, however, the Carter and Reagan administrations opted to employ competitive strategies against the Soviet Union, reversing Nixon and Kissinger's policy. The Carter and Reagan teams displayed confidence that a more competitive strategy would yield a more favorable and enduring position for the United States in the ongoing competition.

Harold Brown, President Jimmy Carter's defense secretary, eagerly implemented Marshall's advice to reinforce U.S. military strengths against specific Soviet weaknesses and vulnerabilities. The Carter administration's pursuit of long-range air-launched and nuclear-armed cruise missiles pressured the USSR to further increase its spending on air defenses, funding that might otherwise have gone to intercontinental missiles and other offensive forces.[9]

Under Brown, the Defense Department expanded research on precision-guided munitions and stealthy radar-avoiding attack aircraft, and expanded antisubmarine forces that would threaten the Soviets' large but noisy new submarines. Finally, Brown made sure Soviet leaders knew that U.S. nuclear-targeting planners knew the locations of the underground bunkers where Soviet leaders planned to hide during a nuclear war against the United States and would promptly destroy those bunkers in the event of a war.[10] Post–Cold War intelligence revealed that this targeting strategy and its communication to Soviet leaders both enhanced deterrence and demoralized Soviet leaders near the end of the competition.[11]

President Ronald Reagan's two defense secretaries, Caspar Weinberger and Frank Carlucci, extended Brown's focus on competitive strategies aimed against Soviet weaknesses and deepened the effort with a surge in defense spending.[12] Marshall's analysis that the Soviet Union was far more burdened by its military spending than previous CIA analyses had calculated encouraged the Reagan administration to believe that time was on the side of the United States and not the Soviet Union, as Nixon and Kissinger had believed.[13] Reagan-era competitive initiatives, many of them extensions from the Carter years, included the B-1B bomber, the B-2 stealthy bomber, antisubmarine systems, precision-guided munitions, and research and acquisition of missile defense systems such as the Patriot tactical interceptor and the Strategic Defense Initiative for countering Soviet intercontinental ballistic missiles. All these initiatives either forced the USSR to spend more resources on territorial defenses or aimed to negate the large investments the Soviet Union had previously made on submarines and long-range ballistic missiles. The pressures imposed by these competitive strategy initiatives, combined with the high burden of Soviet military spending, eventually forced Soviet leaders to grasp at reform and wind down the competition in the Gorbachev era.[14]

Very few U.S. policymakers in the Carter and Reagan administrations foresaw the end of the U.S.-Soviet competition. The goal of the competitive strategy initiative was to sustain deterrence and the competition at an affordable price, mostly by forcing the Soviets to defer spending on further offensive capacities and by deploying new technologies that would negate prior Soviet offensive investments.

We should not expect a competitive or cost-imposing approach to China to result in a collapse of the CCP, as happened to the Soviet Communist Party, and China's subsequent exit from the military competition against the United States and its allies. We should assume, as most U.S. policy-makers did in the 1970s and 1980s, that the military competition will go on indefinitely.

What a competitive strategy against China can accomplish is the sustainment of conventional military deterrence in the U.S.-China military competition at an affordable price for the United States and its allies. And although U.S. and allied planners should never assume a financial or political collapse in China, they can reasonably foresee that the burden of the military competition will become increasingly difficult for China and its society to bear.

A looming collapse in China's workforce combined with a bleak outlook for China's worker productivity compared with the United States portend accelerating challenges for China's leaders and society that will undoubtedly affect the military competition over the long run. According to the UN Department of Economic and Social Affairs, China's working-age population (ages 15–69) peaked in 2015 at 1,022 million potential workers. The department's median projection forecasts this cohort to decline to 579 million potential workers by 2100, resulting in a 43 percent decline in potential annual labor-hours in the Chinese economy by the end of the century.[15] The United States labor force and hours worked, by contrast, will continue to expand over the remainder of the century.[16]

Higher Chinese productivity (output per labor-hour) could in theory offset the impending sharp decline in hours worked. But according to the Penn World Table of global economic indicators, China's total factor productivity in 2019 was only 44 percent of the U.S. level. Further, China's productivity relative to the United States appeared to peak in 2016 and has declined since.[17] Should this trend continue, it would further diminish China's economic potential compared with the United States. The Chinese economy could improve its productivity growth rate with more economically productive investments. But massive debt levels in the Chinese corporate and banking sectors will constrain future investment growth.[18] In addition, greater government micromanagement of the economy and constraints on China's private sector are likely to impair innovation and productive investment spending.[19] We should not expect improving productivity in China to offset the unstoppable collapse in China's workforce, a conclusion also recently reached by researchers at China's central bank.[20]

We have likely seen the end of China's rapid economic growth rate. A sharp increase over the past three decades in China's labor force and a one-time surge in infrastructure and housing investment combined to inflate China's apparent economic growth. China's labor force has now begun an equally sharp decline, with the investment component likely to follow. The result will be a tightening constraint on the resources available to China's leaders as they attempt to maintain China's social stability and the CCP's global ambitions.

Again, U.S. and allied leaders should not assume that financial or political crises in China will bring a sudden end to the strategic competition. But they should have confidence that they will be able to sustain the competition indefinitely against a competitor that will weaken over the remainder of the century. In the medium term and beyond, time should be on the side of the United States and its allies.[21]

Prescription: Match U.S. Strengths against China's Weaknesses

America's strategy for the Indo-Pacific region should be designed to protect U.S. security and economic interests. The United States will accomplish this when it protects the independence and sovereignty of its allies and partners there along with free and open rules and norms of behavior. With China's interests and those of the United States and its partners increasingly in conflict, an attempt should first be made to persuade China's leaders to accept—to China's benefit—the existing order and not to attempt to replace it with an alternative that privileges China over its neighbors.

Developing effective persuasive and dissuasive leverage will require a much deeper understanding of Chinese decision-making than policymakers now have. It will also require assembling a full range of political, diplomatic, economic, and military tools that can provide rewards for favorable Chinese behavior while imposing costs for unfavorable actions. China has interests and vulnerabilities that can be sources of leverage for a competitive strategy. U.S. and allied policymakers and planners need to understand these sources of leverage and design a strategy that takes advantage of them.

This book has focused on the conventional military trends in the Indo-Pacific region and the need for U.S. strategists and policymakers to finally reckon with the implications the current military-technical revolution is having on those trends. Fortunately for the United States and its partners, there are actions they can take to avoid China's cost-imposing strategies and instead impose costs on the PLA and its superiors in the CCP, to match U.S. and allied strengths against China's weaknesses, and to build a competitive and affordable approach to sustaining deterrence.

First, policymakers must accept that air and space power, not maritime power, will dominate military operations in the Indo-Pacific. The now-mature military-technical revolution of battle networks composed of ubiquitous sensors and long-range precision munitions has fundamentally changed the character of warfare, especially in the Indo-Pacific, where the two primary combatants are building these advanced battle networks. Military forces on the surface, especially surface warships, will not be able to hide, and therefore will not be able to avoid targeting and destruction. Regardless of its history, the Indo-Pacific is no longer primarily a naval theater. The United States and its allies should invest immediately and heavily to dominate the air and space domains—they cannot achieve success in any other domain until they dominate air and space. In addition, appointing an Air Force general as the commander of U.S. Indo-Pacific Command would bring aerospace perspective and experience to the command and signal the new conventional military deterrent concept the United States should fashion.

Second, maintaining conventional deterrence by denial should begin by avoiding the exposure of U.S. and allied centers of gravity to the PLA's firepower. U.S. and allied warfighting should not lead with large, manpower-intensive, and politically iconic assemblages of forces that are vulnerable to PLA missile salvos. Doing so is a recipe for losing the war on the first day of hostilities. Warfighting concepts should be designed around raiding with long-range bombers that put at risk only dozens of U.S. lives rather than aircraft carrier strike groups that risk many thousands. The United States and its allies can fight a successful campaign in the region without exposing politically consequential centers of gravity. China will not have this luxury; to achieve a fait accompli objective, such as the seizure of Taiwan, China will have to send out its now politically iconic navy and expose it to destruction.

Third, sustaining deterrence by denial against the PLA should be the organizing principle of U.S. military investments. The most direct way of convincing China's leaders that the United States and its allies can thwart China's military fait accompli plans is to possess the unstoppable capacity to destroy 1,000 major Chinese ships across the Near Seas within a week. These 1,000 ships will include the nearly 500 battle force ships the U.S. Navy estimates the PLAN will have by 2030, about 250 ships in China's militarized coast guard, another roughly 100 in the maritime militia, plus additional large commercial ships the PLA would draft into service during an assault on Taiwan or elsewhere.[22] Destroying the entirety of China's naval power would remove its capacity to execute fait accompli assaults against Taiwan, the Senkakus, or other prospective objectives in the Indo-Pacific region. In addition, the quick destruction of China's naval power would destroy an iconic Chinese center-of-gravity target, perhaps resulting in internal consequences for China's leadership.

Aircraft are the most effective predators of warships, and long-range bombers will rule the Indo-Pacific. Therefore, the U.S. military investment strategy should place bombers, long-range antiship missiles, space and air reconnaissance and communications, and agile and global bomber basing at the top of the investment priority list. Air Force leaders should direct leaders of the bomber forces at Air Force Global Strike Command to make a prospective counter-maritime campaign against the PLAN the command's second planning and training priority, just after the nuclear deterrence mission but ahead of all others.

In the event of kinetic conflict against China, the United States and its allies should not limit ship targeting to just the PLAN's warships. Targets should also include the Chinese coast guard and China's maritime militia, which have been undertaking quasi-military missions across the globe in recent years, thus qualifying them as legal combatants.[23] Destroying these ostensibly civilian but actually military assets would establish a norm against the "gray zone" warfare tactics that rogue actors have employed in recent years.

Fourth, U.S. policymakers should take immediate action to reinforce long-range striking capacity. The United States enjoys superiority in long-range and strategic strike, which is a powerful component to a deterrence-by-denial strategy. Regrettably, U.S. policymakers neglected this capability during the 1990s and 2000s. The resulting capacity shortfall has added to the danger of conflict against China in the Indo-Pacific. However, there are actions today's policymakers can take to quickly increase long-range strike capacity. Congress could appropriate additional funding, perhaps $300 million, to return 10 recently retired B-1 bombers to active service.[24] This would add the capacity to launch an additional 240 JASSMs and LRASMs against the PLAN and other Chinese ships executing a military operation. The Air Force should also acquire at least 2,000 additional LRASM antiship missiles even if that means reducing the planned large purchases of JASSM land-attack missiles. The Air Force will need many more of the antiship missiles for a successful campaign against the PLAN and its auxiliaries.

The Air Force and Congress should enable more rapid production of the B-21 Raider by approving the funding for a second, geographically separate, bomber assembly facility, along with expansions to the aircraft's supply chains. The Air Force and Congress should also fund a redundant JASSM and LRASM assembly facility and supply chain expansions. The 2020s are likely to be the most dangerous decade of the U.S.-China military competition. Accelerating production of the B-21 and its best long-range munitions will shorten this danger period. In addition, the current single facilities for B-21 and LRASM assembly are "single points of failure" in the plan to enhance deterrence by denial. Redundancy, although expensive, would mitigate this risk.

Fifth, the United States should reshape and reset its military forces along the First Island Chain so they can disrupt a prospective PLA assault while avoiding the risk of becoming a center-of-gravity target for the PLA's battle networks. In practice this means the Marine Corps should implement its new warfighting concept fashioned around small missile teams distributed among the islands. The Navy should reshape its

Seventh Fleet around missile frigates and unmanned missile corvettes because the current Seventh Fleet, centered on one aircraft carrier and one amphibious group, will be a liability rather than an asset in a missile war against the PLA. The Air Force should maintain a smaller force of fighter-attack aircraft in the region that will attempt to employ the Agile Combat Employment concept during wartime. And the Army should develop a true intermediate-range ballistic missile able to reach central China from the Second Island Chain, a weapon that does not exist in the Army's current plans. The Army should fit this missile with hypersonic glide vehicles optionally armed with nuclear warheads and aimed at known and suspected CCP and PLA command bunkers.

Together these forces would constitute a force in being that the PLA would have to attack to achieve a fait accompli victory and that would reassure U.S. allies and partners about the U.S. commitment to the region. The force in being would not be designed to defeat the PLA; that would be the mission of the long-range strike forces based outside the PLA's missile engagement zones. Nor would it constitute a vital center of gravity whose destruction would lose the war for the United States. The force would be a critical element of America's deterrence-by-denial posture that the PLA could neither ignore nor attack without suffering a devastating response.

Sixth, the United States should compete with its best competitive advantages while declining to compete where China has an advantage. As discussed in chapter 5, China's massive shipbuilding capacity is far larger than the U.S. naval shipbuilding sector, a fact the Navy's strategy acknowledges.[25] The United States has no chance to keep pace with China in a naval arms race and would be foolish to try. Fortunately, the United States does enjoy major competitive advantages versus China in aircraft and space design, production, and fielding, and it is aerospace power that will dominate the Indo-Pacific battlefield.[26] Prioritizing aerospace technology development and production would bring the United States more and better aerospace capabilities than China's.

Seventh, U.S. strategists and policymakers should appreciate America's dominance in long-range and strategic strike options and capacity. Associated with this dominance is the location of the prospective battlefield along the First Island Chain and China's Near Seas. While this location gives the PLA a tactical advantage, it also means that the battlefield is far away from the U.S. homeland but adjacent to China's, a strategic advantage for the United States. Blackwill and Zelikow (among others) strongly recommended against U.S. attacks against the Chinese homeland, at least as a tenet of initial U.S. war plans. But in a Taiwan invasion scenario, Taiwanese missiles and bombs will strike Chinese coastal cities, bringing the war to China's population with uncertain political consequences.

The PLA possesses a very limited capacity to conduct conventional strikes on the U.S. homeland, probably no more than a symbolic one-off nuisance attack. According to the Director of National Intelligence, China could employ cyber weapons to cause "localized and temporary disruptions" of critical infrastructure inside the United States,[27] a well-known threat that is unlikely to be decisive if employed. But if China did employ cyber weapons against U.S. homeland civilian infrastructure, that would free the United States to retaliate against China's homeland with either cyber or kinetic weapons. The United States, with its strategic airpower, submarine-based land-attack cruise missiles, and its own offensive cyber weapons, would enjoy clear escalation dominance in such an exchange. Deterrence-by-denial targets would include PLAN ships in port, the PLAN's naval bases, the PLA's counterspace assets, PLA command nodes, and PLAAF air bases. If the United States found it necessary to escalate to deterrence-by-punishment targets, these could include attacks against China's internal security forces and the personal assets of China's leaders. China would have little if any capacity for a sustained campaign against similar targets inside the U.S. homeland.

How Would It End? Winding Down a Missile War

The goal of the reforms just discussed is to strengthen conventional military deterrence by denial in the Indo-Pacific region. The success of any deterrence strategy relies on the adversary's perceptions and analysis and requires the adversary to draw the conclusions the defender has planned for. There is always the chance that the best crafted and executed deterrence strategy could still fail due to misperceptions, poor analysis, or perverse incentives that lead to seemingly illogical conclusions and actions. But even as history is littered with such examples, conventional military deterrence by denial is still the preferred course of action for the United States and its security partners in the region.

War over Taiwan or other Chinese goals could occur anyway. In that event, any description of a missile war between China and a U.S.-led coalition is highly speculative. War always takes unexpected paths, and no one can know in advance how well weapons will perform, how commanders will lead, or what policymakers will decide given the conflicting pressures they will be under. That said, a missile war in the western Pacific between advanced battle networks would likely result in the destruction of hundreds of ships, aircraft, facilities, and perhaps spacecraft within days. The death toll to the combatants would be ghastly. After a year, such a war could reduce U.S. economic output by 5–10 percent. China's output loss after a year could total 25–35 percent.[28]

Let us assume that U.S. military planners implement the reforms described above. After a week, U.S. and allied commanders should expect to see major damage at their main air and naval bases along the First and Second Island Chains. Losses to their tactical aircraft at these bases and outlying dispersal airfields would be heavy but less than would have been the case with the legacy strategy that relied more on tactical airpower and based more of it in the region. Commanders should also expect the PLA to have located and struck most of the Marine Corps missile forces along the First Island Chain, although the Marines would first have some success striking PLA ships in the Near Seas. There would not likely be much left of the frigate and unmanned missile ship force in being in the Near Seas. But U.S. aircraft carrier and amphibious strike groups would be intact because they did not participate in the conflict. Finally, the PLA's air defenses would have shot down at least a few of the Air Force's bombers, even if those aircraft employed long-range stand-off munitions such as JASSMs and LRASMs. But the U.S. bomber force would remain intact, with the capacity to continue against additional targets. The bomber force would have largely expended its stockpile of antiship missiles but would still have many of its JASSMs remaining to attack land-based targets.

On the other side of the ledger, if U.S. preparations had focused on countering the PLAN and its auxiliaries, as this book recommends, the U.S. bomber and allied submarine forces should during the first week have sunk a thousand Chinese warships, major coast guard vessels, major members of China's maritime militia, and large commercial ships enlisted to support the PLAN. Those losses would remove the PLA's capacity for amphibious assaults and the PLAN's capacity to reinforce, supply, relocate, or evacuate PLA island and overseas garrisons.

What then? The PLA would still have its land-based antinavy missile and airpower. It would thus still have the capacity to harass U.S. and allied ships in the western Pacific and to restrike allied air bases and Taiwan. The Near Seas would remain a contested war zone even if China had no more significant surface ships to sail on them. Relief convoys for Taiwan would still be in danger. The PLA would have no capacity for offensive initiative, but it would still be able to disrupt U.S. and allied military operations on the Near Seas.

What would this week of missile combat have achieved? A fundamental purpose of war is to provide information to the combatants that they did not possess, or agree on, prior to the war. The war would presumably have begun because both sides thought they could achieve their military objectives. That is, they disagreed on which of them was stronger.[29] A week of missile combat could provide new information to the combatants about which was stronger and which was weaker. The clearer the message, the greater the chance of ending the conflict. Unfortunately, war is often a muddled and inefficient generator of the information policymakers on both sides will need to make their decisions on either ending or continuing the war.[30]

Destroying China's maritime power would presumably have thwarted the PLA's goal of changing the de facto sovereignty of Taiwan, the status of the Senkaku Islands, or some similar goal. From that position, U.S. and allied policymakers would likely favor a ceasefire and an armistice. With China's land-based antinavy military power still intact, freedom of navigation in the western Pacific, another allied goal, would still be in question. But a negotiated armistice would lead the PLA to cease fire and work to restore commercial shipping in the region, which would be in

China's interest. The allies' counter-maritime strategy would presumably have resulted in limited missile strikes on mainland China, perhaps almost all from Taiwan's defense forces. If so, China's leaders could take the "off ramp" being offered if the few missile strikes on Chinese territory have not compelled them into a face-saving escalation.

The loss of China's naval power and the failure of its military campaign would likely result in Taiwan declaring its independence. Taiwan has not so far declared independence for fear of China using force in response. After the PLA's failed assault, that would no longer be an issue. The loss of China's maritime power would also likely mean the isolation and then abandonment of the features China has occupied in the South China Sea.

In this scenario, it would be up to China's leaders to take or not take the off ramp to end the conflict. The survival of the party and its continued command over Chinese society would remain the CCP's paramount objectives. The loss of the PLAN, an iconic center-of-gravity target, and Taiwan's independence declaration would put China's leaders in a dangerous internal political position, regardless of the level of damage inflicted on mainland China by limited missile strikes. China's leaders would have to weigh two risks: (1) whether accepting the truce and in essence admitting defeat would be riskier to the CCP's internal position compared to continuing the missile war with the PLA's remaining land-based forces, knowing that harassment would be the best they could accomplish militarily and that China's import and export economy would remain largely closed; and (2) that the U.S. capacity for strategic strikes against China's homeland would still be intact.

There would presumably be a strong case among China's leaders for accepting a truce and then turning to the task of reconstituting the PLA with a goal of revisiting the Taiwan issue and China's other external security issues in a decade or two. These leaders would see reconstitution as a straightforward technical and production task that would benefit from lessons learned from the missile war. The leaders could also hope that possible economic and political turmoil inside the United States or elsewhere among its security partners would weaken the coalition during China's reconstitution period.

In a darker case, internal political pressures might compel China's leaders to continue the war, even from the weak position in which China would find itself after the first week. China's theory of success in this case would be that an open-ended, low-intensity harassment war conducted with missiles and submarine torpedoes would weaken the resolve of the U.S. public, as has happened with America's other guerilla wars over the past six decades. This course would be an exceptional gamble for China's leaders, but one they might consider unavoidable.

The U.S. response in this case would include China's economic and financial isolation; continued U.S. and allied missile strikes on China's shipbuilding enterprise to delay China's naval reconstitution; a political warfare campaign aimed to separate the Chinese population from the CCP; and attacks on the assets of China's leaders with a goal of inciting factional fighting within the CCP. U.S. airpower could employ large volleys of air-launched low-cost autonomous attack weapons (discussed in chapter 7) to periodically suppress the PLA's land-based antinavy missile and airpower in southeast China, permitting relief convoys to arrive in Taiwan.[31]

In sum, should deterrence by denial fail and a missile war occur, the reforms discussed in this chapter will increase the odds of the United States and its allies successfully defending their territory and sovereignty from Chinese aggression. But just a week of high-intensity missile combat would be shocking and immensely costly. China's leaders, fearful of their internal position, might feel compelled to continue the war even from a much-weakened position.

With the path so unpredictable, U.S. policymakers and planners would do best to build a military force centered on flexible long-range capabilities that could strike an adversary without exposing a critical center of gravity. U.S. and allied leaders should plan for a war that could last years at various levels of intensity. This will require generous aerospace capacity, munition stockpiles, and the capacity to regenerate military power in a sustainable fashion. A U.S. military strategy centered on aerospace power would play to U.S. competitive advantages for these requirements.

By the mid-2030s, the planned force of at least one hundred B-21 Raider bombers should be the leading component of a deterrence-by-denial strategy against the PLA. The B-21's arrival in service will give U.S. and allied policymakers flexible and survivable capabilities and will greatly strengthen deterrence against China. Under conservative assumptions this force could precisely strike ten thousand aim points per week anywhere inside China and sustain this rate for months if necessary, with little the PLA could do against the advanced stealthy aircraft.[32] If the destruction of China's maritime power were insufficient to end a conflict, the B-21-led campaign could ignore the PLA's ground forces to focus on leadership and command targets, space and counterspace forces, the PLA's missile and airpower, shipbuilding enterprises, and China's internal security forces. The B-21 force could suppress and destroy the PLA's antinavy forces in southeast China, reopening air and sea access to Taiwan.

Confidence and Leadership Can Overcome Resistance to Innovation

Bureaucratic and institutional interests that resist changes to the defense program are the greatest barrier to a better U.S. military strategy for the Indo-Pacific. As chapters 3 and 5 discussed, large government defense bureaucracies, industrial contractors, military bases, local constituencies, and supporting interest groups have grown up around the current defense posture and will resist substantial changes to it. Surface naval forces, short-range tactical airpower, and ground forces are increasingly becoming irrelevant in the military competition against the PLA, but these forces receive the lion's share of the resources allocated by the Defense Department's current program of record. In theory, if the same defense dollars were allocated to more useful programs and systems, existing contractors and communities could transition to those new programs and systems. But that reassuring message will not forestall bureaucratic and political resistance from risk-averse interests that fear change.

Overcoming these barriers to change will require persistent and bipartisan leadership from top civilian political leaders and policymakers at the White House, the Pentagon, and on Capitol Hill. These civilian leaders have the authority to overcome institutional resistance and accomplish the necessary changes, disruptive as they will be to some sectors.

There are historical precedents for top-level leadership compelling dramatic changes in U.S. defense policy. The most striking example was led by President Dwight Eisenhower following the Korean War. Eisenhower's two terms coincided with some of the most intense and unstable years of the U.S.-Soviet security competition. Eisenhower was determined to resist Soviet expansionism and the Warsaw Pact's conventional military superiority in Europe, but to do so both affordably and in a way that would not change the United States into a virtually militarized society.

Even though Eisenhower was a West Point graduate and a former five-star Army general, his defense program slashed spending on the Army after the Korean War and capped funding for the Navy. Eisenhower poured the diverted funds into the Air Force, recently created as a separate service. The Army's share of the total defense budget fell from 38 percent during the Korean War (which ended in 1953) to 25 percent during the remainder of Eisenhower's presidency, which ended in 1961. The Navy's budget share was flat during the 1950s at about 29 percent. The Air Force, however, saw its budget share rise from 33 percent during the Korean War to 45 percent during the rest of the Eisenhower presidency, a level no service has reached since then.[33]

The huge jump in the Air Force's budget share during the Eisenhower era was a direct result of Eisenhower's strategy for competing against the Soviet Union in an affordable manner. Eisenhower's "New Look" approach heavily funded the U.S. competitive advantage—long-range strategic airpower armed with nuclear weapons—against a major Soviet vulnerability, its immense and indefensible borders and air space, and its concentrations of military and industrial capabilities. The resulting "Massive Retaliation" doctrine of the Eisenhower era implemented deterrence by punishment to counter the threat of a possible Warsaw Pact attack into Western Europe. New Look was a quintessential competitive strategy that deliberately spared the U.S. economy and culture from having to match the Soviet Union soldier for soldier and tank for tank in Europe and elsewhere.[34]

As the strategic situation changed, future administrations replaced New Look with more flexible doctrines that included greater roles for the other military services. The Eisenhower era is proof, however, that strong civilian leadership, led by an informed and curious president, can develop a comprehensive strategy and work with Congress to implement dramatic changes on the defense bureaucracy.

Eisenhower, with his pedigree as a war-winning theater commander and strategic planner, brought immense prestige to the task of pushing major funding reallocations through Congress and the defense bureaucracy. But Eisenhower is not unique in that regard. President Jimmy Carter—a Naval Academy graduate, nuclear submarine officer, and engineer—also engaged in the details of defense strategy and budgeting and personally promoted his reforms of strategic forces and new technologies.[35] President Ronald Reagan did the same with his defense program, which involved not only large across-the-board funding increases but also specific competitive strategy components such as recapitalization of the bomber force and strategic missile defense, and he personally lobbied Congress for funding for these programs.[36]

It will take similar leadership from today's top civilian policymakers to implement the reforms urgently needed to reinforce deterrence in the Indo-Pacific region. Top leaders must engage with members of Congress to promote these controversial reforms if they are to receive funding for them.

By making the right choices the United States and its allies can deter China and maintain peace and freedom in the Indo-Pacific region. Policymakers and citizens in these countries should have confidence in their capacity to do so, and at a reasonable cost. With a good strategy built around the most useful and effective concepts and systems, the United States can deter war and meet its other global defense obligations for about 3 percent of its annual economic output, less than the spending rate during the Cold War against the Soviet Union.

Policymakers and citizens should also understand that the United States is not a declining power. Its working population, skills, technology, and productivity will continue to increase during the remainder of this century. China's working population has already begun a steep decline that will continue during the remainder of the century. China still struggles to improve its economic productivity compared with that of the United States, and the CCP's micromanagement of the Chinese economy will ensure that struggle continues. In the 2030s and beyond, China will be increasingly hard-pressed to continue the security competition against the United States and its allies.

The present decade, however, will be dangerous. Programs such as the B-21 Raider and new long-range missiles can redress the previous neglect, but the United States and its allies will have to pass through a perilous period while commanders in the Pacific wait for them to arrive.

It will take until near the end of this decade for the United States to bring some of its new stealthy bombers to combat-ready status, to refashion its naval forces in the Pacific so they will not be a vulnerable center-of-gravity target, and to reorganize and arm the Marine Corps and Army for their roles as missile-armed barriers along the western Pacific island chains. During this dangerous decade, U.S. defense planners should look for ways to accelerate improvements to the most critical deterrence capabilities, such as the bomber force and its readiness for war.

The reforms discussed here will greatly strengthen conventional military deterrence against the PLA. But until they are in place, U.S. and allied commanders will have to cope with the prospect of meeting PLA aggression with the forces as they are. China's leaders will similarly decide whether the 2020s will be their last opportunity to seize the initiative before U.S. defenses improve and China's demographic decline compounds. Should China's leaders decide to strike in the next few years, success for the United States and its allies will greatly depend on the creativity and virtuosity of the field commanders who will fight the battle without the capabilities earlier policymakers should have provided for them.

Once past this decade, the United States and its friends in the Indo-Pacific should look forward to a century of peace, freedom, and opportunity. China, hopefully deterred from aggression, can also participate in an era that includes development and prosperity for all. Getting there will require today's policymakers to make difficult decisions that many interests will resist. But these decisions and the defense reforms they bring are worth fighting for.

NOTES

Introduction

1. Robert Blackwill and Philip Zelikow, "The United States, China, and Taiwan: A Strategy to Prevent War," Council on Foreign Relations, February 2021, 31, accessed March 15, 2021, https://cdn.cfr.org/sites/default/files/report_pdf /csr90_1.pdf.

2. Mallory Shelbourne, "Davidson: China Could Try to Take Control of Taiwan in 'Next Six Years,'" *U.S. Naval Institute News*, March 9, 2021, accessed April 26, 2021, https://news.usni.org/2021/03/09/davidson-china-could-try-to-take -control-of-taiwan-in-next-six-years?utm_source=USNI+News&utm _campaign=c90c40efa7-USNI_NEWS_DAILY&utm_medium=email&utm _term=0_0dd4a1450b-c90c40efa7-230370089&ct=t(USNI_NEWS _DAILY)&mc_cid=c90c40efa7&mc_eid=acace2ab92.

3. Lingling Wei and Bob Davis, "China's Message to America: We're an Equal Now," *Wall Street Journal*, April 12, 2021, accessed April 26, 2021, https://www.wsj .com/articles/america-china-policy-biden-xi-11617896117?mod=searchresults _pos4&page=1.

4. Jacqueline Deal, "China Could Soon Outgun the U.S.," *Politico* China Watcher, May 27, 2021, accessed May 27, 2021, https://www.politico.com/newsletters /politico-china-watcher/2021/05/27/china-could-soon-outgun-the-us-493014.

5. "SIPRI Military Expenditure Database," Stockholm International Peace Research Institute, accessed February 8, 2021, https://sipri.org/databases /milex.

6. Deal, "China Could Soon Outgun the U.S."

7. Henry Kissinger, *Diplomacy* (New York: Simon and Shuster, 1994), 826.

8. Kevin Rudd, "A Maritime Balkans of the 21st Century?," *Foreign Policy*, January 30, 2013, accessed April 26, 2021, https://foreignpolicy.com/2013/01/30/a-maritime-balkans-of-the-21st-century/.

9. Kurt Campbell, "Threats to Peace Are Lurking in the East China Sea," *Financial Times*, June 25, 2013, accessed April 26, 2021, https://www.ft.com/content/b924cc56-dda1-11e2-a756-00144feab7de#axzz2ZtGart72.

10. Blackwill and Zelikow, "The United States, China, and Taiwan," 47–49.

11. Kurt Campbell and Jake Sullivan, "Competition without Catastrophe: How America Can Both Challenge and Coexist with China," *Foreign Affairs*, September/October 2019, accessed April 27, 2021, https://www.foreignaffairs.com/articles/china/competition-with-china-without-catastrophe.

12. Lara Seligman and Connor O'Brien, "Austin Wants to Pivot to China. But Can He Pay for It?," Politico, March 3, 2021, accessed April 27, 2021, https://fwww.politico.com/news/2021/03/03/lloyd-austin-china-pentagon-473405.

13. Geoffrey Blainey, *The Causes of War* (New York: Free Press, 1973), 122–23.

Chapter 1. A Four-Decade Drive to a Collision

1. Robert C. Feenstra, Robert Inklaar, and Marcel P. Timmer, "The Next Generation of the Penn World Table," *American Economic Review* 105, no. 10 (2015): 3150–82, available for download at http://www.ggdc.net/pwt.

2. Feenstra, Inklaar, and Timmer.

3. *The World Factbook: China*, U.S. Central Intelligence Agency, "Economy" tab, accessed January 12, 2021, https://www.cia.gov/the-world-factbook/countries/china/#economy.

4. *The World Factbook: China*.

5. Feenstra, Inklaar, and Timmer, "The Next Generation of the Penn World Table."

6. *The World Factbook: China*.

7. "China Analysis," U.S. Energy Information Administration, U.S. Department of Energy, "China Data" tab, accessed May 3, 2021, https://www.eia.gov/international/data/country/CHN.

8. "China—Oil and Gas," U.S. Department of Commerce, Export.gov, July 30, 2019, accessed January 13, 2021, https://www.export.gov/apex/article2?id=China-Oil-and-Gas.

9. *Annual Report to Congress: Military and Security Developments Involving the People's Republic of China 2020* (Washington, DC: Office of the Secretary of Defense, 2020), 133, accessed January 13, 2021, https://media.defense

.gov/2020/Sep/01/2002488689/-1/-1/1/2020-DOD-CHINA-MILITARY-POWER
-REPORT-FINAL.PDF.

10. *Military and Security Developments Involving the People's Republic of China 2020*, 1.

11. Josh Chin, "China Spends More on Domestic Security as Xi's Powers Grow," *Wall Street Journal*, March 6, 2018, accessed January 13, 2021, https://www.wsj
.com/articles/china-spends-more-on-domestic-security-as-xis-powers-grow
-1520358522.

12. Hal Brands, "Regime Realism and Chinese Grand Strategy," American Enterprise Institute, November 2020, 2, accessed January 13, 2021, https://www.aei.org/wp
-content/uploads/2020/11/Regime-Realism-and-Chinese-Grand-Strategy.pdf.

13. John J. Mearsheimer, "China's Unpeaceful Rise," *Current History*, April 2006, 160. See also Mearsheimer, *The Tragedy of Great Power Politics* (New York: W. W. Norton, 2001), 401–2.

14. Henry Kissinger, *On China* (New York: Penguin Press, 2011), chap. 1.

15. *Annual Report to Congress: Military and Security Developments Involving the People's Republic of China 2011* (Washington, DC: Office of the Secretary of Defense, 2011), 15, accessed May 4, 2021, https://dod.defense.gov/Portals/1/Documents
/pubs/2011_CMPR_Final.pdf.

16. Ronald O'Rourke, "China Naval Modernization: Implications for U.S. Navy Capabilities—Background and Issues for Congress," Congressional Research Service, March 9, 2021, 8–10, accessed May 4, 2021, https://crsreports.congress.gov
/product/pdf/RL/RL33153.

17. Brands, "Regime Realism and Chinese Grand Strategy," 3–6.

18. Michael Pillsbury, *The Hundred-Year Marathon: China's Secret Strategy to Replace America as the Global Superpower* (New York: Henry Holt, 2015), 27–30.

19. "South China Sea," U.S. Energy Information Administration, U.S. Department of Energy, October 15, 2019, accessed January 14, 2021, https://www.eia.gov
/international/analysis/regions-of-interest/South_China_Sea.

20. "East China Sea," U.S. Energy Information Administration, U.S. Department of Energy, September 17, 2014, accessed January 14, 2021, https://www.eia.gov
/international/analysis/regions-of-interest/East_China_Sea.

21. See the Penn World Table for international comparisons of real per capita income growth since 1950, in Feenstra, Inklaar, and Timmer, "The Next Generation of the Penn World Table."

22. China Power Team, "How Much Trade Transits the South China Sea?," *China Power*, Center for Strategic and International Studies, August 2, 2017, updated

August 26, 2020, accessed January 15, 2021, https://chinapower.csis.org/much -trade-transits-south-china-sea/.

23. *Annual Report to Congress: Military and Security Developments Involving the People's Republic of China 2013* (Washington, DC: Office of the Secretary of Defense, 2013), 22, accessed January 15, 2021, http://www.defense.gov/pubs /pdfs/2013_CMPR_Final.pdf.

24. U.S. Department of State, *Treaties in Force: A List of Treaties and Other International Agreements of the United States in Force on January 1, 2020*, accessed January 15, 2021, https://www.state.gov/treaties-in-force/.

25. U.S. Department of State, *Treaties in Force*.

26. Simon Denyer and Eva Dou, "Biden Vows to Defend U.S. Allies as China Asserts Power in Asia," *Washington Post*, November 12, 2020, accessed January 15, 2021, https://www.washingtonpost.com/world/asia_pacific/biden-china-japan -korea-allies/2020/11/12/6cf6e212–24af-11eb-9c4a-0dc6242c4814_story.html.

27. Calculated as a percentage of U.S. 2019 current-dollar gross domestic product of $21,433 billion and the U.S. population employed of 158.735 million in December 2019. See "International Trade in Goods and Services" and "Gross Domestic Product," U.S. Department of Commerce, Bureau of Economic Analysis; "Employment Situation," U.S. Department of Labor, Bureau of Labor Statistics, accessed January 15, 2021, https://www.bea.gov/data/intl-trade -investment/international-trade-goods-and-services, https://www.bea.gov /data/gdp/gross-domestic-product, https://www.bls.gov/news.release/empsit .toc.htm.

28. *Military and Security Developments Involving the People's Republic of China 2011*, 17.

29. *Military and Security Developments Involving the People's Republic of China 2011*, 16.

30. Xi Jinping, "Secure a Decisive Victory in Building a Moderately Prosperous Society in All Respects and Strive for the Great Success of Socialism with Chinese Characteristics for a New Era," Report to the Nineteenth National Congress of the Communist Party of China, October 18, 2017, accessed January 16, 2021, http://www.xinhuanet.com/english/download/Xi_Jinping's_report _at_19th_CPC_National_Congress.pdf.

31. Xi Jinping.

32. "China's National Defense in the New Era," State Council Information Office of the People's Republic of China, Xinhua, July 2019, accessed January 16, 2021, http://english.www.gov.cn/archive/whitepaper/201907/24/content_ WS5d3941ddc6d08408f502283d.html.

33. Edward N. Luttwak, *The Rise of China vs. the Logic of Strategy* (Cambridge: Belknap Press of Harvard University Press, 2012).

34. See Edward Luttwak's presentation at the Center for Strategic and International Studies on February 25, 2013, https://www.csis.org/events/book-event -rise-china-vs-logic-strategy; accessed May 4, 2021.

35. Jeremy Page, "How the U.S. Misread China's Xi: Hoping for a Globalist, It Got an Autocrat," *Wall Street Journal*, December 23, 2020, accessed January 18, 2021, https://www.wsj.com/articles/xi-jinping-globalist-autocrat-misread -11608735769?mod=hp_lead_pos10.

36. See Luttwak's presentation at the Center for Strategic and International Studies on February 25, 2013.

37. *Military and Security Developments Involving the People's Republic of China 2011*, 14.

38. Jacqueline Newmyer Deal, "China's Nationalist Heritage," *National Interest*, January–February 2013, accessed May 4, 2021, https://nationalinterest.org /article/chinas-nationalist-heritage-7885. In Newmyer Deal's view, China's current form of nationalism displays the elite's insecurities and is a disturbing zero-sum view of China's interactions with outside actors.

39. See Luttwak's presentation at the Center for Strategic and International Studies.

40. *Military and Security Developments Involving the People's Republic of China 2011*, 15; M. Taylor Fravel, "Regime Insecurity and International Cooperation: Explaining China's Compromises in Territorial Disputes," *International Security* 30, no. 2 (fall 2005): 46–47, http://www.mitpressjournals.org/doi/ pdf/10.1162/016228805775124534.

Chapter 2. It Matters Who Runs the Pacific

1. See, for example, Barry R. Posen, "Pull Back: The Case for a Less Activist Foreign Policy," *Foreign Affairs*, January–February 2013, accessed May 5, 2021, https://www.foreignaffairs.com/articles/united-states/2013-01-01/pull -back?page=show; Christopher Layne, *The Peace of Illusions: American Grand Strategy from 1940 to the Present* (Ithaca: Cornell University Press, 2007); and Justin Logan, "China, America, and the Pivot to Asia," CATO Institute, Policy Analysis No. 717, January 8, 2013, accessed May 5, 2021, https://www.cato.org /policy-analysis/china-america-pivot-asia.

2. National Intelligence Council, *Global Trends 2030: Alternative Worlds* (Washington, DC: Office of Director of National Intelligence, 2012), cover letter,

accessed May 5, 2021, https://www.dni.gov/files/documents/GlobalTrends _2030.pdf.

3. National Intelligence Council, 76–78.

4. See Edward Luttwak's presentation at the Center for Strategic and International Studies.

5. John Garnaut, "Xi's War Drums," *Foreign Policy*, May–June 2013, 4, accessed May 5, 2021, https://foreignpolicy.com/2013/04/29/xis-war-drums/.

6. Xi Jinping, "Secure a Decisive Victory in Building a Moderately Prosperous Society in All Respects and Strive for the Great Success of Socialism with Chinese Characteristics for a New Era."

7. Kissinger, *On China*, chap. 1.

8. John Lee, "Lonely Power, Staying Power: The Rise of China and the Resilience of US Pre-eminence," Hudson Institute, October 11, 2011, accessed May 5, 2021, https://www.hudson.org/content/researchattachments/attachment/938 /the_rise_of_china_and_the_resilience_of_us_preeminence.pdf.

9. Jay Solomon and Miho Inada, "Japan's Nuclear Plan Unsettles U.S.," *Wall Street Journal*, May 1, 2013, accessed May 5, 2021, https://www.wsj.com/articles /SB10001424127887324582004578456943867189804.

10. Solomon and Inada.

11. Vincent Fournier, "Surveying Safeguarded Material 24/7," International Atomic Energy Agency, September 12, 2016, accessed January 19, 2021, https:// www.iaea.org/newscenter/news/surveying-safeguarded-material-24/7.

12. "JAXA History," Japan Aerospace Exploration Agency, accessed January 20, 2021, https://global.jaxa.jp/about/history/index.html.

13. "H-11A Launch Vehicle," Japan Aerospace Exploration Agency, accessed January 20, 2021, https://global.jaxa.jp/activity/pr/brochure/files/rocket01 .pdf.

14. Michelle Ye Hee Lee, "More Than Ever, South Koreans Want Their Own Nuclear Weapons," *Washington Post*, September 13, 2017, accessed January 21, 2021, https://www.washingtonpost.com/news/worldviews/wp/2017/09/13/most -south-koreans-dont-think-the-north-will-start-a-war-but-they-still-want -their-own-nuclear-weapons/.

15. Jay Solomon, "Seoul Seeks Ability to Make Nuclear Fuel," *Wall Street Journal*, April 3, 2013, accessed May 5, 2021, https://www.wsj.com/articles/SB100014 24127887324883604578399053942895628.

16. "Nuclear Power in South Korea," World Nuclear Association fact sheet, November 2020, accessed January 21, 2021, https://world-nuclear.org/information -library/country-profiles/countries-o-s/south-korea.aspx#:~:text=Fuel%20

cycle%20South%20Korea%20has%20always%20had%20an,(see%20 section%20below%20on%20Korea-US%20Atomic%20Energy%20Agreement).

17. Missile Defense Project, "Missiles of South Korea," *Missile Threat*, Center for Strategic and International Studies, July 30, 2020, accessed January 21, 2021, https://missilethreat.csis.org/country/south-korea/.

18. International Institute for Strategic Studies, *The Military Balance: 2021* (London: Routledge, 2021), 344–45.

19. "Arms Control and Proliferation Profile: India," Arms Control Association, January 2018, accessed January 21, 2021, https://www.armscontrol.org/factsheets /indiaprofile.

20. Missile Defense Project, "Missiles of India," *Missile Threat*, Center for Strategic and International Studies, June 14, 2018, accessed January 21, 2021, https:// missilethreat.csis.org/country/india/.

21. Frank von Hippel, "Plutonium, Proliferation and Radioactive-Waste Politics in East Asia," Nonproliferation Policy Education Center, January 3, 2011, accessed May 5, 2021, http://www.npolicy.org/article.php?aid=44&rt=~2~6~&key =proliferation%20japan&sec=article&author=.

22. Missile Defense Project, "Missiles of Taiwan," *Missile Threat*, Center for Strategic and International Studies, July 16, 2020, accessed January 21, 2021, https:// missilethreat.csis.org/country/taiwan/.

23. Layne, *The Peace of Illusions*, 160.

24. Layne, 160.

25. Layne, 178.

26. Layne, 178.

27. Hugh White, *The China Choice: Why America Should Share Power* (Collingswood, Australia: Black, 2012).

28. Hugh White, "The China Choice: A Bold Vision for U.S.-China Relations," *The Diplomat*, August 17, 2012, accessed May 5, 2021, https://thediplomat .com/2012/08/the-china-choice-a-bold-vision-for-u-s-china-relations/.

29. Brands, "Regime Realism and Chinese Grand Strategy," 5–7.

30. Chris Buckley, "China Takes Aim at Western Ideas," *New York Times*, August 19, 2013, accessed June 6, 2021, https://www.nytimes.com/2013/08/20/world /asia/chinas-new-leadership-takes-hard-line-in-secret-memo.html.

31. Jude Blanchette, "Beijing's Visions of American Decline," *Politico* China Watcher, March 11, 2021, accessed May 5, 2021, https://www.politico.com /newsletters/politico-china-watcher/2021/03/11/beijings-visions-of -american-decline-492064.

32. Blackwill and Zelikow, "The United States, China, and Taiwan," 14–17.

33. Max Hastings, "America Is Headed to a Showdown over Taiwan, and China Might Win," Bloomberg, March 14, 2021, accessed March 17, 2021, https://www.bloomberg.com/opinion/articles/2021-03-14/max-hastings-china-might-defeat-america-in-war-over-taiwan.

34. U.S. Energy Information Administration, *International Energy Outlook 2019*, September 24, 2019, tables A5, G2, and F13, accessed January 23, 2021, https://www.eia.gov/outlooks/archive/ieo19/tables_ref.php.

35. Alastair Gale and Chieko Tsuneoka, "As China-Taiwan Tensions Rise, Japan Begins Preparing for Possible Conflict," *Wall Street Journal*, August 27, 2021, accessed October 13, 2021, https://www.wsj.com/articles/as-china-taiwan-tensions-rise-japan-begins-preparing-for-possible-conflict-11630067601?mod=world_major_1_pos1.

36. Blackwill and Zelikow, "The United States, China, and Taiwan," 46.

37. Eliot Cohen, *The Big Stick: The Limits of Soft Power and the Necessity of Military Force* (New York: Basic Books, 2016), 26.

38. David Pierson, "Military Spending Is Soaring in the Asia-Pacific Region. Here's Why," *Los Angeles Times*, June 7, 2019, accessed January 23, 2021, https://www.latimes.com/world/asia/la-fg-asia-defense-industry-20190607-story.html.

Chapter 3. The Origins of America's Archaic Military Machine in the Pacific

1. *Military and Security Developments Involving the People's Republic of China 2020*.

2. Stacie L. Pettyjohn, *U.S. Global Defense Posture, 1783–2011* (Santa Monica: RAND Corporation, 2012), 50–54, accessed May 6, 2021, https://www.rand.org/pubs/monographs/MG1244.html.

3. Pettyjohn, 54.

4. Pettyjohn, 51.

5. Pettyjohn, 51–52.

6. Pettyjohn, 52.

7. Pettyjohn, 52–53.

8. Pettyjohn, 52–53.

9. Pettyjohn, 62–63.

10. Pettyjohn, 64.

11. Pettyjohn, 75.

12. Pettyjohn, 67–69, table 9.1.

13. Pettyjohn, 72.

14. Pettyjohn, 51–52.

15. John B. Hattendorf, *The Evolution of the U.S. Navy's Maritime Strategy, 1977–1986* (Newport: Naval War College Press, 2004), 17–20.

16. Hattendorf, 21.

17. *Indo-Pacific Strategy Report: Preparedness, Partnerships, and Promoting a Networked Region*, U.S. Department of Defense, June 1, 2019, 26–30, accessed January 26, 2021, https://media.defense.gov/2019/Jul/01/2002152311/-1/-1/1 /department-of-defense-indo-pacific-strategy-report-2019.PDF.

18. *Indo-Pacific Strategy Report*, 23.

19. Thomas P. Ehrhard and Robert O. Work, *Range, Persistence, Stealth, and Networking: The Case for a Carrier-Based Unmanned Combat Air System* (Washington, DC: Center for Strategic and Budgetary Assessments, 2008), chap. 5, accessed May 6, 2021, https://csbaonline.org/uploads/documents/The -Case-for-A-Carrier-Based-Unmanned-Combat-Air-System.pdf.

20. For historical U.S. Air Force aircraft inventories, see James C. Ruehrmund Jr. and Christopher J. Bowie, "Arsenal of Airpower: USAF Aircraft Inventory 1950–2016," Mitchell Institute for Aerospace Studies, February 2018, app. B, accessed January 26, 2021, https://www.mitchellaerospacepower.org/single-post/2018/02/22 /Arsenal-of-Airpower-USAF-Aircraft-Inventory-1950–2016.

21. Jeremiah Gertler, "Defense Primer: United States Airpower," Congressional Research Service, December 15, 2020, accessed January 26, 2021, https:// crsreports.congress.gov/product/pdf/IF/IF10546.

22. John A. Warden III, *The Air Campaign: Planning for Combat* (Washington DC: National Defense University Press, 1988), chap. 1, accessed May 6, 2021, https://archive.org/details/DTIC_ADA259303/page/n7/mode/2up.

23. Warden, chap. 1.

24. Alan Vick, *Snakes in the Eagle's Nest: A History of Ground Attacks on Air Bases*, (Santa Monica, CA: RAND Corporation, 1995), accessed May 6, 2021, https://www .rand.org/pubs/monograph_reports/MR553.html.

25. Ehrhard and Work, *Range, Persistence, Stealth, and Networking*, 35.

26. "America's Navy—About—Mission," U.S. Navy, accessed January 27, 2021, https://www.navy.mil/About/Mission/.

27. Kevin Lewis, "National Security Spending and Budget Trends since World War II," RAND Corporation, June 1990, 88, accessed April 29, 2021, https://apps.dtic .mil/dtic/tr/fulltext/u2/a238854.pdf.

28. Edward J. Marolda, *Ready Seapower: A History of the U.S. Seventh Fleet* (Washington, DC: Department of the Navy, Naval History and Heritage Command, 2012), 23–26, accessed May 6, 2021, https://www.history.navy.mil/content/dam /nhhc/research/publications/Publication-PDF/ReadySeapower.pdf.

29. Marolda, 30.

30. Marolda, 59.

31. Marolda, 104–8.

32. Ehrhard and Work, *Range, Persistence, Stealth, and Networking*, 74–75.

33. Ehrhard and Work, 86–89.

34. David H. Buss, William F. Moran, and Thomas J. Moore, "Why America Still Needs Aircraft Carriers," *Foreign Policy*, April 26, 2013, accessed May 6, 2021, https://foreignpolicy.com/2013/04/26/why-america-still-needs-aircraft-carriers/.

35. "Tomahawk Cruise Missile," U.S. Navy Fact File, April 26, 2018, accessed January 28, 2021, https://www.navy.mil/Resources/Fact-Files/Display-FactFiles/Article/2169229/tomohawk-cruise-missile/.

36. See the U.S. Navy Fact Files for weapons data and home ports for its surface ships and submarines, https://www.navy.mil/Resources/Fact-Files/.

37. U.S. Navy Fact Files.

38. Bryan G. McGrath and Timothy A. Walton, "The Time for Lasers Is Now," U.S. Naval Institute *Proceedings* 139, no. 4 (April 2013): 64–69, accessed May 7, 2021, https://www.usni.org/magazines/proceedings/2013/april/time-lasers-now.

39. Kyle Mizokami, "The Navy Needs a Way to Reload Missile Silos at Sea," *Popular Mechanics*, July 6, 2017, accessed January 28, 2021, https://www.popularmechanics.com/military/navy-ships/a27205/navy-reload-missile-silos-at-sea/.

40. Thomas A. Keaney and Eliot A. Cohen, *Gulf War Air Power Survey Summary Report*, 1993, 65, accessed May 6, 2021, https://media.defense.gov/2010/Sep/27/2001329801/-1/-1/0/gulf_war_air_power_survey-summary.pdf.

41. Marolda, *Ready Seapower*, 62.

42. Gordon S. Barrass, "U.S. Competitive Strategy during the Cold War," in *Competitive Strategies for the 21st Century*, ed. Thomas G. Mahnken (Stanford: Stanford Security Studies, 2012), 71–89.

43. Bureau of Arms Control, Verification and Compliance, "Treaty between the United States of America and the Union of Soviet Socialist Republics on the Elimination of Their Intermediate-Range and Shorter-Range Missiles (INF Treaty)," U.S. Department of State, accessed May 7, 2021, https://2009-2017.state.gov/t/avc/trty/102360.htm.

44. C. Todd Lopez, "U.S. Withdraws from Intermediate-Range Nuclear Forces Treaty," U.S. Department of Defense news release, August 2, 2019, accessed January 28, 2021, https://www.defense.gov/Explore/News/Article/Article/1924779/us-withdraws-from-intermediate-range-nuclear-forces-treaty/.

45. Krepinevich and Watts, *The Last Warrior*, 198–202.

46. *Quadrennial Defense Review Report*, Office of the Secretary of Defense, September 30, 2001, 4, accessed January 29, 2021, https://archive.defense.gov/pubs/qdr2001.pdf.

47. *Quadrennial Defense Review Report*, 2001, 31.

48. *Quadrennial Defense Review Report*, Office of the Secretary of Defense, February 6, 2006, 29, accessed May 7, 2021, https://archive.defense.gov/pubs/pdfs/QDR20060203.pdf.

49. *Quadrennial Defense Review Report*, Office of the Secretary of Defense, February 2010, 31, accessed May 7, 2021, https://dod.defense.gov/Portals/1/features/defenseReviews/QDR/QDR_as_of_29JAN10_1600.pdf.

50. *Quadrennial Defense Review Report*, February 2010, 32.

51. Michael Pillsbury, *The Hundred-Year Marathon: China's Secret Strategy to Replace America as the Global Superpower* (New York: Henry Holt, 2015), 7–12.

52. Bill Clinton, *My Life* (New York: Alfred A. Knopf, 2004), 794.

53. Clinton, 768.

54. George W. Bush, *Decision Points* (New York: Crown Publishers, 2010), 427.

55. Susan Rice, "National Security Advisor Susan E. Rice's As Prepared Remarks on the U.S.-China Relationship at George Washington University," The White House, Office of the Press Secretary, September 21, 2015, accessed February 2, 2021, https://obamawhitehouse.archives.gov/the-press-office/2015/09/21/national-security-advisor-susan-e-rices-prepared-remarks-us-china.

56. Robert Gates, *Duty* (New York: Alfred A. Knopf, 2014), 142–46.

57. Gates, 144.

58. "The China Syndrome," *The Economist*, June 9, 2012, accessed May 7, 2021, https://www.economist.com/united-states/2012/06/09/the-china-syndrome.

59. Bryan Bender, "Chief of US Pacific Forces Calls Climate Biggest Worry," *Boston Globe*, March 9, 2013, accessed February 1, 2021, https://www.bostonglobe.com/news/nation/2013/03/09/admiral-samuel-locklear-commander-pacific-forces-warns-that-climate-change-top-threat/BHdPVCLrWEMxRe9IXJZcHL/story.html.

60. "F-22 Raptor," U.S. Air Force Fact Sheet, September 2015, accessed May 7, 2021, https://www.af.mil/About-Us/Fact-Sheets/Display/Article/104506/f-22-raptor/.

61. "F-15E Strike Eagle," U.S. Air Force Fact Sheet, April 2019, accessed May 7, 2021, https://www.af.mil/About-Us/Fact-Sheets/Display/Article/104499/f-15e-strike-eagle/;"General Dynamics F-111F," National Museum of the U.S. Air Force Fact Sheet, July 28, 2015, accessed May 7, 2021, https://www

.nationalmuseum.af.mil/Visit/Museum-Exhibits/Fact-Sheets/Display
/Article/195859/general-dynamics-f-111f-aardvark/.

62. Mark Gunzinger, "Long-Range Strike: Resetting the Balance of Stand-in and
Stand-off Forces," Mitchell Institute for Aerospace Studies, June 18–19, 2020,
accessed February 21, 2021, https://a2dd917a-65ab-41f1-ab11–5f1897e16299
.usrfiles.com/ugd/a2dd91_4f2e5df4b4b2464ca6d50d0dcd9ea04f.pdf.

Chapter 4. China's Strategy

1. Andrew S. Erickson and Adam P. Liff, "China's Military Development, Beyond
the Numbers," *The Diplomat*, March 12, 2013, 2, accessed May 8, 2021,
https://thediplomat.com/2013/03/chinas-military-development-beyond-the
-numbers/.

2. "SIPRI Military Expenditure Database," Stockholm International Peace
Research Institute, accessed February 8, 2021, https://sipri.org/databases
/milex.

3. *Military and Security Developments Involving the People's Republic of China
2020*, 18–23.

4. MacGregor Knox and Williamson Murray, eds., *The Dynamics of Military
Revolution, 1300–2050* (Cambridge: Cambridge University Press, 2001), chap.
10.

5. For the Defense Department's formal definitions of "anti-access" and "area
denial," see U.S. Department of Defense, *Joint Operational Access Concept,
Version 1.0* (Arlington, VA: Department of Defense, 2011), 6, accessed May 9,
2021, https://dod.defense.gov/Portals/1/Documents/pubs/JOAC_Jan%202012
_Signed.pdf.

6. Andrew S. Erickson, "Are China's Near Seas 'Anti-Navy' Capabilities Aimed
Directly at the United States?," *Information Dissemination*, June 14, 2012,
accessed May 9, 2021, http://www.informationdissemination.net/2012/06
/are-chinas-near-seas-anti-navy.html.

7. For examples, see various projected missile and warships costs from *Program
Acquisition Cost by Weapon System*, Office of the Under Secretary of Defense
(Comptroller)/Chief Financial Officer, U.S. Department of Defense, February
2020, 5–6, 6–5, 6–11, accessed February 8, 2021, https://comptroller.defense.gov
/Portals/45/Documents/defbudget/fy2021/fy2021_Weapons.pdf.

8. *Program Acquisition Cost by Weapon System*.

9. *2010 Report to Congress of the U.S.-China Economic and Security Review Commission*, November 2010, 89–90, accessed May 9, 2021, https://www.uscc.gov
/sites/default/files/annual_reports/2010-Report-to-Congress.pdf.

10. Christopher J. Bowie, "The Lessons of Salty Demo," *Air Force* magazine, March 2009, accessed May 9, 2021, https://www.airforcemag.com/article/0309salty/.

11. *2010 Report to Congress of the U.S.-China Economic and Security Review Commission*, 89–90. See also Eric Stephen Gons, "Access Challenges and Implications for Airpower in the Western Pacific" (PhD diss., Pardee RAND Graduate School, 2011), 63–65, accessed February 11, 2021, http://www.rand.org/pubs/rgs_dissertations/RGSD267.html.

12. Roger Cliff, *China's Military Power* (New York: Cambridge University Press, 2015), 197.

13. *Military and Security Developments Involving the People's Republic of China 2020*, 55.

14. *Military and Security Developments Involving the People's Republic of China 2020*, 55–56.

15. *Military and Security Developments Involving the People's Republic of China 2020*, 59–60.

16. *Military and Security Developments Involving the People's Republic of China 2020*, 59.

17. Thomas R. McCabe, "Air and Space Power with Chinese Characteristics: China's Military Revolution," *Air and Space Power Journal* 34 (spring 2020): 23, accessed October 31, 2021, https://www.airuniversity.af.edu/Portals/10/ASPJ/journals/Volume-34_Issue-1/F-McCabe.pdf.

18. Dylan B. Ross and Jimmy A. Harmon, "New Navy Fighting Machine in the South China Sea" (master's thesis, Naval Postgraduate School, Monterey, CA, 2012), 31, accessed May 9, 2021, https://apps.dtic.mil/dtic/tr/fulltext/u2/a563777.pdf.

19. An essay written by a former U.S. Navy surface warfare officer explains how U.S. naval strike group commanders can employ deception and electronic support to disrupt adversary reconnaissance and targeting efforts. Although possibly practicable in a single case where policymakers and commanders were willing to take a high risk for a particular objective, there now seems little prospect of U.S. strike group commanders sustaining such deception and concealment against the PLA in the Near Seas. See Jonathan F. Solomon, "Maritime Deception and Concealment: Concepts for Defeating Wide-Area Oceanic Surveillance-Reconnaissance-Strike Networks," *Naval War College Review* 66, no. 4, art. 7, accessed April 3, 2021, https://digital-commons.usnwc.edu/nwc-review/vol66/iss4/7/.

20. *Military and Security Developments Involving the People's Republic of China 2020*, 63–64.

21. International Institute for Strategic Studies, *The Military Balance: 2021* (London: Routledge, 2021), 250.

22. *Military and Security Developments Involving the People's Republic of China 2020*, 65.

23. Mark Stokes, Gabriel Alvarado, Emily Weinstein, and Ian Easton, "China's Space and Counterspace Capabilities and Activities," U.S.-China Economic and Security Review Commission, March 30, 2020, 28–34, accessed February 10, 2021, https://www.uscc.gov/sites/default/files/2020–05/China_Space_and_Counterspace_Activities.pdf.

24. Stokes, Alvarado, Weinstein, and Easton, 35–36.

25. Andrew Jones, "Chinese Partnership to Create Tianxian SAR Satellite Constellation," *Space News*, October 8, 2021, accessed October 20, 2021, https://spacenews.com/chinese-partnership-to-create-tianxian-sar-satellite-constellation/.

26. Stokes, Alvarado, Weinstein, and Easton, "China's Space and Counterspace Capabilities and Activities," 51–57.

27. *Military and Security Developments Involving the People's Republic of China 2020*, 65.

28. *Military and Security Developments Involving the People's Republic of China 2020*, 52.

29. McCabe, "Air and Space Power with Chinese Characteristics," 26.

30. *Military and Security Developments Involving the People's Republic of China 2020*, 52.

31. *Military and Security Developments Involving the People's Republic of China 2020*, 50.

32. *The Military Balance: 2021*, 253–55.

33. McCabe, "Air and Space Power with Chinese Characteristics," 24.

34. *Military and Security Developments Involving the People's Republic of China 2020*, 50–51.

35. *2012 Report to Congress of the U.S.-China Economic and Security Review Commission*, November 2012, 129, accessed May 9, 2021, https://www.uscc.gov/sites/default/files/annual_reports/2012-Report-to-Congress.pdf.

36. International Institute for Strategic Studies, *The Military Balance: 2018* (London: Routledge, 2018), 9.

37. *The Military Balance: 2021*, 253–55.

38. *Military and Security Developments Involving the People's Republic of China 2020*, 51.

39. McCabe, "Air and Space Power with Chinese Characteristics," 22–25.

40. *Military and Security Developments Involving the People's Republic of China 2020*, 51.

41. *The Military Balance: 2021*, 253–55.

42. *Military and Security Developments Involving the People's Republic of China 2020*, 44.

43. Ronald O'Rourke, "China Naval Modernization: Implications for U.S. Navy Capabilities—Background and Issues for Congress," Congressional Research Service, January 27, 2021, accessed February 12, 2021, https://crsreports.congress.gov/product/pdf/RL/RL33153.

44. O'Rourke, 2–3.

45. O'Rourke, 4.

46. *Military and Security Developments Involving the People's Republic of China 2020*, 44.

47. O'Rourke, "China Naval Modernization," 3.

48. *Military and Security Developments Involving the People's Republic of China 2020*, 46.

49. *Military and Security Developments Involving the People's Republic of China 2020*, 46–47.

50. O'Rourke, "China Naval Modernization," 22–27.

51. *Military and Security Developments Involving the People's Republic of China 2020*, 48.

52. Gregory B. Poling, "The Conventional Wisdom on China's Island Bases Is Dangerously Wrong," War on the Rocks, January 10, 2020, accessed February 13, 2021, https://warontherocks.com/2020/01/the-conventional-wisdom-on-chinas-island-bases-is-dangerously-wrong/.

53. *Military and Security Developments Involving the People's Republic of China 2020*, 101–2.

54. Xi Jinping, "Secure a Decisive Victory in Building a Moderately Prosperous Society in All Respects and Strive for the Great Success of Socialism with Chinese Characteristics for a New Era," Report to the Nineteenth National Congress of the Communist Party of China, October 18, 2017.

55. Patrick Gerard Buchan and Benjamin Rimland, "Defining the Diamond: The Past, Present, and Future of the Quadrilateral Security Dialogue," Center for Strategic and International Studies, March 16, 2020, accessed February 14, 2021, https://www.csis.org/analysis/defining-diamond-past-present-and-future-quadrilateral-security-dialogue.

56. O'Rourke, "China Naval Modernization," 35.

57. Kerry K. Gershaneck, *Political Warfare: Strategies for Combating China's Plan to "Win without Fighting"* (Quantico, VA: Marine Corps University Press, 2020), chap. 2.

58. Christina Zhou and Bang Xiao, "China's Social Credit System Is Pegged to Be Fully Operational by 2020—but What Will It Look Like?," Australian Broadcast Corporation, January 1, 2020, accessed January 17, 2021, https://www.abc.net.au /news/2020–01–02/china-social-credit-system-operational-by-2020/11764740.

59. Lingling Wei, "China's Xi Ramps Up Control of Private Sector. 'We Have No Choice but to Follow the Party,'" *Wall Street Journal*, December 10, 2020, accessed January 18, 2021, https://www.wsj.com/articles/china-xi-clampdown-private -sector-communist-party-11607612531.

60. Chao Deng, "China Razed Thousands of Xinjiang Mosques in Assimilation Push, Report Says," *Wall Street Journal*, September 25, 2020, accessed January 17, 2021, https://www.wsj.com/articles/china-razed-thousands-of-xinjiang -mosques-in-assimilation-push-report-says-11601049531?mod=searchresults _pos10&page=3.

61. Natasha Khan, "Hong Kong Police Arrest 53 Opposition Figures over Alleged Subversion," *Wall Street Journal*, January 6, 2021, accessed January 17, 2021, https://www.wsj.com/articles/hong-kong-police-arrest-dozens-of-opposition -politicians-over-alleged-subversion11609895177?mod=searchresults _pos12&page=1.

62. *The PRC in International Organizations*, U.S.-China Economic and Security Review Commission, April 20, 2020, accessed January 17, 2021, https://www .uscc.gov/prc-international-orgs.

63. Kurt M. Campbell and Rush Doshi, "How America Can Shore Up Asian Order," *Foreign Affairs*, January 12, 2021, accessed January 18, 2021, https://www .foreignaffairs.com/articles/united-states/2021–01–12/how-america-can -shore-asian-order.

64. Tim Kelly, "Japan Sets Record $52 Billion Military Budget with Stealth Jets, Long-Range Missiles," Reuters, December 20, 2020, accessed January 18, 2021, https:// www.reuters.com/article/japan-defence-budget/japan-sets-record-52-billion -military-budget-with-stealth-jets-long-range-missiles-idUSKBN28V03X.

65. Jade Macmillan and Andrew Greene, "Australia to Spend $270b Building Larger Military to Prepare for 'Poorer, More Dangerous' World and Rise of China," Australian Broadcast Corporation, July 1, 2020, accessed January 18, 2021, https://www.abc.net.au/news/2020–06–30/australia-unveils-10-year-defence -strategy/12408232.

66. "Brussels Summit Communiqué," North Atlantic Treaty Organization press release, June 14, 2021, accessed June 22, 2021, https://www.nato.int/cps/en/natohq/news_185000.htm?selectedLocale=en.

67. Laura Silver, Kat Devlin, and Christine Huang, "Unfavorable Views of China Reach Historic Highs in Many Countries," Pew Research Center, October 6, 2020, accessed January 18, 2021, https://www.pewresearch.org/global/2020/10/06/unfavorable-views-of-china-reach-historic-highs-in-many-countries/.

68. Jeremy Page, "How the U.S. Misread China's Xi: Hoping for a Globalist, It Got an Autocrat," *Wall Street Journal*, December 23, 2020, accessed January 18, 2021, https://www.wsj.com/articles/xi-jinping-globalist-autocrat-misread-11608735769?mod=hp_lead_pos10.

69. *Military and Security Developments Involving the People's Republic of China 2020*, 80.

70. *Military and Security Developments Involving the People's Republic of China 2020*, 78.

71. *Military and Security Developments Involving the People's Republic of China 2020*, 79.

72. *Military and Security Developments Involving the People's Republic of China 2020*, 81.

73. *Military and Security Developments Involving the People's Republic of China 2020*, 81–84.

74. *Military and Security Developments Involving the People's Republic of China 2020*, 31–33.

Chapter 5. America Pivots to Asia, Then Stumbles

1. *Quadrennial Defense Review Report, 2010*, 31–32.

2. U.S. Department of Defense, *Joint Operational Access Concept, Version 1.0*, foreword.

3. Barry D. Watts, *The Maturing Revolution in Military Affairs* (Washington, DC: Center for Strategic and Budgetary Assessments, 2011), 1–2, accessed May 10, 2021, https://csbaonline.org/research/publications/the-maturing-revolution-in-military-affairs/.

4. *Joint Operational Access Concept, Version 1.0*, foreword.

5. *Joint Operational Access Concept, Version 1.0*, ii.

6. *Joint Operational Access Concept, Version 1.0*, ii.

7. *Joint Operational Access Concept, Version 1.0*, 9.

8. *Joint Operational Access Concept, Version 1.0*, 17.

9. *Joint Operational Access Concept, Version 1.0*, 33–36.

10. *Joint Operational Access Concept, Version 1.0*, 36–38.

11. *Quadrennial Defense Review Report, 2010*, 32.

12. Gen. Norton A. Schwartz and Adm. Jonathan W. Greenert, "Air-Sea Battle," *American Interest*, February 20, 2012, accessed May 10, 2021, https://www.the -american-interest.com/2012/02/20/air-sea-battle/.

13. Keaney and Cohen, *Gulf War Air Power Survey Summary Report*.

14. Ronald O'Rourke, "Navy Lasers, Railgun, and Gun-Launched Guided Projectile: Background and Issues for Congress," Congressional Research Service, January 12, 2021, accessed February 17, 2021, https://crsreports.congress.gov/product /pdf/R/R44175.

15. Harry Kazianis, "Air-Sea Battle's Next Step: JAM-GC on Deck," National Interest, November 25, 2015, accessed February 17, 2021, https://nationalinterest.org /feature/air-sea-battles-next-step-jam-gc-deck-14440.

16. Marcus Hand, "Malacca Strait Transits Grow 2% to Record in 2015, Box-ships See Dip in H2," *Seatrade Maritime News*, March 7, 2016, accessed February 19, 2021, https://www.seatrade-maritime.com/asia/malacca-strait -transits-grow-2-record-2015-boxships-see-dip-h2.

17. Gabriel B. Collins and William S. Murray, "No Oil for the Lamps of China?," *Naval War College Review* 61, no. 2 (spring 2008): 84–85, accessed February 19, 2021, https://digital-commons.usnwc.edu/nwc-review/vol61/iss2/10/.

18. U.S. Navy Fact Files, accessed February 19, 2021, https://www.navy.mil /Resources/Fact-Files/.

19. Collins and Murray, "No Oil for the Lamps of China?," 81.

20. *Summary of the 2018 National Defense Strategy of the United States of America: Sharpening the American Military's Competitive Edge*, Office of the U.S. Secretary of Defense, January 19, 2018, 2, accessed February 20, 2021, https://dod. defense.gov/Portals/1/Documents/pubs/2018-National-Defense-Strategy -Summary.pdf.

21. *Summary of the 2018 National Defense Strategy*, 1.

22. Russell Wicke, "Gen. Moseley: New Long-Range Bomber on Horizon for 2018," U.S. Air Force Air Combat Command Public Affairs, July 26, 2006, accessed February 20, 2021, https://www.af.mil/News/Article-Display/Article/130296 /gen-moseley-new-long-range-bomber-on-horizon-for-2018/.

23. John Tirpak, "First of 17 B-1Bs Heads to the Boneyard," *Air Force* magazine, February 17, 2021, accessed February 21, 2021, https://www.airforcemag.com /first-of-17-b-1bs-heads-to-the-boneyard/.

24. Gunzinger, "Long-Range Strike," 3.

25. John Tirpak, "Schwartz, in Memoir, Says F-22 Was Traded for B-21 Bomber," *Air Force* magazine, April 26, 2018, accessed February 21, 2021, https://www.airforcemag.com/schwartz-in-memoir-says-f-22-was-traded-for-b-21-bomber/.

26. Gates, *Duty*, 457.

27. "JASSM-ER Fact Sheet," Lockheed-Martin Corporation, accessed February 22, 2021, https://www.lockheedmartin.com/content/dam/lockheed-martin/mfc/pc/jassm/mfc-jassm-er-pc.pdf.

28. Garrett Reim, "USAF Aims to Double Long-Term JASSM Production up to 10,000 Units," FlightGlobal, September 27, 2019, accessed February 22, 2021, https://www.flightglobal.com/fixed-wing/usaf-aims-to-double-long-term-jassm-production-up-to-10000-units/134510.article.

29. John Hoehn and Samuel Ryder, "Precision-Guided Munitions: Background and Issues for Congress," Congressional Research Service, June 26, 2020, 17, accessed February 22, 2021, https://crsreports.congress.gov/product/pdf/R/R45996.

30. Reim, "USAF Aims to Double Long-Term JASSM Production."

31. "Long Range Anti-Ship Missile Fact Sheet," Lockheed-Martin Corporation, accessed February 22, 2021, https://www.lockheedmartin.com/content/dam/lockheed-martin/mfc/pc/long-range-anti-ship-missile/mfc-lrasm-pc-01.pdf.

32. Jennifer Hlad and Amy McCullough, "ACE-ing the Test," *Air Force* magazine, May 1, 2020, accessed February 23, 2021, https://www.airforcemag.com/article/ace-ing-the-test/.

33. Hlad and McCullough.

34. Brian Everstine, "PACAF Surveyed Every 'Piece of Concrete' in the Pacific for Agile Combat Employment," *Air Force* magazine, November 25, 2020, accessed February 23, 2021, https://www.airforcemag.com/pacaf-surveyed-every-piece-of-concrete-in-the-pacific-for-agile-combat-employment/.

35. Gons, "Access Challenges and Implications for Airpower in the Western Pacific," 67–70.

36. See O'Rourke, "Navy Lasers, Railgun, and Gun-Launched Guided Projectile."

37. Ronald O'Rourke, "Navy Force Structure and Shipbuilding Plans: Background and Issues for Congress," Congressional Research Service, January 26, 2021, 10–11, accessed February 24, 2021, https://crsreports.congress.gov/product/pdf/RL/RL32665.

38. See U.S. Navy Fact File for fixed-wing aircraft, accessed May 10, 2021, https://www.navy.mil/Resources/Fact-Files/ http://www.navy.mil/navydata/fact_display.asp?cid=1100&tid=1200&ct=1.

39. Sam LaGrone, "New Age in Carrier Aviation Takes Off with X-47B Landing," *U.S. Naval Institute News*, July 10, 2013, accessed May 10, 2021, https://news.usni.org/2013/07/10/new-carrier-age-in-carrier-aviation-takes-off-with-x-47b-landing.

40. "MQ-25A Stingray," U.S. Navy Fact File, February 21, 2019, accessed January 27, 2021, https://www.navy.mil/Resources/Fact-Files/Display-FactFiles/Article/2160662/mq-25a-stingray/.

41. Wayne P. Hughes Jr., *The New Navy Fighting Machine: A Study of the Connections between Contemporary Policy, Strategy, Sea Power, Naval Operations, and the Composition of the United States Fleet* (Monterey, CA: Naval Postgraduate School, 2009), 11, 48, accessed April 3, 2021, https://docs.google.com/file/d/0B4aOmucPTb-IYjY3OTRkODMtN2NjZSooMWFmLWFhOTUtMDcoNjQzNGQxODYo/edit?pli=1.

42. Phillip E. Pournelle, "The Rise of the Missile Carriers," U.S. Naval Institute *Proceedings*, May 2013, 32, accessed April 4, 2021, https://www.usni.org/magazines/proceedings/2013/may/rise-missile-carriers.

43. Thomas Hamilton, "Comparing the Cost of Penetrating Bombers to Expendable Missiles over Thirty Years," RAND Corporation (WR-778-AF), 2011, accessed May 17, 2021, https://www.rand.org/pubs/working_papers/WR778.html.

44. O'Rourke, "Navy Force Structure and Shipbuilding Plans," 2.

45. Paul McLeary, "Congress Applauds VP Pence's Surprise Nixing of *Truman* Retirement," *Breaking Defense*, April 30, 2019, accessed February 24, 2021, https://breakingdefense.com/2019/04/vp-pences-surprise-nixing-of-truman-retirement-navy-modernization/.

46. O'Rourke, "Navy Force Structure and Shipbuilding Plans," 46–47.

47. O'Rourke, "Navy Force Structure and Shipbuilding Plans," 47–48.

48. O'Rourke, "Navy Force Structure and Shipbuilding Plans," 6.

49. "An Analysis of the Navy's Fiscal 2022 Shipbuilding Plan," Congressional Budget Office, September 2021, 2, accessed October 29, 2021, https://www.cbo.gov/system/files/2021-09/57414-Shipbuilding_1.pdf.

50. "An Analysis of the Navy's Fiscal 2022 Shipbuilding Plan," Congressional Budget Office, 6.

51. Christian Steidl, Laurent Daniel, and Cenk Yildiran, "Shipbuilding Market Developments Q2 2018," Organization of Economic Cooperation and Development (OECD), May 15, 2018, 17, accessed February 25, 2021, http://www.oecd.org/sti/ind/shipbuilding-market-developments-Q2-2018.pdf.

52. David Berger, "Commandant's Planning Guidance: 38th Commandant of the Marine Corps," Headquarters, U.S. Marine Corps, July 17, 2019, accessed February

25, 2021, https://www.marines.mil/Portals/1/Publications/Commandant's %20Planning%20Guidance_2019.pdf?ver=2019-07-17-090732-937.

53. David Berger, "Force Design 2030," Headquarters, U.S. Marine Corps, March 2020, 3, accessed February 25, 2021, https://www.hqmc.marines.mil/Portals /142/Docs/CMC38%20Force%20Design%202030%20Report%20Phase%20 I%20and%20II.pdf?ver=2020-03-26-121328-460.

54. Berger, "Force Design 2030," 5.

55. Berger, "Force Design 2030,"7.

56. Berger, "Force Design 2030,"5.

57. Berger, "Force Design 2030,"10, 12.

58. Berger, "Commandant's Planning Guidance," 3.

59. Berger, "Force Design 2030," 5.

60. John Hoehn, "Joint All-Domain Command and Control (JADC2)," Congressional Research Service, December 9, 2020, accessed March 1, 2021, https://crsreports .congress.gov/product/pdf/IF/IF11493.

61. Kelley Sayler, "Hypersonic Weapons: Background and Issues for Congress," Congressional Research Service, December 1, 2020, 5-6, accessed March 1, 2021, https://crsreports.congress.gov/product/pdf/R/R45811.

62. Mark Gunzinger, Lukas Autenried, and Bryan Clark, "Understanding the Long-Range Strike Debate," Mitchell Institute for Aerospace Studies, April 2021, 4, accessed May 11, 2021, https://a2dd917a-65ab-41f1-ab11-5f1897e16299 .usrfiles.com/ugd/a2dd91_584d2a721b0f44babobf7d25986ea40d.pdf.

Chapter 6. Designing a Competitive Strategy for the Indo-Pacific

1. Richard Rumelt, *Good Strategy/Bad Strategy: The Difference and Why It Matters* (New York: Crown Business, 2011), 6.

2. Rumelt, 33-37; see also U.S. Government, *National Security Strategy*, December 2017, accessed March 3, 2021, https://trumpwhitehouse.archives.gov/wp -content/uploads/2017/12/NSS-Final-12-18-2017-0905.pdf.

3. Henry Kissinger, *Diplomacy* (New York: Simon and Shuster, 1994), 201-6.

4. Bob Woodward, *Obama's Wars* (New York: Simon and Schuster, 2010), 278-83.

5. National Intelligence Council, *Global Trends 2040: A More Contested World*, Office of Director of National Intelligence, March 2021, accessed May 12, 2021, https://www.dni.gov/index.php/global-trends-home.

6. Rumelt, *Good Strategy/Bad Strategy*, 32, 41-44.

7. Rumelt, 32, 54-57.

8. "X" (George F. Kennan), "The Sources of Soviet Conduct," *Foreign Affairs*, July 1947, accessed May 12, 2021, https://www.foreignaffairs.com/articles

/russian-federation/1947-07-01/sources-soviet-conduct; *NSC 68: United States Objectives and Programs for National Security*, Federation of American Scientists, April 7, 1950, accessed May 12, 2021, https://fas.org/irp/offdocs/nsc-hst/nsc-68.htm.

9. Kennan, "The Sources of Soviet Conduct."

10. *NSC 68*, "Conclusions" and "Recommendations."

11. See, for example, Peter Beinart, "Biden's Taiwan Policy Is Truly, Deeply Reckless," *New York Times*, May 5, 2021, accessed June 11, 2021, https://www.nytimes.com/2021/05/05/opinion/biden-taiwan-china.html.

12. *Joint Publication 5-0: Joint Planning*, U.S. Department of Defense, December 1, 2020, IV-22, accessed March 9, 2021, https://www.jcs.mil/Portals/36/Documents/Doctrine/pubs/jp5_0.pdf?ver=ztDG06paGvpQRrLxThNZUw%3d%3d.

13. *Joint Publication 5-0*, IV-26.

14. Lawrence Freedman, *Deterrence* (Cambridge, UK: Polity Press, 2004), 37–39.

15. Thomas Schelling, *Arms and Influence* (New Haven, CT: Yale University Press, 2008), 47–48.

16. Blackwill and Zelikow, "The United States, China, and Taiwan," 45–46.

17. Freedman, *Deterrence*, 37–40.

18. Michael Pillsbury, "The Sixteen Fears: China's Strategic Psychology," *Survival: Global Politics and Strategy* 54, no. 5 (October–November 2012): 149–82, accessed March 9, 2021, https://iiss.tandfonline.com/doi/full/10.1080/00396338.2012.728351#.YEfbFrCSmUk.

19. *Military and Security Developments Involving the People's Republic of China 2020*, 29.

20. Benjamin Lambeth, *NATO's Air War for Kosovo: A Strategic and Operational Assessment* (Santa Monica, CA: RAND Corporation, 2001), 68–72, accessed May 12, 2021, https://www.rand.org/pubs/monograph_reports/MR1365.html.

21. See Gordon S. Barrass, "U.S. Competitive Strategy during the Cold War," in *Competitive Strategies for the 21st Century*, ed. Thomas G. Mahnken (Palo Alto: Stanford Security Studies, 2012), 71–89; and Gordon S. Barrass, *The Great Cold War: A Journey through the Hall of Mirrors* (Palo Alto: Stanford University Press, 2009).

22. Thomas Mahnken, "Cost-Imposing Strategies: A Brief Primer," Center for a New American Security, November 2014, 10, accessed April 9, 2021, https://s3.us-east-1.amazonaws.com/files.cnas.org/documents/CNAS_Maritime4_Mahnken.pdf?mtime=20160906081628&focal=none.

23. Barrass, "U.S. Competitive Strategy during the Cold War," 83–85.

Chapter 7. Thwarting a Chinese Fait Accompli

1. *Military and Security Developments Involving the People's Republic of China 2020*, 165.

2. Lee His-min and Eric Lee, "Taiwan's Overall Defense Concept, Explained," *The Diplomat*, November 3, 2020, accessed March 17, 2021, https://thediplomat .com/2020/11/taiwans-overall-defense-concept-explained/.

3. Blackwill and Zelikow, "The United States, China, and Taiwan," 27–28.

4. Blackwill and Zelikow, 35–37.

5. Max Hastings, "America Is Headed to a Showdown over Taiwan, and China Might Win," Bloomberg, March 14, 2021, accessed March 17, 2021, https://www .bloomberg.com/opinion/articles/2021-03-14/max-hastings-china-might -defeat-america-in-war-over-taiwan.

6. *Military and Security Developments Involving the People's Republic of China 2020*, 24.

7. Ian Easton, *The Chinese Invasion Threat: Taiwan's Defense and American Strategy in Asia* (Manchester, UK: Eastbridge Books, 2019), chaps. 5 and 6.

8. Joyu Wang and Alastair Gale, "Does Taiwan's Military Stand a Chance against China? Few Think So," *Wall Street Journal*, October 26, 2021, accessed October 26, 2021, https://www.wsj.com/articles/taiwan-military-readiness-china-threat -us-defense-11635174187?mod=articletype_trending_now_article_pos5.

9. *The Military Balance: 2021*, 301–2.

10. Tanner Greer, "Taiwan Can Win a War with China," *Foreign Policy*, September 25, 2018, accessed March 17, 2021, https://foreignpolicy.com/2018/09/25 /taiwan-can-win-a-war-with-china/.

11. Blackwill and Zelikow, "The United States, China, and Taiwan," 44–47.

12. Michèle Flournoy, "How to Prevent a War in Asia," *Foreign Affairs*, June 18, 2020, accessed March 18, 2021, http://foreignaffairs.com/articles/united -states/2020-06-18/how-prevent-war-asia. For Robert Work's view, see Sydney Freedberg Jr., "US 'Gets Its Ass Handed to It' in Wargames: Here's a $24 Billion Fix," Breaking Defense, March 7, 2019, accessed March 18, 2021, http://breaking-defense.com/2019/03/us-gets-its-ass-handed-to-it-in-wargames-heres -a-24-billion-fix.

13. David Deptula, "Bombers for Maritime Strike: An Asymmetric Counter to China's Navy," Mitchell Institute for Aerospace Studies, February 2019, 1, accessed March 19, 2021, http://docs.wixstatic.com/ugd/a2dd91_546d5ed9 b4424fd780887be1146f9ac2.pdf.

14. Paul Johnson, *Modern Times* (New York: HarperCollins, 1991), 394–96.

15. Joint Army-Navy Assessment Committee, "Japanese Naval and Merchant Shipping Losses during World War II by All Causes," U.S. Navy History and Heritage Command, February 1947, accessed March 19, 2021, https://www.history.navy.mil/research/library/online-reading-room/title-list-alphabetically/j/japanese-naval-merchant-shipping-losses-wwii.html.

16. Max Hastings and Simon Jenkins, *The Battle for the Falklands* (New York: W. W. Norton, 1983), 316–19, 346–49.

17. Deptula, "Bombers for Maritime Strike," 3.

18. Mark Barrett and Mace Carpenter, "Survivability in the Digital Age: The Imperative for Stealth," Mitchell Institute for Aerospace Studies, July 2017, 14, accessed March 21, 2021, http://docs.wixstatic.com/ugd/a2dd91_cd5494417b644d1fa7d7aacb9295324d.pdf.

19. Gunzinger, "Long-Range Strike," 30–32.

20. Gunzinger, 14.

21. John Tirpak, "B-21 Temporary Shelters Could Also Shelter B-2s," *Air Force* magazine, March 5, 2021, accessed March 21, 2021, https://www.airforcemag.com/b-21-temporary-shelters-could-also-shelter-b-2s/.

22. John Tirpak, "The Raider Comes out of the Black," *Air Force* magazine, February 19, 2021, accessed March 21, 2021, https://www.airforcemag.com/article/the-raider-comes-out-of-the-black/.

23. Gunzinger, "Long-Range Strike," 17–18.

24. Deptula, "Bombers for Maritime Strike," 10.

25. Christopher Dougherty, "The Pentagon Needs a Plan to Get Punched in the Mouth," C4ISR Net, May 20, 2021, accessed October 28, 2021, https://www.c4isrnet.com/thought-leadership/2021/05/20/the-pentagon-needs-a-plan-to-get-punched-in-the-mouth/.

26. "Advanced Extremely High Frequency System Fact Sheet," U.S. Space Force, March 22, 2017, accessed October 28, 2021, https://www.spaceforce.mil/About-Us/Fact-Sheets/Article/2197713/advanced-extremely-high-frequency-system/.

27. Glen VanHerck, "NORAD-USNORTHCOM Commander's Senate Armed Services Committee Statement," U.S. Northern Command, March 16, 2021, accessed March 22, 2021, https://www.northcom.mil/Newsroom/Transcripts/Transcript/Article/2541921/norad-usnorthcom-commanders-senate-armed-services-committee-statement/.

28. Todd Harrison, Kaitlyn Johnson, and Makena Young, "Defense against the Dark Arts in Space: Protecting Space Systems from Counterspace Weapons," Center for Strategic and International Studies, February 25, 2021, 3, accessed

March 23, 2021, https://www.csis.org/analysis/defense-against-dark-arts
-space-protecting-space-systems-counterspace-weapons.

29. David Deptula, William LaPlante, and Robert Haddick, "Modernizing U.S.
Nuclear Command, Control, and Communications," Mitchell Institute for
Aerospace Studies, February 2019, 26, accessed March 23, 2021, http://docs
.wixstatic.com/ugd/a2dd91_ed45cfd71de2457eba3bcce4d0657196.pdf.

30. "SpaceX Mission," Space Exploration Technologies, accessed March 24, 2021,
https://www.spacex.com/mission/.

31. "Our Constellation," Planet Labs company, accessed March 24, 2021, https://
storage.googleapis.com/planet-ditl/day-in-the-life/index.html.

32. "SAR Made Easy," Capella Space, accessed March 24, 2021, https://www.
capellaspace.com/.

33. Amanda Miller, "SDA Outlines Missile Tracking Satellite Plan," *Air Force*
magazine, April 16, 2021, accessed May 21, 2021, https://www.airforcemag.com
/sda-outlines-missile-tracking-satellite-plan/.

34. "USAF Unit Moves Reveal Clues to RQ-180 Ops Debut," Aviation Week Network, October 24, 2019, accessed March 24, 2021, https://aviationweek.com
/defense-space/usaf-unit-moves-reveal-clues-rq-180-ops-debut.

35. Blackwill and Zelikow, "The United States, China, and Taiwan," 45–47, 49–50.

36. Blackwill and Zelikow, 45–47, 49–50.

37. Blackwill and Zelikow, 50.

38. *Military and Security Developments Involving the People's Republic of China
2020*, 91.

39. Jeff Hagen, "The U.S. Air Force and the Chinese Aerospace Challenge,"
in *Chinese Aerospace Power*, ed. Andrew S. Erickson and Lyle J. Goldstein
(Annapolis, MD: Naval Institute Press, 2011), 469–71; see also Gons, "Access
Challenges and Implications for Airpower in the Western Pacific," 154–83.

40. James R. FitzSimonds, "Cultural Barriers to Implementing a Competitive
Strategy," in *Competitive Strategies for the 21st Century* (Stanford, CA: Stanford
Security Studies, 2012), 290–92.

41. FitzSimonds, 291.

42. FitzSimonds, 291–92.

43. "Low Cost Autonomous Attack System (LOCAAS) Miniature Munition Capability," Federation of American Scientists, November 29, 1999, accessed May
13, 2021, https://fas.org/man/dod-101/sys/smart/locaas.htm.

44. "Miniature Air Launched Decoy (MALD) Flight Vehicle," Air Force Technology, accessed March 28, 2021, https://www.airforce-technology.com/projects
/miniature-air-launched-decoy-mald-flight-vehicle/.

45. Robert Haddick, "Stopping Mobile Missiles: Top Picks for Offset Strategy," Breaking Defense, January 23, 2015, accessed March 28, 2021, https://breakingdefense .com/2015/01/stopping-mobile-missiles-top-picks-for-offset-strategy/.

46. Haddick.

Chapter 8. Roles for Naval Power in the Sensor and Missile Age

1. David C. Gompert, Astrid Stuth Cevallos, and Cristina L. Garafola, "War with China: Thinking Through the Unthinkable," RAND Corporation, 2016, 41–50, accessed May 27, 2021, https://www.rand.org/pubs/research_reports /RR1140.html.

2. David C. Gompert, "Sea Power and American Interests in the Western Pacific," RAND Corporation 2013, 186–88, accessed April 5, 2021, https://www.rand .org/pubs/research_reports/RR151.html#abstract.

3. See Eliot Cohen and John Gooch, *Military Misfortunes: The Anatomy of Failure in War* (New York: Free Press, 1990).

4. U.S. Department of the Navy and U.S. Coast Guard, "Advantage at Sea: Prevailing with Integrated All-Domain Naval Power," December 2020, 9–14, accessed April 3, 2021, https://media.defense.gov/2020/Dec/17/2002553481 /-1/-1/0/TRISERVICESTRATEGY.PDF/TRISERVICESTRATEGY.PDF.

5. "Advantage at Sea," 13–14.

6. Wayne P. Hughes Jr., *The New Navy Fighting Machine: A Study of the Connections between Contemporary Policy, Strategy, Sea Power, Naval Operations, and the Composition of the United States Fleet* (Monterey, CA: Naval Postgraduate School, 2009), 46–47.

7. Hughes, vii–viii.

8. Hughes, 5.

9. Hughes, viii–ix.

10. Hughes, 5.

11. Robert C. Rubel, "Cede No Water: Strategy, Littorals, and Flotillas," U.S. Naval Institute *Proceedings*, September 2013, 41, accessed April 5, 2021, https:// www.usni.org/magazines/proceedings/2013/september/cede-no-water -strategy-littorals-and-flotillas.

12. Rubel, 43–45.

13. See "SAR Made Easy," Capella Space, accessed March 24, 2021, https://www .capellaspace.com/.

14. Gompert, "Sea Power and American Interests in the Western Pacific," 148.

15. Unit cost from *Program Acquisition Cost by Weapon System*, Office of the Under Secretary of Defense (Comptroller)/Chief Financial Officer, February 2020, 6-6.

16. "Advantage at Sea," 16, 21.

17. Pournelle, "The Rise of the Missile Carriers," 31–32.

18. Hoehn and Ryder, "Precision-Guided Munitions," 24.

19. Sayler, "Hypersonic Weapons," 5.

20. O'Rourke, "Navy Force Structure and Shipbuilding Plans," 2–14.

21. Ronald O'Rourke, "Navy Large Unmanned Surface and Undersea Vehicles: Background and Issues for Congress," Congressional Research Service, March 25, 2021, 18–21, accessed April 7, 2021, https://crsreports.congress.gov/product /pdf/R/R45757.

22. Berger, "Commandant's Planning Guidance: 38th Commandant of the Marine Corps," 4–5.

23. Berger, 4–5.

24. Mahnken, "Cost-Imposing Strategies," 6–11.

25. Ronald O'Rourke, "Navy Constellation (FFG-62) Class Frigate [Previously FFG(X)] Program: Background and Issues for Congress," Congressional Research Service, February 11, 2021, 7, accessed April 10, 2021, https://crsreports .congress.gov/product/pdf/R/R44972.

26. O'Rourke, "Navy Large Unmanned Surface and Undersea Vehicles," 11.

27. O'Rourke, "Navy Large Unmanned Surface and Undersea Vehicles," 9.

28. O'Rourke, "Navy Large Unmanned Surface and Undersea Vehicles," 11–12.

29. See U.S. Navy Fact File for surface ships, accessed May 14, 2021, https://www .navy.mil/Resources/Fact-Files/ http://www.navy.mil/navydata/fact_display .asp?cid=1100&tid=1200&ct=1.

30. U.S. Navy Fact File for surface ships.

31. *Program Acquisition Cost by Weapon System*, 6-6.

32. "Defense Acquisitions Annual Assessment," U.S. Government Accountability Office, June 2020, 119; *Program Acquisition Cost by Weapon System*, 6-5.

33. Joseph Biden, "Interim National Security Strategic Guidance," The White House, Washington, March 2021, 7–10, 20, accessed April 11, 2021, https://www .whitehouse.gov/wp-content/uploads/2021/03/NSC-1v2.pdf.

34. Edward S. Miller, *War Plan Orange: The U.S. Strategy to Defeat Japan, 1897–1945* (Annapolis, MD: Naval Institute Press, 1991), 10.

Chapter 9. How to Win the Long Marathon in the Indo-Pacific

1. Paul Kennedy, *The Rise and Fall of the Great Powers* (New York: Random House, 1987), 355, table 35.

2. Barrass, "U.S. Competitive Strategy during the Cold War," 83–85.

3. Joseph Bosco, "Entrapment and Abandonment in Asia," *National Interest*, July 8, 2013, accessed May 15, 2021, https://nationalinterest.org/commentary /entrapment-abandonment-asia-8697.

4. "U.S. Public, Experts Differ on China Policies," Pew Research Center, September 18, 2012, accessed April 21, 2021, https://www.pewresearch.org/global /2012/09/18/u-s-public-experts-differ-on-china-policies/.

5. Laura Silver, Kat Devlin, and Christine Huang, "Most Americans Support Tough Stance toward China on Human Rights, Economic Issues," Pew Research Center, March 4, 2021, accessed April 21, 2021, https://www.pewresearch.org /global/2021/03/04/most-americans-support-tough-stance-toward-china -on-human-rights-economic-issues/.

6. J. J. Moncus and Laura Silver, "Americans' Views of Asia-Pacific Nations Have Not Changed since 2018—with the Exception of China," Pew Research Center, April 12, 2021, accessed April 21, 2021, https://www.pewresearch.org /fact-tank/2021/04/12/americans-views-of-asia-pacific-nations-have-not -changed-since-2018-with-the-exception-of-china/.

7. Bonnie Glaser and Mathew Funaiole, "Poll Shows Increase in American Support for Defending Taiwan," *The Diplomat*, October 23, 2020, accessed April 24, 2021, https://thediplomat.com/2020/10/poll-shows-increase-in-american -support-for-defending-taiwan/.

8. Barrass, "U.S. Competitive Strategy during the Cold War," 71–89.

9. Krepinevich and Watts, *The Last Warrior*, 130–34.

10. Krepinevich and Watts, 135–36.

11. Barrass, "U.S. Competitive Strategy during the Cold War," 71–89.

12. Krepinevich and Watts, *The Last Warrior*, 166–67.

13. Krepinevich and Watts, 149–51.

14. Barrass, "U.S. Competitive Strategy during the Cold War," 71–89.

15. "World Population Prospects 2019," UN Department of Economic and Social Affairs, China tab, accessed June 9, 2021, https://population.un.org/wpp /DataQuery/.

16. "World Population Prospects 2019."

17. Feenstra, Inklaar, and Timmer, "The Next Generation of the Penn World Table."

18. Amanda Lee, "China Debt: How Big Is It and Who Owns It?," Reuters, May 19, 2020, accessed April 23, 2021, https://www.scmp.com/economy/china-economy /article/3084979/china-debt-how-big-it-who-owns-it-and-what-next.

19. Lingling Wei, "China's Economic Recovery Belies a Lingering Productivity Challenge," *Wall Street Journal*, January 17, 2021, accessed June 22, 2021, https://www .wsj.com/articles/chinas-economic-recovery-belies-a-lingering-productivity -challenge-11610884800?mod=hp_lista_pos2.

20. Liyan Qi, "China's Census Highlights Its Looming Population Problem," *Wall Street Journal*, May 11, 2021, accessed May 15, 2021, https://www.wsj.com/articles /china-says-its-population-rose-slightly-in-2020-11620698964?mod=article _inline.

21. See also Walter Russell Mead, "Strengthen Asia to Weaken Beijing," *Wall Street Journal*, May 10, 2021, accessed May 15, 2021, https://www.wsj.com/articles /strengthen-asia-to-weaken-beijing-11620684893?mod=opinion_lead_pos10.

22. "Advantage at Sea," 4.

23. Chui-Wei Yap, "China's Fishing Fleet, the World's Largest, Drives Beijing's Global Ambitions," *Wall Street Journal*, April 21, 2021, accessed April 26, 2021, https://www.wsj.com/articles/chinas-fishing-fleet-the-worlds-largest -drives-beijings-global-ambitions-11619015507?mod=searchresults_pos1 &page=1.

24. Tirpak, "First of 17 B-1Bs Heads to the Boneyard."

25. "Advantage at Sea," 4.

26. Robert Haddick, "Competitive Mobilization: How Would We Fare against China?," War on the Rocks, March 15, 2016, accessed April 26, 2021, https:// warontherocks.com/2016/03/competitive-mobilization-how-would-we -fare-against-china/.

27. Office of the Director of National Intelligence, "Annual Threat Assessment of the U.S. Intelligence Community," April 9, 2021, 8, accessed April 26, 2021, https:// www.dni.gov/files/ODNI/documents/assessments/ATA-2021-Unclassified -Report.pdf.

28. Gompert, Cevallos, and Garafola, "War with China," 48.

29. Blainey, *The Causes of War*, 122–23.

30. Dan Reiter, *How Wars End* (Princeton: Princeton University Press, 2009), 220–22.

31. Lonnie Henley, "PLA Operational Concepts and Centers of Gravity in a Taiwan Conflict," testimony before the U.S.-China Economic and Security Review Commission, February 18, 2021, accessed June 22, 2021, https://www.uscc.gov /sites/default/files/2021–02/Lonnie_Henley_Testimony.pdf.

32. Gunzinger, Autenried, and Clark, "Understanding the Long-Range Strike Debate," 6. The calculation assumes thirty B-21 sorties per day with each aircraft carrying fifty precision-guided weapons.

33. Lewis, "National Security Spending and Budget Trends since World War II," 88.

34. Lewis, 139.

35. Krepinevich and Watts, *The Last Warrior*, 131–36.

36. Barrass, "U.S. Competitive Strategy during the Cold War," 71–89.

SELECTED BIBLIOGRAPHY

Air Force Technology. "Miniature Air Launched Decoy (MALD) Flight Vehicle." Accessed March 28, 2021, https://www.airforce-technology.com/projects/miniature-air-launched-decoy-mald-flight-vehicle/.

Allison, Graham, and Philip Zelikow. *Essence of Decision: Explaining the Cuban Missile Crisis*. New York: Addison-Wesley, 1999.

Angell, Norman. *The Great Illusion: A Study of the Relation of Military Power to National Advantage*. 1901. Reprint, New York: Cosimo, 2007.

Arms Control Association. "Arms Control and Proliferation Profile: India." Accessed January 21, 2021, https://www.armscontrol.org/factsheets/indiaprofile.

Atkinson, Rick. *Crusade: The Untold Story of the Persian Gulf War*. Boston: Houghton Mifflin, 1993.

Aviation Week Network. "USAF Unit Moves Reveal Clues to RQ-180 Ops Debut." October 24, 2019. Accessed March 24, 2021, https://aviationweek.com/defense-space/usaf-unit-moves-reveal-clues-rq-180-ops-debut.

Barrass, Gordon S. *The Great Cold War: A Journey through the Hall of Mirrors*. Palo Alto, CA: Stanford University Press, 2009.

———. "U.S. Competitive Strategy during the Cold War." In *Competitive Strategies for the 21st Century*, ed. Thomas G. Mahnken, 71–89. Stanford, CA: Stanford Security Studies, 2012.

Barrett, Mark, and Mace Carpenter. "Survivability in the Digital Age: The Imperative for Stealth." Mitchell Institute for Aerospace Studies, July 2017. Accessed March 21, 2021, http://docs.wixstatic.com/ugd/a2dd91_cd5494417b644d1fa7d7aacb9295324d.pdf.

Beinart, Peter. "Biden's Taiwan Policy Is Truly, Deeply Reckless." *New York Times*, May 5, 2021. Accessed June 11, 2021, https://www.nytimes.com/2021/05/05/opinion/biden-taiwan-china.html.

Bender, Bryan. "Chief of US Pacific Forces Calls Climate Biggest Worry." *Boston Globe*, March 9, 2013. Accessed February 1, 2021, https://www.bostonglobe.com/news/nation/2013/03/09/admiral-samuel-locklear-commander-pacific-forces-warns-that-climate-change-top-threat/BHdPVCLrWEMxRe9IXJZcHL/story.html.

Berger, David. "Commandant's Planning Guidance: 38th Commandant of the Marine Corps." Headquarters, U.S. Marine Corps, July 17, 2019. Accessed February 25, 2021, https://www.marines.mil/Portals/1/Publications/Commandant's%20Planning%20Guidance_2019.pdf?ver=2019-07-17-090732-937.

———. "Force Design 2030." Headquarters, U.S. Marine Corps, March 2020. Accessed February 25, 2021, https://www.hqmc.marines.mil/Portals/142/Docs/CMC38%20Force%20Design%202030%20Report%20Phase%20I%20and%20II.pdf?ver=2020-03-26-121328-460.

Biden, Joseph. "Interim National Security Strategic Guidance." The White House, Washington, DC, March 2021. Accessed April 11, 2021, https://www.whitehouse.gov/wp-content/uploads/2021/03/NSC-1v2.pdf.

Blackwill, Robert, and Philip Zelikow. "The United States, China, and Taiwan: A Strategy to Prevent War." Council on Foreign Relations, February 2021. Accessed March 15, 2021, https://cdn.cfr.org/sites/default/files/report_pdf/csr90_1.pdf.

Blainey, Geoffrey. *The Causes of War*. New York: Free Press, 1973.

Blanchette, Jude. "Beijing's Visions of American Decline." *Politico* China Watcher, March 11, 2021. Accessed May 5, 2021, https://www.politico.com/newsletters/politico-china-watcher/2021/03/11/beijings-visions-of-american-decline-492064.

Blumenthal, Dan, and Phillip Swagel. *An Awkward Embrace: The United States and China in the 21st Century*. Washington, DC: AEI Press, 2012.

Bosco, Joseph. "Entrapment and Abandonment in Asia." *National Interest*, July 8, 2013. Accessed May 15, 2021, https://nationalinterest.org/commentary/entrapment-abandonment-asia-8697.

Bowie, Christopher J. "The Lessons of Salty Demo." *Air Force* magazine, March 2009. Accessed May 9, 2021, https://www.airforcemag.com/article/0309salty/.

Brands, Hal. "Regime Realism and Chinese Grand Strategy." American Enterprise Institute, November 2020. Accessed January 13, 2021, https://www.aei.org/wp-content/uploads/2020/11/Regime-Realism-and-Chinese-Grand-Strategy.pdf.

Buchan, Patrick Gerard, and Benjamin Rimland. "Defining the Diamond: The Past, Present, and Future of the Quadrilateral Security Dialogue." Center for

Strategic and International Studies, March 16, 2020. Accessed February 14, 2021, https://www.csis.org/analysis/defining-diamond-past-present-and-future-quadrilateral-security-dialogue.

Buckley, Chris. "China Takes Aim at Western Ideas." *New York Times*, August 19, 2013. Accessed June 6, 2021, https://www.nytimes.com/2013/08/20/world/asia/chinas-new-leadership-takes-hard-line-in-secret-memo.html.

Bush, George W. *Decision Points*. New York: Crown Publishers, 2010.

Buss, David H., William F. Moran, and Thomas J. Moore. "Why America Still Needs Aircraft Carriers." *Foreign Policy*, April 26, 2013. Accessed May 6, 2021, https://foreignpolicy.com/2013/04/26/why-america-still-needs-aircraft-carriers/.

Campbell, Kurt. "Threats to Peace Are Lurking in the East China Sea." *Financial Times*, June 25, 2013. Accessed April 26, 2021, https://www.ft.com/content/b924cc56-dda1-11e2-a756-00144feab7de#axzz2ZtGart72.

Campbell, Kurt M., and Rush Doshi. "How America Can Shore Up Asian Order." *Foreign Affairs*, January 12, 2021. Accessed January 18, 2021, https://www.foreignaffairs.com/articles/united-states/2021-01-12/how-america-can-shore-asian-order.

Campbell, Kurt, and Jake Sullivan. "Competition without Catastrophe: How America Can Both Challenge and Coexist with China." *Foreign Affairs*, September/October 2019. Accessed April 27, 2021, https://www.foreignaffairs.com/articles/china/competition-with-china-without-catastrophe.

Chin, Josh. "China Spends More on Domestic Security as Xi's Powers Grow." *Wall Street Journal*, March 6, 2018. Accessed January 13, 2021, https://www.wsj.com/articles/china-spends-more-on-domestic-security-as-xis-powers-grow-1520358522.

China Power Team. "How Much Trade Transits the South China Sea?" *China Power*, August 2, 2017; updated August 26, 2020. Accessed January 15, 2021. https://chinapower.csis.org/much-trade-transits-south-china-sea/.

Cliff, Roger. *China's Military Power*. New York: Cambridge University Press, 2015.

Clinton, Bill. *My Life*. New York: Alfred A. Knopf, 2004.

Cohen, Eliot. *The Big Stick: The Limits of Soft Power and the Necessity of Military Force*. New York: Basic Books, 2016.

Cohen, Eliot, and John Gooch. *Military Misfortunes: The Anatomy of Failure in War*. New York: Free Press, 1990.

Collins, Gabriel B., and William S. Murray. "No Oil for the Lamps of China?" *Naval War College Review* 61, no. 2 (2008): 79–95.

Congressional Budget Office. "An Analysis of the Navy's Fiscal Year 2022 Shipbuilding Plan." September 2021. Accessed October 29, 2021, https://www.cbo.gov/system/files/2021-09/57414-Shipbuilding_1.pdf.

Coté, Owen R., Jr. "Assessing the Undersea Balance between the United States and China." In *Competitive Strategies for the 21st Century*, ed. Thomas G. Mahnken, 184–205. Stanford, CA: Stanford Security Studies, 2012.

Deal, Jacqueline. "China Could Soon Outgun the U.S." *Politico* China Watcher, May 27, 2021. Accessed May 27, 2021, https://www.politico.com/newsletters /politico-china-watcher/2021/05/27/china-could-soon-outgun-the-us-493014.

Deng, Chao. "China Razed Thousands of Xinjiang Mosques in Assimilation Push, Report Says." *Wall Street Journal*, September 25, 2020. Accessed January 17, 2021, https://www.wsj.com/articles/china-razed-thousands-of-xinjiang -mosques-in-assimilation-push-report-says-11601049531?mod=searchresults _pos10&page=3.

Denyer, Simon, and Eva Dou. "Biden Vows to Defend U.S. Allies as China Asserts Power in Asia." *Washington Post*, November 12, 2020. Accessed January 15, 2021, https://www.washingtonpost.com/world/asia_pacific/biden-china-japan -korea-allies/2020/11/12/6cf6e212-24af-11eb-9c4a-0dc6242c4814_story.html.

Deptula, David. "Bombers for Maritime Strike: An Asymmetric Counter to China's Navy." Mitchell Institute for Aerospace Studies, February 2019. Accessed March 19, 2021, http://docs.wixstatic.com/ugd/a2dd91_546d5ed9b4424fd780887be1 146f9ac2.pdf.

Deptula, David, William LaPlante, and Robert Haddick. "Modernizing U.S. Nuclear Command, Control, and Communications." Mitchell Institute for Aerospace Studies, February 2019. Accessed March 23, 2021, http://docs.wixstatic .com/ugd/a2dd91_ed45cfd71de2457eba3bcce4d0657196.pdf

Dougherty, Christopher. "The Pentagon Needs a Plan to Get Punched in the Mouth." C4ISR Net, May 20, 2021. Accessed October 28, 2021, https://www .c4isrnet.com/thought-leadership/2021/05/20/the-pentagon-needs-a-plan-to -get-punched-in-the-mouth/.

Easton, Ian. *The Chinese Invasion Threat: Taiwan's Defense and American Strategy in Asia*. Manchester, UK: Eastbridge Books, 2019.

Ehrhard, Thomas P., and Robert O. Work. *Range, Persistence, Stealth, and Networking: The Case for a Carrier-Based Unmanned Combat Air System*. Center for Strategic and Budgetary Assessments, 2008. Accessed May 6, 2021, https://csbaonline.org/uploads/documents/The-Case-for-A-Carrier-Based -Unmanned-Combat-Air-System.pdf.

Erickson, Andrew S. "Are China's Near Seas 'Anti-Navy' Capabilities Aimed Directly at the United States?" *Information Dissemination*, June 14, 2012. Accessed May 9, 2021, http://www.informationdissemination.net/2012/06/are -chinas-near-seas-anti-navy.html.

————. "China's Modernization of Its Naval and Air Power Capabilities." In *Strategic Asia 2012–2013: China's Military Challenge*, ed. Ashley Tellis and Travis Tanner, 61–126. Washington DC: National Bureau of Asian Research, 2012.

Erickson, Andrew S., and Adam P. Liff. "China's Military Development, Beyond the Numbers." *The Diplomat*, March 12, 2013. Accessed May 8, 2021, https://thediplomat.com/2013/03/chinas-military-development-beyond-the-numbers/.

Everstine, Brian. "PACAF Surveyed Every 'Piece of Concrete' in the Pacific for Agile Combat Employment." *Air Force* magazine, November 25, 2020. Accessed February 23, 2021, https://www.airforcemag.com/pacaf-surveyed-every-piece-of-concrete-in-the-pacific-for-agile-combat-employment/.

Federation of American Scientists. "Low Cost Autonomous Attack System (LOCAAS) Miniature Munition Capability." November 29, 1999. Accessed May 13, 2021, https://fas.org/man/dod-101/sys/smart/locaas.htm.

————. "NSC 68: United States Objectives and Programs for National Security." April 7, 1950. Accessed May 12, 2021, https://fas.org/irp/offdocs/nsc-hst/nsc-68.htm.

Feenstra, Robert C., Robert Inklaar, and Marcel P. Timmer. "The Next Generation of the Penn World Table." *American Economic Review* 105, no. 10 (2015): 3150–82. Available for download at www.ggdc.net/pwt.

Fisher, Richard D., Jr. "Maritime Employment of PLA Unmanned Aerial Vehicles." In *Chinese Aerospace Power*, ed. Andrew S. Erickson and Lyle J. Goldstein, 108–29. Annapolis, MD: Naval Institute Press, 2011.

FitzSimonds, James R. "Cultural Barriers to Implementing a Competitive Strategy." In *Competitive Strategies for the 21st Century*, ed. Thomas G. Mahnken, 289–300. Stanford, CA: Stanford Security Studies, 2012.

Flournoy, Michèle. "How to Prevent a War in Asia." *Foreign Affairs*, June 18, 2020. Accessed March 18, 2021, http://foreignaffairs.com/articles/united-states/2020-06-18/how-prevent-war-asia.

Fravel, M. Taylor. "Regime Insecurity and International Cooperation: Explaining China's Compromises in Territorial Disputes." *International Security* 30, no. 2 (2005): 46–83.

Freedberg, Sydney, Jr. "US 'Gets Its Ass Handed to It' in Wargames: Here's a $24 Billion Fix." Breaking Defense, March 7, 2019. Accessed March 18, 2021, http://breakingdefense.com/2019/03/us-gets-its-ass-handed-to-it-in-wargames-heres-a-24-billion-fix.

Freedman, Lawrence. *Deterrence*. Cambridge, UK: Polity Press, 2004.

Friedberg, Aaron L. *A Contest for Supremacy: China, America, and the Struggle for Mastery in Asia*. New York: W. W. Norton, 2011.

Fromkin, David. *Europe's Last Summer: Who Started the Great War in 1914?* New York: Alfred A. Knopf, 2004.

Fournier, Vincent. "Surveying Safeguarded Material 24/7." International Atomic Energy Agency, September 12, 2016. Accessed January 19, 2021, https://www.iaea.org/newscenter/news/surveying-safeguarded-material-24/7.

Gale, Alastair, and Chieko Tsuneoka. "As China-Taiwan Tensions Rise, Japan Begins Preparing for Possible Conflict." *Wall Street Journal*, August 27, 2021. Accessed October 13, 2021, https://www.wsj.com/articles/as-china-taiwan-tensions-rise-japan-begins-preparing-for-possible-conflict-11630067601?mod=world_major_1_pos1.

Garnaut, John. "Xi's War Drums." *Foreign Policy*, May–June 2013. Accessed May 5, 2021, https://foreignpolicy.com/2013/04/29/xis-war-drums/.

Gates, Robert. *Duty*. New York: Alfred A. Knopf, 2014.

Gershaneck, Kerry K. *Political Warfare: Strategies for Combating China's Plan to "Win without Fighting."* Quantico, VA: Marine Corps University Press, 2020.

Gertler, Jeremiah. "Defense Primer: United States Airpower." Congressional Research Service, December 15, 2020. Accessed January 26, 2021, https://crsreports.congress.gov/product/pdf/IF/IF10546.

Glaser, Bonnie, and Mathew Funaiole. "Poll Shows Increase in American Support for Defending Taiwan." *The Diplomat*, October 23, 2020. Accessed April 24, 2021, https://thediplomat.com/2020/10/poll-shows-increase-in-american-support-for-defending-taiwan/.

Gompert, David C. "Sea Power and American Interests in the Western Pacific." RAND Corporation, 2013. Accessed April 5, 2021, https://www.rand.org/pubs/research_reports/RR151.html#abstract.

Gompert, David C., Astrid Stuth Cevallos, and Cristina L. Garafola. "War with China: Thinking Through the Unthinkable." RAND Corporation, 2016. Accessed May 27, 2021, https://www.rand.org/pubs/research_reports/RR1140.html.

Gons, Eric Stephen. "Access Challenges and Implications for Airpower in the Western Pacific." PhD diss., Pardee RAND Graduate School, 2011.

Gordon, Michael R., and James Marson. "NATO Should Expand Its Focus to Include China, Report Says." *Wall Street Journal*, December 1, 2020. Accessed January 18, 2021, https://www.wsj.com/articles/nato-should-expand-its-focus-to-include-china-report-says-11606820403?mod=lead_feature_below_a_pos1.

Greer, Tanner. "Taiwan Can Win a War with China." *Foreign Policy*, September 25, 2018. Accessed March 17, 2021, https://foreignpolicy.com/2018/09/25/taiwan-can-win-a-war-with-china/.

Gunzinger, Mark. "Long-Range Strike: Resetting the Balance of Stand-in and Stand-off Forces." Mitchell Institute for Aerospace Studies, June 2020. Accessed February 21, 2021, https://a2dd917a-65ab-41f1-ab11–5f1897e16299.usrfiles.com /ugd/a2dd91_4f2e5df4b4b2464ca6d50d0dcd9ea04f.pdf.

Gunzinger, Mark, Lukas Autenried, and Bryan Clark. "Understanding the Long-Range Strike Debate." Mitchell Institute for Aerospace Studies, April 2021. Accessed May 11, 2021, https://a2dd917a-65ab-41f1-ab11–5f1897e16299.usrfiles .com/ugd/a2dd91_584d2a721b0f44babobf7d25986ea40d.pdf.

Haddick, Robert. "Competitive Mobilization: How Would We Fare against China?" War on the Rocks, March 15, 2016. Accessed April 26, 2021, https://warontherocks .com/2016/03/competitive-mobilization-how-would-we-fare-against-china/.

———. "Stopping Mobile Missiles: Top Picks for Offset Strategy." Breaking Defense, January 23, 2015. Accessed March 28, 2021, https://breakingdefense.com/2015/01 /stopping-mobile-missiles-top-picks-for-offset-strategy/.

Hagen, Jeff. "The U.S. Air Force and the Chinese Aerospace Challenge." In *Chinese Aerospace Power*, ed. Andrew S. Erickson and Lyle J. Goldstein, 466–76. Annapolis, MD: Naval Institute Press, 2011.

Hagt, Eric. "Integrating China's New Aerospace Power in the Maritime Realm." In *Chinese Aerospace Power*, ed. Andrew S. Erickson and Lyle J. Goldstein, 377–406. Annapolis, MD: Naval Institute Press, 2011.

Hamilton, Thomas. "Comparing the Cost of Penetrating Bombers to Expendable Missiles over Thirty Years." RAND Corporation, 2011. Accessed May 17, 2021, https://www.rand.org/pubs/working_papers/WR778.html.

Hand, Marcus. "Malacca Strait Transits Grow 2% to Record in 2015, Boxships See Dip in H2." *Seatrade Maritime News*, March 7, 2016. Accessed February 19, 2021, https:// www.seatrade-maritime.com/asia/malacca-strait-transits-grow-2-record-2015 -boxships-see-dip-h2.

Harrison, Todd, Kaitlyn Johnson, and Makena Young. "Defense against the Dark Arts in Space: Protecting Space Systems from Counterspace Weapons." Center for Strategic and International Studies, February 25, 2021. Accessed March 23, 2021, https://www.csis.org/analysis/defense-against-dark-arts-space-protecting -space-systems-counterspace-weapons.

Hastings, Max. "America Is Headed to a Showdown over Taiwan, and China Might Win." *Bloomberg*, March 14, 2021. Accessed March 17, 2021, https://www .bloomberg.com/opinion/articles/2021–03–14/max-hastings-china-might -defeat-america-in-war-over-taiwan.

Hastings, Max, and Simon Jenkins. *The Battle for the Falklands*. New York: W. W. Norton, 1983.

Hattendorf, John B. *The Evolution of the U.S. Navy's Maritime Strategy, 1977–1986*. Newport, RI: Naval War College Press, 2004.

Henley, Lonnie. "PLA Operational Concepts and Centers of Gravity in a Taiwan Conflict." Testimony before the U.S.-China Economic and Security Review Commission, February 18, 2021. Accessed June 22, 2021, https://www.uscc .gov/sites/default/files/2021–02/Lonnie_Henley_Testimony.pdf.

Hlad, Jennifer, and Amy McCullough. "ACE-ing the Test." *Air Force* magazine, May 1, 2020. Accessed February 23, 2021, https://www.airforcemag.com/article /ace-ing-the-test/.

Hoehn, John. "Joint All-Domain Command and Control (JADC2)." Congressional Research Service, December 9, 2020. Accessed March 1, 2021, https://crsreports .congress.gov/product/pdf/IF/IF11493.

Hoehn, John, and Samuel Ryder. "Precision-Guided Munitions: Background and Issues for Congress." Congressional Research Service, June 26, 2020. Accessed February 22, 2021, https://crsreports.congress.gov/product/pdf/R/R45996.

Hughes, Wayne P., Jr. *The New Navy Fighting Machine: A Study of the Connections between Contemporary Policy, Strategy, Sea Power, Naval Operations, and the Composition of the United States Fleet*. Monterey, CA: Naval Postgraduate School, 2009.

Ikenberry, G. John. "The Rise of China and the Future of the West." *Foreign Affairs*, January–February 2008. Accessed October 27, 2021, https://www.foreignaffairs .com/articles/asia/2008–01–01/rise-china-and-future-west.

International Institute for Strategic Studies. *The Military Balance: 2018*. London: Routledge, 2018.

———. *The Military Balance: 2021*. London: Routledge, 2021.

Japan Aerospace Exploration Agency. "H-11A Launch Vehicle." Accessed January 20, 2021, https://global.jaxa.jp/activity/pr/brochure/files/rocket01.pdf.

———. *JAXA History*. Accessed January 20, 2021, https://global.jaxa.jp/about/history /index.html.

Joint Army-Navy Assessment Committee. "Japanese Naval and Merchant Shipping Losses during World War II by All Causes." U.S. Navy History and Heritage Command, February 1947. Accessed March 19, 2021, https://www.history.navy .mil/research/library/online-reading-room/title-list-alphabetically/j/japanese -naval-merchant-shipping-losses-wwii.html.

Johnson, Paul. *Modern Times*. New York: HarperCollins, 1991.

Jones, Andrew. "Chinese Partnership to Create Tianxian SAR Satellite Constellation." *Space News*, October 8, 2021. Accessed October 20, 2021, https://spacenews .com/chinese-partnership-to-create-tianxian-sar-satellite-constellation/.

Kazianis, Harry. "Air-Sea Battle's Next Step: JAM-GC on Deck." *National Interest*, November 25, 2015. Accessed February 17, 2021, https://nationalinterest.org /feature/air-sea-battles-next-step-jam-gc-deck-14440.

Keaney, Thomas A., and Eliot A. Cohen. *Gulf War Air Power Survey Summary Report*. Washington, DC: U.S. Air Force, 1993. Accessed May 7, 2021, https://media .defense.gov/2010/Sep/27/2001329801/-1/-1/0/gulf_war_air_power_survey -summary.pdf.

Kelly, Tim. "Japan Sets Record $52 Billion Military Budget with Stealth Jets, Long-Range Missiles." Reuters, December 20, 2020. Accessed January 18, 2021, https:// www.reuters.com/article/japan-defence-budget/japan-sets-record-52-billion -military-budget-with-stealth-jets-long-range-missiles-idUSKBN28V03X.

Kennedy, Paul. *The Rise and Fall of the Great Powers*. New York: Random House, 1987.

Khan, Natasha. "Hong Kong Police Arrest 53 Opposition Figures over Alleged Subversion." *Wall Street Journal*, January 6, 2021. Accessed January 17, 2021, https://www.wsj.com/articles/hong-kong-police-arrest-dozens-of-opposition -politicians-over-alleged-subversion-11609895177?mod=searchresults_pos12 &page=1.

Kissinger, Henry. *Diplomacy*. New York: Simon and Shuster, 1994.

———. *On China*. New York: Penguin Press, 2011.

Knox, MacGregor, and Williamson Murry, eds. *The Dynamics of Military Revolution, 1300–2050*. Cambridge, UK: Cambridge University Press, 2001, 175–94.

Krepinevich, Andrew, and Barry Watts. *The Last Warrior*. New York: Basic Books, 2015.

LaGrone, Sam. "New Age in Carrier Aviation Takes Off with X-47B Landing." U.S. Naval Institute News, July 10, 2013. Accessed May 10, 2021, https://news .usni.org/2013/07/10/new-carrier-age-in-carrier-aviation-takes-off-with -x-47b-landing.

Lambert, Benjamin S. *NATO's Air War for Kosovo: A Strategic and Operational Assessment*. Santa Monica, CA: RAND Corporation, 2001. Accessed May 12, 2021, https://www.rand.org/pubs/monograph_reports/MR1365.html.

Layne, Christopher. *The Peace of Illusions: American Grand Strategy from 1940 to the Present*. Ithaca, NY: Cornell University Press, 2007.

Lee, Amanda. "China Debt: How Big Is It and Who Owns It?" Reuters, May 19, 2020. Accessed April 23, 2021, https://www.scmp.com/economy/china-economy /article/3084979/china-debt-how-big-it-who-owns-it-and-what-next.

Lee His-min and Eric Lee. "Taiwan's Overall Defense Concept, Explained." *The Diplomat*, November 3, 2020. Accessed March 17, 2021, https://thediplomat .com/2020/11/taiwans-overall-defense-concept-explained/.

Lee, John. "Lonely Power, Staying Power: The Rise of China and the Resilience of US Pre-eminence." Hudson Institute, October 11, 2011. Accessed May 5, 2021, https://www.hudson.org/content/researchattachments/attachment/938/the_rise_of_china_and_the_resilience_of_us_preeminence.pdf.

Lee, Michelle Ye Hee. "More than Ever, South Koreans Want Their Own Nuclear Weapons." *Washington Post*, September 13, 2017. Accessed January 21, 2021, https://www.washingtonpost.com/news/worldviews/wp/2017/09/13/most-south-koreans-dont-think-the-north-will-start-a-war-but-they-still-want-their-own-nuclear-weapons/.

Lewis, Kevin. "National Security Spending and Budget Trends since World War II." RAND Corporation, June 1990. Accessed April 29, 2021, https://apps.dtic.mil/dtic/tr/fulltext/u2/a238854.pdf.

Lockheed Martin Corporation. "JASSM-ER Fact Sheet." Accessed February 22, 2021, https://www.lockheedmartin.com/content/dam/lockheed-martin/mfc/pc/jassm/mfc-jassm-er-pc.pdf.

———. "Long Range Anti-Ship Missile Fact Sheet." Accessed February 22, 2021, https://www.lockheedmartin.com/content/dam/lockheed-martin/mfc/pc/long-range-anti-ship-missile/mfc-lrasm-pc-01.pdf.

Logan, Justin. "China, America, and the Pivot to Asia." CATO Institute, Policy Analysis no. 71, January 8, 2013. Accessed May 5, 2021, https://www.cato.org/policy-analysis/china-america-pivot-asia.

Lopez, C. Todd. "U.S. Withdraws from Intermediate-Range Nuclear Forces Treaty." U.S. Department of Defense news release, August 2, 2019. Accessed January 28, 2021, https://www.defense.gov/Explore/News/Article/Article/1924779/us-withdraws-from-intermediate-range-nuclear-forces-treaty/.

Luttwak, Edward N. *The Rise of China vs. the Logic of Strategy.* Cambridge, MA: Belknap Press of Harvard University Press, 2012.

Macmillan, Jade, and Andrew Greene. "Australia to Spend $270B Building Larger Military to Prepare for 'Poorer, More Dangerous' World and Rise of China." Australian Broadcast Corporation, July 1, 2020. Accessed January 18, 2021, https://www.abc.net.au/news/2020–06–30/australia-unveils-10-year-defence-strategy/12408232.

Mahnken, Thomas. "Cost-Imposing Strategies: A Brief Primer." Center for a New American Security, November 2014. Accessed April 9, 2021, https://s3.us-east-1.amazonaws.com/files.cnas.org/documents/CNAS_Maritime4_Mahnken.pdf?mtime=20160906081628&focal=none.

Marolda, Edward J. *Ready Seapower: A History of the U.S. Seventh Fleet.* Washington DC: Department of the Navy, Naval History and Heritage Command,

2012. Accessed May 6, 2021, https://www.history.navy.mil/content/dam/nhhc /research/publications/Publication-PDF/ReadySeapower.pdf.

McCabe, Thomas R. "Air and Space Power with Chinese Characteristics: China's Military Revolution." *Air and Space Power Journal* 34, no. 1 (spring 2020). Accessed February 9, 2021, https://www.airuniversity.af.edu/Portals/10/ASPJ/journals /Volume-34_Issue-1/F-McCabe.pdf.

McGrath, Bryan G., and Timothy A. Walton. "The Time for Lasers Is Now." U.S. Naval Institute *Proceedings*, April 2013. Accessed May 7, 2021, https://www .usni.org/magazines/proceedings/2013/april/time-lasers-now.

McLeary, Paul. "Congress Applauds VP Pence's Surprise Nixing of *Truman* Retirement." Breaking Defense, April 30, 2019. Accessed February 24, 2021, https://breakingdefense.com/2019/04/vp-pences-surprise-nixing-of-truman -retirement-navy-modernization/.

Mead, Walter Russell. "Strengthen Asia to Weaken Beijing." *Wall Street Journal*, May 10, 2021. Accessed May 15, 2021, https://www.wsj.com/articles /strengthen-asia-to-weaken-beijing-11620684893?mod=opinion_lead_pos10.

Mearsheimer, John J. "China's Unpeaceful Rise." *Current History*, April 2006, 160–62.

———. *The Tragedy of Great Power Politics.* New York: W. W. Norton, 2001.

Miller, Amanda. "SDA Outlines Missile Tracking Satellite Plan." *Air Force* magazine, April 16, 2021. Accessed May 21, 2021, https://www.airforcemag.com/sda -outlines-missile-tracking-satellite-plan/.

Miller, Edward S. *War Plan Orange: The U.S. Strategy to Defeat Japan, 1897–1945.* Annapolis, MD: Naval Institute Press, 1991.

Missile Defense Project. "Missiles of India." *Missile Threat,* Center for Strategic and International Studies, October 29, 2020. Accessed January 21, 2021, https:// missilethreat.csis.org/country/india/.

———. "Missiles of South Korea." *Missile Threat*, Center for Strategic and International Studies, July 30, 2020. Accessed January 21, 2021, https://missilethreat .csis.org/country/south-korea/.

———. "Missiles of Taiwan." *Missile Threat*, Center for Strategic and International Studies, July 16, 2020. Accessed January 21, 2021, https://missilethreat.csis.org /country/taiwan/.

Mizokami, Kyle. "The Navy Needs a Way to Reload Missile Silos at Sea." *Popular Mechanics*, July 6, 2017. Accessed January 28, 2021, https://www. popularmechanics.com/military/navy-ships/a27205/navy-reload-missile -silos-at-sea/.

Moncus, J. J., and Laura Silver. "Americans' Views of Asia-Pacific Nations Have Not Changed since 2018—with the Exception of China." Pew Research Center, April 12, 2021. Accessed April 21, 2021, https://www.pewresearch.org/fact-tank /2021/04/12/americans-views-of-asia-pacific-nations-have-not-changed-since -2018-with-the-exception-of-china/.

National Intelligence Council. *Global Trends 2030: Alternative Worlds*. Washington, DC: Office of the Director of National Intelligence, 2012. Accessed May 5, 2021, https://www.dni.gov/files/documents/GlobalTrends_2030.pdf.

———. *Global Trends 2040: A More Contested World*. Office of Director of National Intelligence, March 2021. Accessed May 12, 2021, https://www.dni.gov/index .php/global-trends-home.

National Museum of the U.S. Air Force. "General Dynamics F-111F." National Museum of the U.S. Air Force Fact Sheet. July 28, 2015. Accessed May 7, 2021, https://www.nationalmuseum.af.mil/Visit/Museum-Exhibits/Fact-Sheets /Display/Article/195859/general-dynamics-f-111f-aardvark/.

Neustadt, Richard, and Ernest R. May. *Thinking in Time: The Uses of History for Decision Makers*. New York: Macmillan USA, 1986.

Newmyer Deal, Jacqueline. "China's Approach to Strategy and Long-term Competition." In *Competitive Strategies for the 21st Century*, ed. Thomas G. Mahnken, 147–67. Stanford, CA: Stanford Security Studies, 2012.

———. "China's Nationalist Heritage." *National Interest*, January–February 2013. Accessed May 4, 2021, https://nationalinterest.org/article/chinas-nationalist -heritage-7885.

North Atlantic Treaty Organization. "Brussels Summit Communiqué." Press release, June 14, 2021. Accessed June 22, 2021, https://www.nato.int/cps/en/natohq/news _185000.htm?selectedLocale=en.

Office of the Director of National Intelligence. "Annual Threat Assessment of the U.S. Intelligence Community," April 9, 2021. Accessed April 26, 2021, https:// www.dni.gov/files/ODNI/documents/assessments/ATA-2021-Unclassified -Report.pdf.

Office of the U.S. Secretary of Defense. *Summary of the 2018 National Defense Strategy of the United States of American: Sharpening the American Military's Competitive Edge*, January 19, 2018. Accessed February 20, 2021, https://dod.defense .gov/Portals/1/Documents/pubs/2018-National-Defense-Strategy-Summary .pdf.

O'Rourke, Ronald. "China Naval Modernization: Implications for U.S. Navy Capabilities—Background and Issues for Congress." Congressional Research

Service, March 9, 2021. Accessed May 4, 2021, https://crsreports.congress.gov /product/pdf/RL/RL33153.

———. "Navy Constellation (FFG-62) Class Frigate (Previously FFG[X]) Program: Background and Issues for Congress." Congressional Research Service, February 11, 2021. Accessed April 10, 2021, https://crsreports.congress.gov/product /pdf/R/R44972.

———. "Navy Force Structure and Shipbuilding Plans: Background and Issues for Congress." Congressional Research Service, January 26, 2021. Accessed February 24, 2021, https://crsreports.congress.gov/product/pdf/RL/RL32665.

———. "Navy Large Unmanned Surface and Undersea Vehicles: Background and Issues for Congress." Congressional Research Service, March 25, 2021. Accessed April 7, 2021, https://crsreports.congress.gov/product/pdf/R/R45757.

———. "Navy Lasers, Railgun, and Gun-Launched Guided Projectile: Background and Issues for Congress." Congressional Research Service, January 12, 2021, accessed February 17, 2021, https://crsreports.congress.gov/product/pdf/R /R44175.

———. "Precision-Guided Munitions: Background and Issues for Congress." Congressional Research Service, June 26, 2020. Accessed April 3, 2021, https:// crsreports.congress.gov/product/pdf/R/R45996.

Page, Jeremy. "How the U.S. Misread China's Xi: Hoping for a Globalist, It Got an Autocrat." *Wall Street Journal*, December 23, 2020. Accessed January 18, 2021, https://www.wsj.com/articles/xi-jinping-globalist-autocrat-misread -11608735769?mod=hp_lead_pos10.

People's Republic of China, State Council. "China's National Defense in the New Era." Xinhua, July 2019. Accessed January 16, 2021, http://english.www.gov .cn/archive/whitepaper/201907/24/content_WS5d3941ddc6d08408f502283d .html.

Pettyjohn, Stacie L. *U.S. Global Defense Posture, 1783–2011.* Santa Monica, CA: RAND Corporation, 2012. Accessed May 6, 2021, https://www.rand.org/pubs /monographs/MG1244.html.

Pew Research Center. *U.S. Public, Experts Differ on China Policies.* September 18, 2012. Accessed April 21, 2021, https://www.pewresearch.org /global/2012/09/18/u-s-public-experts-differ-on-china-policies/.

Pierson, David. "Military Spending Is Soaring in the Asia-Pacific Region. Here's Why." *Los Angeles Times*, June 7, 2019. Accessed January 23, 2021, https://www .latimes.com/world/asia/la-fg-asia-defense-industry-20190607-story.html.

Pillsbury, Michael. *The Hundred-Year Marathon: China's Secret Strategy to Replace America as the Global Superpower.* New York: Henry Holt, 2015.

———. "The Sixteen Fears: China's Strategic Psychology." *Survival: Global Politics and Strategy* 54, no. 5 (October–November 2012): 149–82.

PlanetLabs. "Our Constellation." Accessed March 24, 2021, https://storage.googleapis.com/planet-ditl/day-in-the-life/index.html.

Poling, Gregory B. "The Conventional Wisdom on China's Island Bases Is Dangerously Wrong." War on the Rocks, January 10, 2020. Accessed February 13, 2021, https://warontherocks.com/2020/01/the-conventional-wisdom-on-chinas-island-bases-is-dangerously-wrong/.

Posen, Barry R. "Pull Back: The Case for a Less Activist Foreign Policy." *Foreign Affairs*, January–February 2013. Accessed May 5, 2021, https://www.foreignaffairs.com/articles/united-states/2013-01-01/pull-back?page=show.

Pournelle, Phillip E. "The Rise of the Missile Carriers." U.S. Naval Institute *Proceedings*, May 2013. Accessed April 4, 2021, https://www.usni.org/magazines/proceedings/2013/may/rise-missile-carriers.

Pradun, Vitaliy O. "From Bottle Rockets to Lightning Bolts: China's Missile Revolution and PLA Strategy against U.S. Military Intervention." *Naval War College Review* 64, no. 2 (2011): 7–39.

Qi, Liyan. "China's Census Highlights Its Looming Population Problem." *Wall Street Journal*, May 11, 2021. Accessed May 15, 2021, https://www.wsj.com/articles/china-says-its-population-rose-slightly-in-2020-11620698964?mod=article_inline.

Reim, Garrett. "USAF Aims to Double Long-Term JASSM Production up to 10,000 Units." FlightGlobal, September 27, 2019. Accessed February 22, 2021, https://www.flightglobal.com/fixed-wing/usaf-aims-to-double-long-term-jassm-production-up-to-10000-units/134510.article.

Reiter, Dan. *How Wars End*. Princeton: Princeton University Press, 2009.

Rice, Susan. "National Security Advisor Susan E. Rice's As Prepared Remarks on the U.S.-China Relationship at George Washington University." The White House, Office of the Press Secretary, September 21, 2015. Accessed February 2, 2021, https://obamawhitehouse.archives.gov/the-press-office/2015/09/21/national-security-advisor-susan-e-rices-prepared-remarks-us-china.

Ross, Dylan B., and Jimmy A. Harmon. "New Navy Fighting Machine in the South China Sea." Master's thesis, Naval Postgraduate School, Monterey, CA, 2012. Accessed May 9, 2021, https://apps.dtic.mil/dtic/tr/fulltext/u2/a563777.pdf.

Rubel, Robert C. "Cede No Water: Strategy, Littorals, and Flotillas." U.S. Naval Institute *Proceedings*, September 2013. Accessed April 5, 2021, https://www.usni.org/magazines/proceedings/2013/septembercede-no-water-strategy-littorals-and-flotillas.

Rudd, Kevin. "A Maritime Balkans of the 21st Century?" *Foreign Policy*, January 30, 2013. Accessed April 26, 2021, https://foreignpolicy.com/2013/01/30/a-maritime-balkans-of-the-21st-century/.

Ruehrmund, James C. Jr., and Christopher J. Bowie. "Arsenal of Airpower: USAF Aircraft Inventory 1950–2016." Mitchell Institute for Aerospace Studies, February 2018. Accessed January 26, 2021, https://www.mitchellaerospacepower.org/single-post/2018/02/22/Arsenal-of-Airpower-USAF-Aircraft-Inventory-1950–2016.

Rumelt, Richard. *Good Strategy/Bad Strategy: The Difference and Why It Matters.* New York: Crown Business, 2011.

"SAR Made Easy." Capella Space. Accessed March 24, 2021, https://www.capellaspace.com/.

Sayler, Kelley. "Hypersonic Weapons: Background and Issues for Congress." Congressional Research Service, December 1, 2020. Accessed March 1, 2021, https://crsreports.congress.gov/product/pdf/R/R45811.

Schelling, Thomas. *Arms and Influence*. New Haven: Yale University Press, 2008.

Schwartz, Norton A., and Jonathan W. Greenert. "Air-Sea Battle." *The American Interest*, February 20, 2012. Accessed May 10, 2021, https://www.the-american-interest.com/2012/02/20/air-sea-battle/.

Seligman, Lara, and Connor O'Brien. "Austin Wants to Pivot to China. But Can He Pay for It?" *Politico*, March 3, 2021. Accessed April 27, 2021, https://www.politico.com/news/2021/03/03/lloyd-austin-china-pentagon-473405.

Shelbourne, Mallory. "Davidson: China Could Try to Take Control of Taiwan in 'Next Six Years.'" *U.S. Naval Institute News*, March 9, 2021. Accessed April 26, 2021, https://news.usni.org/2021/03/09/davidson-china-could-try-to-take-control-of-taiwan-in-next-six-years?utm_source=USNI+News&utm_campaign=c90c40efa7-USNI_NEWS_DAILY&utm_medium=email&utm_term=0_0dd4a1450b-c90c40efa7-230370089&ct=t(USNI_NEWS_DAILY)&mc_cid=c90c40efa7&mc_eid=acace2ab92.

Silver, Laura, Kat Devlin, and Christine Huang. "Most Americans Support Tough Stance toward China on Human Rights, Economic Issues." Pew Research Center, March 4, 2021. Accessed April 21, 2021, https://www.pewresearch.org/global/2021/03/04/most-americans-support-tough-stance-toward-china-on-human-rights-economic-issues/.

———. "Unfavorable Views of China Reach Historic Highs in Many Countries." Pew Research Center, October 6, 2020. Accessed January 18, 2021, https://www.pewresearch.org/global/2020/10/06/unfavorable-views-of-china-reach-historic-highs-in-many-countries/.

Solomon, Jay. "Seoul Seeks Ability to Make Nuclear Fuel." *Wall Street Journal,* April 3, 2013. Accessed May 5, 2021, https://www.wsj.com/articles/SB1000142 412788732488360457839905394289 5628.

Solomon, Jay, and Miho Inada. "Japan's Nuclear Plan Unsettles U.S." *Wall Street Journal,* May 1, 2013. Accessed May 5, 2021, https://www.wsj.com/articles/SB1 000142412788732458200457845694386 7189804.

Solomon, Jonathan F. "Maritime Deception and Concealment: Concepts for Defeating Wide-Area Oceanic Surveillance-Reconnaissance-Strike Networks." *Naval War College Review* 66, no. 4 (2013): 87–116.

Space Exploration Technologies. "SpaceX Mission." Accessed March 24, 2021, https://www.spacex.com/mission/.

Steidl, Christian, Laurent Daniel, and Cenk Yildiran. "Shipbuilding Market Developments Q2 2018." Organization of Economic Cooperation and Development (OECD), May 15, 2018. Accessed February 25, 2021, http://www.oecd.org/sti /ind/shipbuilding-market-developments-Q2–2018.pdf.

Stockholm International Peace Research Institute. "SIPRI Military Expenditure Database." Accessed February 8, 2021, https://sipri.org/databases/milex.

Stokes, Mark, Gabriel Alvarado, Emily Weinstein, and Ian Easton. "China's Space and Counterspace Capabilities and Activities." U.S.-China Economic and Security Review Commission, March 30, 2020. Accessed February 10, 2021, https:// www.uscc.gov/sites/default/files/2020–05/China_Space_and_Counterspace _Activities.pdf.

Tirpak, John. "B-21 Temporary Shelters Could Also Shelter B-2s." *Air Force* magazine, March 5, 2021. Accessed March 21, 2021, https://www.airforcemag .com/b-21-temporary-shelters-could-also-shelter-b-2s/.

———. "First of 17 B-1Bs Heads to the Boneyard." *Air Force* magazine, February 17, 2021. Accessed February 21, 2021, https://www.airforcemag.com/first-of-17-b-1bs -heads-to-the-boneyard/.

———. "The Raider Comes out of the Black." *Air Force* magazine, February 19, 2021. Accessed March 21, 2021, https://www.airforcemag.com/article/the -raider-comes-out-of-the-black/.

———. "Schwartz, in Memoir, Says F-22 Was Traded for B-21 Bomber." *Air Force* magazine, April 26, 2018. Accessed February 21, 2021, https://www.airforcemag .com/schwartz-in-memoir-says-f-22-was-traded-for-b-21-bomber/.

United Nations Department of Economic and Social Affairs. "World Population Prospects 2019." China tab. Accessed April 23, 2021, https://population.un.org /wpp/Graphs/Probabilistic/POP/20–69/156.

U.S. Air Force. "F-15E Strike Eagle Fact Sheet." April 2019. Accessed May 7, 2021, https://www.af.mil/About-Us/Fact-Sheets/Display/Article/104499/f-15e-strike -eagle/.

———. "F-22 Raptor Fact Sheet." September 2015. Accessed May 7, 2021, https:// www.af.mil/About-Us/Fact-Sheets/Display/Article/104506/f-22-raptor/.

———. *A Report on Technology Horizons: A Vision for Air Force Science and Technology during 2010–2030*. Washington, DC: U.S. Air Force, 2011.

U.S. Central Intelligence Agency. *The World Factbook: China*. Economy tab. Accessed January 12, 2021, https://www.cia.gov/the-world-factbook/countries /china/#economy.

U.S.-China Economic and Security Review Commission. *The PRC in International Organizations*. April 20, 2020. Accessed January 17, 2021, https://www.uscc.gov /prc-international-orgs.

———. *2010 Report to Congress of the U.S.-China Economic and Security Review Commission*. November 2010. Accessed May 9, 2021, https://www.uscc.gov /sites/default/files/annual_reports/2010-Report-to-Congress.pdf.

———. *2011 Report to Congress of the U.S.-China Economic and Security Review Commission*. November 2011. Accessed May 9, 2021, https://www.uscc.gov /sites/default/files/annual_reports/annual_report_full_11.pdf.

———. *2012 Report to Congress of the U.S.-China Economic and Security Review Commission*. November 2012. Accessed May 9, 2021, https://www.uscc.gov /sites/default/files/annual_reports/2012-Report-to-Congress.pdf.

U.S. Department of Commerce, Bureau of Economic Analysis. *China—Oil and Gas*. Export.gov. July 30, 2019. Accessed January 13, 2021, https://www.export .gov/apex/article2?id=China-Oil-and-Gas.

———. *Gross Domestic Product*. Accessed January 15, 2021, https://www.bea.gov /data/gdp/gross-domestic-product.

———. *International Trade in Goods and Services*. Accessed January 15, 2021, https://www.bea.gov/data/intl-trade-investment/international-trade-goods -and-services.

U.S. Department of Defense. *Annual Report to Congress: Military and Security Developments Involving the People's Republic of China 2011*. Accessed May 5, 2021, https://dod.defense.gov/Portals/1/Documents/pubs/2011_CMPR_Final .pdf.

———. *Annual Report to Congress: Military and Security Developments Involving the People's Republic of China 2013*. Accessed January 15, 2021, http://www.defense .gov/pubs/pdfs/2013_CMPR_Final.pdf.

———. *Annual Report to Congress: Military and Security Developments Involving the People's Republic of China 2020*. Accessed January 13, 2021, https://media. defense.gov/2020/Sep/01/2002488689/-1/-1/1/2020-DOD-CHINA-MILITARY -POWER-REPORT-FINAL.PDF.

———. *Indo-Pacific Strategy Report: Preparedness, Partnerships, and Promoting a Networked Region*. June 1, 2019. Accessed January 26, 2021, https://media.defense. gov/2019/Jul/01/2002152311/-1/-1/1/DEPARTMENT-OF-DEFENSE-INDO -PACIFIC-STRATEGY-REPORT-2019.PDF.

———. *Joint Operational Access Concept, Version 1.0*. 2012. Accessed May 9, 2021, https://dod.defense.gov/Portals/1/Documents/pubs/JOAC_Jan%202012 _Signed.pdf.

———. *Joint Publication 5-0: Joint Planning*. December 1, 2020. Accessed March 9, 2021, https://www.jcs.mil/Portals/36/Documents/Doctrine/pubs/jp5_0.pdf ?ver=ztDGo6paGvpQRrLxThNZUw%3d%3d.

———. *Program Acquisition Cost by Weapon System*. Office of the Under Secretary of Defense (Comptroller)/Chief Financial Officer, U.S. Department of Defense. February 2020. Accessed February 8, 2021, https://comptroller.defense.gov/Portals /45/Documents/defbudget/fy2021/fy2021_Weapons.pdf.

———. *Quadrennial Defense Review Report, 2001*. Accessed January 29, 2021, https://archive.defense.gov/pubs/qdr2001.pdf.

———. *Quadrennial Defense Review Report, 2006*. Accessed May 7, 2021, https:// archive.defense.gov/pubs/pdfs/QDR20060203.pdf.

———. *Quadrennial Defense Review Report, 2010*. Accessed May 7, 2021, https://dod .defense.gov/Portals/1/features/defenseReviews/QDR/QDR_as_of_29JAN10 _1600.pdf.

U.S. Department of Energy, U.S. Energy Information Administration. *China Analysis*. China Data tab. Accessed May 3, 2021, https://www.eia.gov/international /data/country/CHN.

———. *East China Sea*. September 17, 2014. Accessed January 14, 2021, https:// www.eia.gov/international/analysis/regions-of-interest/East_China_Sea.

———. *International Energy Outlook 2019*. September 24, 2019. Tables A5, G2, and F13. Accessed January 23, 2021, https://www.eia.gov/outlooks/archive /ieo19/tables_ref.php.

———. *South China Sea*. October 15, 2019. Accessed January 14, 2021, https:// www.eia.gov/international/analysis/regions-of-interest/South_China_Sea.

U.S. Department of Labor. Bureau of Labor Statistics. *Employment Situation*. Accessed January 15, 2021, https://www.bls.gov/news.release/empsit.toc.htm.

U.S. Department of State. *Treaties in Force: A List of Treaties and Other International Agreements of the United States in Force on January 1, 2020*. 2020. Accessed January 15, 2021, https://www.state.gov/treaties-in-force/.

———. *Treaty between the United States of America and the Union of Soviet Socialist Republics on the Elimination of Their Intermediate-Range and Shorter-Range Missiles (INF Treaty)*. Accessed May 7, 2021, https://2009–2017.state.gov/t/avc/trty/102360.htm.

U.S. Department of the Navy and the U.S. Coast Guard. "Advantage at Sea: Prevailing with Integrated All-Domain Naval Power." December 2020. Accessed April 3, 2021, https://media.defense.gov/2020/Dec/17/2002553481/-1/-1/0/TRISERVICESTRATEGY.PDF/TRISERVICESTRATEGY.PDF.

U.S. Government. *National Security Strategy*. December 2017. Accessed March 3, 2021, https://trumpwhitehouse.archives.gov/wp-content/uploads/2017/12/NSS-Final-12-18-2017-0905.pdf.

———. *NSC 68: United States Objectives and Programs for National Security*. April 14, 1950. Accessed May 12, 2021, https://fas.org/irp/offdocs/nsc-hst/nsc-68.htm.

U.S. Government Accountability Office. *Defense Acquisitions Annual Assessment*. June 2020. Accessed March 21, 2021, https://www.gao.gov/assets/gao-20-439.pdf.

U.S. Navy. *America's Navy—About—Mission*. U.S. Navy. Accessed January 27, 2021, https://www.navy.mil/About/Mission/.

———. "MQ-25A Stingray." Fact File, February 21, 2019. Accessed January 27, 2021, https://www.navy.mil/Resources/Fact-Files/Display-FactFiles/Article/2160662/mq-25a-stingray/.

———. "Tomahawk Cruise Missile." Fact File, April 26, 2018. Accessed January 28, 2021, https://www.navy.mil/Resources/Fact-Files/Display-FactFiles/Article/2169229/tomohawk-cruise-missile/.

U.S. Space Force. "Advanced Extremely High Frequency System Fact Sheet." March 22, 2017. Accessed October 28, 2021, https://www.spaceforce.mil/About-Us/Fact-Sheets/Article/2197713/advanced-extremely-high-frequency-system/.

VanHerck, Glen. "NORAD-USNORTHCOM Commander's Senate Armed Services Committee Statement." U.S. Northern Command, March 16, 2021. Accessed March 22, 2021, https://www.northcom.mil/Newsroom/Transcripts/Transcript/Article/2541921/norad-usnorthcom-commanders-senate-armed-services-committee-statement/.

Vick, Alan. *Snakes in the Eagle's Nest: A History of Ground Attacks on Air Bases*. Santa Monica, CA: RAND Corporation, 1995. Accessed May 6, 2021, https://www.rand.org/pubs/monograph_reports/MR553.html.

von Hippel, Frank. "Plutonium, Proliferation and Radioactive-Waste Politics in East Asia." Nonproliferation Policy Education Center, January 3, 2011. Accessed May 5, 2021, http://www.npolicy.org/article.php?aid=44&rt=~2~6~&key=proliferation%20japan&sec=article&author=.

Wang, Joyu, and Alastair Gale. "Does Taiwan's Military Stand a Chance against China? Few Think So." *Wall Street Journal*, October 26, 2021. Accessed October 26, 2021, https://www.wsj.com/articles/taiwan-military-readiness-china-threat-us-defense-11635174187?mod=articletype_trending_now_article_pos5.

Warden, John A., III. *The Air Campaign: Planning for Combat*. Washington DC: National Defense University Press, 1988. Accessed May 6, 2021, https://archive.org/details/DTIC_ADA259303/page/n7/mode/2up.

———. "Strategy and Airpower." *Air and Space Power Journal* 25, no. 1 (2011): 64–77.

Watts, Barry D. *The Maturing Revolution in Military Affairs*. Washington, DC: Center for Strategic and Budgetary Assessments, 2011. Accessed May 10, 2021, https://csbaonline.org/research/publications/the-maturing-revolution-in-military-affairs/.

Wei, Lingling. "China's Economic Recovery Belies a Lingering Productivity Challenge." *Wall Street Journal*, January 17, 2021. Accessed June 22, 2021, https://www.wsj.com/articles/chinas-economic-recovery-belies-a-lingering-productivity-challenge-11610884800?mod=hp_lista_pos2.

———. "China's Xi Ramps Up Control of Private Sector. 'We Have No Choice but to Follow the Party.'" *Wall Street Journal*, December 10, 2020. Accessed January 18, 2021, https://www.wsj.com/articles/china-xi-clampdown-private-sector-communist-party-11607612531.

Wei, Lingling, and Bob Davis. "China's Message to America: We're an Equal Now." *Wall Street Journal*, April 12, 2021. Accessed April 26, 2021, https://www.wsj.com/articles/america-china-policy-biden-xi-11617896117?mod=searchresults_pos4&page=1.

White, Hugh. "The China Choice: A Bold Vision for U.S-China Relations." *The Diplomat*, August 17, 2012. Accessed May 5, 2021, https://thediplomat.com/2012/08/the-china-choice-a-bold-vision-for-u-s-china-relations/.

———. *The China Choice: Why America Should Share Power*. Collingswood, Australia: Black Inc., 2012.

Wicke, Russell. "Gen. Moseley: New Long-Range Bomber on Horizon for 2018." U.S. Air Force Air Combat Command Public Affairs, July 26, 2006. Accessed February 20, 2021, https://www.af.mil/News/Article-Display/Article/130296/gen-moseley-new-long-range-bomber-on-horizon-for-2018/.

Woodward, Bob. *Obama's Wars*. New York: Simon and Schuster, 2010.

World Nuclear Association. "Nuclear Power in South Korea." November 2020. Accessed January 21, 2021, https://world-nuclear.org/information-library /country-profiles/countries-o-s/south-korea.aspx#:~:text=Fuel%20cycle %20South%20Korea%20has%20always%20had%20an,(see%20section %20below%20on%20Korea-US%20Atomic%20Energy%20Agreement).

"X" (George F. Kennan). "The Sources of Soviet Conduct." *Foreign Affairs*, July 1947. Accessed May 12, 2021, https://www.foreignaffairs.com/articles/russian -federation/1947-07-01/sources-soviet-conduct.

Xi Jinping. "Secure a Decisive Victory in Building a Moderately Prosperous Society in All Respects and Strive for the Great Success of Socialism with Chinese Characteristics for a New Era." Report to the Nineteenth National Congress of the Communist Party of China, October 18, 2017. Xinhua. Accessed January 16, 2021, http://www.xinhuanet.com/english/download/Xi_Jinping's_report _at_19th_CPC_National_Congress.pdf.

Yap, Chui-Wei. "China's Fishing Fleet, the World's Largest, Drives Beijing's Global Ambitions." *Wall Street Journal*, April 21, 2021. Accessed April 26, 2021, https:// www.wsj.com/articles/chinas-fishing-fleet-the-worlds-largest-drives-beijings -global-ambitions-11619015507?mod=searchresults_pos1&page=1.

Zhou, Christina, and Bang Xiao. "China's Social Credit System Is Pegged to Be Fully Operational by 2020—but What Will It Look Like?" Australian Broadcast Corporation, January 1, 2020. Accessed January 17, 2021, https://www.abc.net.au /news/2020-01-02/china-social-credit-system-operational-by-2020/11764740.

INDEX

ABOUT THE AUTHOR

Robert Haddick is a visiting senior fellow at the Mitchell Institute for Aerospace Studies, Air Force Association. He is a former U.S. Marine Corps officer with experience in East Asia and Africa. Haddick was a contractor for U.S. Special Operations Command and performed research for the Pentagon's Office of Net Assessment. He was a national security columnist at *Foreign Policy* magazine and has delivered lectures on strategy across the U.S. government.